This study provides an accessible and authoritative account of poverty and deviance during the early modern period, informed by those new perspectives on the role of the poor themselves in the provision of welfare services characteristic of much recent social history. In this introductory text Robert Jütte looks at how the poor shaped their own world, and how the notions of poverty and social deviance that preoccupied much contemporary thought saw their ultimate fruition in the systematic programmes for social welfare that emerged during the nineteenth century. Contrary to the once-traditional historical emphasis on the ameliorative role of individual reformers, Professor Jütte's account looks much more closely at the poor themselves, and the complex network of social and communal relationships they inhabited. He examines the lives not only of poor relief recipients but of the vast number of destitute individuals who had to find other means to stay alive, and how these people formed their own patterns of survival within given communities. Attractively illustrated with contemporary engravings, the work includes numerous features to aid the student reader, including a chronology, brief biographies of key individuals and extensive notes on further reading.

Poverty and Deviance
in Early Modern Europe

NEW APPROACHES TO EUROPEAN HISTORY

Series editors
WILLIAM BEIK *Emory University*
T. C. W. BLANNING *Sidney Sussex College, Cambridge*

New Approaches to European History is an important textbook series, which provides concise but authoritative surveys of major themes and problems in European history since the Renaissance. Written at a level and length accessible to advanced school students and undergraduates, each book in the series addresses topics or themes that students of European history encounter daily: the series will embrace both some of the more 'traditional' subjects of study, and those cultural and social issues to which increasing numbers of school and college courses are devoted. A particular effort is made to consider the wider international implications of the subject under scrutiny.

To aid the student reader scholarly apparatus and annotation is light, but each work has full supplementary bibliographies and notes for further reading: where appropriate chronologies, maps, diagrams and other illustrative material are also provided.

For a list of titles published in the series, please see end of book.

Poverty and Deviance
in Early Modern Europe

ROBERT JÜTTE

*Professor of History, Institut für Geschichte
der Medizin der Robert Bosch Stiftung,
Stuttgart*

CAMBRIDGE
UNIVERSITY PRESS

PUBLISHED BY THE PRESS SYNDICATE OF THE UNIVERSITY OF CAMBRIDGE
The Pitt Building, Trumpington Street, Cambridge, United Kingdom

CAMBRIDGE UNIVERSITY PRESS
The Edinburgh Building, Cambridge CB2 2RU, UK
40 West 20th Street, New York, NY 10011–4211, USA
477 Williamstown Road, Port Melbourne, VIC 3207, Australia
Ruiz de Alarcón 13, 28014 Madrid, Spain
Dock House, The Waterfront, Cape Town 8001, South Africa

http://www.cambridge.org

First published 1994
Reprinted 1996, 1999, 2001

Printed in the United Kingdom at the University Press, Cambridge

A catalogue record for this book is available from the British Library

Library of Congress Cataloguing in Publication data
Jütte, Robert.
Poverty and deviance in early modern Europe / Robert Jütte
   p.   cm. – (New approaches to European history)
Includes bibliographical references.
ISBN 0 521 41169 6 (hb.). – ISBN 0 521 42322 8 (pbk.)
1. Poor – Europe – History.   2. Marginality, Social – Europe –
History.   3. Crime – Europe – History.   I. Title.   II. Series.
HV6174.J88   1994
362.5'094–dc20   93-2577   CIP

ISBN 0 521 41169 6 hardback
ISBN 0 521 42322 8 paperback

TAG

Let not ambition mock their useful toil,
Their homely joys, and destiny obscure;
Nor grandeur hear with a disdainful smile
The short and simple annals of the poor.

Thomas Gray (1716–71),
Elegy Written in a Country Churchyard

In memory of my grandfather
Bernhard Volpert (1878–1973)
who initiated me into the
'economy of makeshifts'.

Contents

Illustrations

Tables

Preface

This book has been written in the belief that the problem of poverty and deviance in early modern Europe is of interest to a modern readership. The fact that the lives of the poor that are here chronicled ended more than two hundred years ago does not diminish their significance. In addition, the vicissitudes marking the lives of the poor in the past should be relevant to our own attitudes and actions because the foundations of our welfare state are built on their experience.

Parts of this work are written directly from my own research, and much depends on others, because the aim of a textbook is to offer an overview of a whole period. My debts to published works will be appreciated from the select bibliography. I cannot acknowledge all my obligations personally as a high proportion of my conversations with dozens of friends, fellow researchers and collaborators, colleagues and students over the past fifteen years has contributed to my understanding of the subject. Nonetheless, it would be indecent, if not dishonest, to fail to express my gratitude to some of them.

Archives and libraries are the laboratories of historical research, and the scholar depends very much on the knowledge and helpfulness of the staff. I wish to thank especially Dipl. Bibl. Beate Schleh of the Institute for the History of Medicine of the Robert Bosch Foundation in Stuttgart for her aid in providing books and articles by inter-library loan. I hope that those archivists and librarians acknowledged in my previous books for the debt which I still owe them will accept this time a more general assurance.

Many anonymous readers commented on the first three outlines of this study or on particular chapters. I hope that they will be pleased to recognize that they have strengthened it with their criticism and suggestions. Special thanks must go to Dr Martin Dinges, Stuttgart, who carefully read and criticized my work, pointing out several previously unnoted difficulties at an early stage. I wish to express my gratitude also to other members of the staff at the Institute for the History of Medicine of the Robert Bosch Foundation. During the gestation of this project, they showed patient support and unquenchable spirit. Their good humour and excellent work in the face of a director who had for two years become engrossed in writing this book are a testimony to their professionalism.

Many thanks go to the editors of this series, who have entrusted me with the task of writing this book. They provided sympathetic encouragement as well as guidance throughout the project. Finally, I wish to express my gratitude to Richard Fisher, editor in the Social Sciences Division at Cambridge University Press, and to Frances Brown, subeditor. Their careful editing and patience in waiting for me to produce such a general survey became absolute prerequisites for the successful completion of this textbook.

Authors usually thank their families for tolerance at being neglected during the writing of a book. In my case the neglect is chronic; whatever subject I wrote on in the past, my wife and my son found themselves drawn into the work.

1 Introduction

Research and sources

Historians of early modern Europe have in recent years made great efforts to study the causes and the extent of impoverishment in Europe before 1800. Although most publications refer to specific areas – usually individual towns or provinces – they nevertheless provide us with new perspectives and insights. Despite several attempts (e.g. by C. Lis/H. Soly, J.-P. Gutton, B. Geremek, W. Fischer, Th. Riis, St. Woolf) to sum up recent research in this field, we still lack a comprehensive survey and a general study on the strategies which the poor adopted for survival, providing comparisons between various European regions and countries in the early modern period (1450–1800). While the major case-studies so far have a slight western and central European bias, an attempt is here made to draw also on research of poor relief in urban and rural communities in northern and southern Europe.

The bulk of historiographical work on the poor in the nineteenth and early twentieth century deals with the variations in attitude towards the poor taken by Protestant and Catholic governments – with major differences stemming from Luther's belief that alms-giving as a traditional Christian form of doing 'good works' did not necessarily lead to the salvation of the giver's soul. Further, laicization and rationalization of poor relief were regarded as an outcome of the Reformation. In the past few decades, however, historians have emphasized that the actual social policy of European local and national governments cut across religious boundaries and followed a pattern which was adjusted to local conditions. French, English, American and German scholars have delineated in detail the similarities and divergences in urban Catholic and Protestant programmes of relief. And there is almost a consensus among historians nowadays that the reform of poor relief took place at the local, for the most part municipal, level, and that even in England, where the reform of poor relief was undertaken at the national level, the towns played an important part in the preliminary stages of what was later known as the

'Old Poor Law'. That a poor relief scheme had to be flexible is not only a result of modern political and social thought. The contemporaries who witnessed the paramount changes and reform projects of the early sixteenth century were already familiar with this idea. The eminent Spanish writer Juan de Medina, for example, noted: 'The poverty of people is of many kinds, and we cannot indicate a certain way of provision for them, because the change in time and in customs requires different kinds of provision: as it is the case in all other matters of government.'

By the end of Middle Ages, the faces of the poor were many in kind and in number. The poor no longer included only the traditional groups (widows, orphans, the blind, the lame) but also comprised newer kinds as well. As a large number of urban wage-earners, cottagers and day-labourers lived in circumstances which even contemporaries admitted to be extremely precarious, larger, structural and cyclical changes, such as economy, war, climate, could accelerate the impoverishment processes which had attained such enormous proportions in the sixteenth century and which remained at work throughout the early modern period. The new features of poverty awakened the curiosity as much as the fear of contemporaries. At the time the social extent of the problem grew so great that traditional charity institutions could no longer cope with this tidal wave of people in need of relief. The new quantity and quality of poverty demanded a radical departure from the beaten tracks of medieval charity. The religious and social values associated with poverty changed, although poverty and poor relief was in neither Catholic nor Protestant communities completely severed from its former strong religious connotations.

The perspective presented in this general survey has been deeply influenced by my own archival research as well as by a group of social historians whose contributions to historical demography and historical anthropology moved them away from viewing the emergence of the welfare state as the work of some reformers and governments and turned their attention instead to the rather complex role of the community and the poor themselves in the growth and development of the welfare state. Since 1980 scholars have begun to look more closely at the poor themselves and their living conditions, shedding light not only on the recipients of poor relief but also on the vast number of poor people who had to find other means to stay alive. They have managed to look directly at the lives of the poor, instead of seeing them through the eyes of governments, theologians, poor relief administrators, or alms-givers and philanthropists. While welfare historians relied in the past to a large extent on archival material that inadvertently but inevitably led to studies tracing the rise of charitable institutions and major social legislation, this new school of historians looks for additional sources which, for example, can tell us something about the material culture of the poor and which can also help us to explain the strategies of survival of the nearly 60 to 80 per cent of the population below or close to the poverty line.

Despite our desire to give equal space to the life of the 'ordinary poor', a substantial share of this book must necessarily be devoted to a study of the instruments of social policy as well as to the concomitants of poverty, deviance in general and vagrancy in particular. The reason is very simple. Much of the scholarship on the poor in early modern Europe has focused so far on the institutions and the politics of relief. This focus may help to explain why even the most laudable attempt to bring new perspectives into the history of poverty and deviance cannot avoid referring to the problem in terms of governmental regulation and social control.

This book is by no means a definitive or even comprehensive account of the entire field or period; to cover all aspects of the subject would require more space than a textbook allows. Rather, it is a brief review of the living conditions of the poor as well as of the poor relief policies and practices in Europe from the early sixteenth century to the end of the *ancien régime*. It attempts to bridge the gap between a collective work of many scholars and a monographic study consisting of more than one volume. Naturally some developments and phenomena are alluded to only briefly, such as the informal attempts at relief and philanthropical projects, and others had to be omitted, particularly the care for the poor within certain ethnic or religious communities (Jews, Anabaptists, Quakers, etc.). Still the book embodies what I believe to be the essence of the present state of knowledge on poor relief, poverty and deviance in early modern Europe. On the broad basis of my own extensive reading and research in this field, which I started in 1977, I have tried mainly to assemble, assimilate and synthesize the vast literature that already exists in this field; there is little here that is completely new. Writing this textbook was nevertheless an impressive, intellectually rewarding experience. I hope that it fills a major gap in the literature by combining judicious use of archival material and results of recent research with the approaches of social historians to a number of topics, such as the family, migration, voluntary associations, work, crime, neighbourhood, social segregation and mentalities.

Themes

I have chosen to follow individual themes over time, rather than to organize the material chronologically. This method enables the historian to show the long-term development within particular sectors, without losing sight of the social context and running the risk that the nature and significance of the overall structure of poverty in the early modern period remains elusive.

Recent developments in the history of poverty open tempting vistas. Much depends, however, on the expressiveness and informational value of the available sources. Abundant official records survive – poor law disbursements, hospital administration registers, petitions and judicial files – sufficiently rich to hold out hopes of systematic and even statistical analysis. However, when attempting to diverge from a history seen through the eyes of legislators, reformers, pedagogues, theologians and the like, one normally comes across sources which pose grave interpretative problems. How does one disentangle, for example, the experience of the poor from the language of the recording agency, be he poor relief administrator or hospital official? Before we can describe how socio-economic problems and poor relief related to each other, we must therefore examine the perceptions of poverty and the poor during the transition from the Middle Ages to the early modern period. That will be the task of Chapter 2, which will deal with images of the poor. Images can be produced and promoted by various means; language is only one of them. Although there is always some dissonance between language and social reality, the analysis of vocabulary used to describe the various degrees of poverty and indigence, taken in conjunction with other facts, may focus attention upon a less well-known dimension of the overall and perennial problem. Like linguistic evidence, visual images of the poor attest the increasing interest of the public in poverty and poor relief from the Middle Ages onwards. The variety of roles represented by the poor in the various media suggests therefore a complex perception of the social order in the period under study. According to recent research in this field there can be no doubt that the language of poverty and pictorial evidence should be taken seriously, both as an insight into the mentality of the ruling classes and as a realistic reflection of the world of destitution and marginality.

Poverty had many faces and causes in a pre-industrial society such as early modern Europe, and we will turn to this in more detail in Chapter 3. Economic fluctuations, wars, illness and natural catastrophes are traditional explanations of poverty. Recent research has emphasized the role of un- and underemployment as a cause for mass impoverishment. One of the most fruitful developments in recent years has been, however, the shift towards a more dynamic conception of poverty, stressing, for example, the importance of the life-cycle ('nuclear hardship hypothesis'). Summing up the discussion of the different causes and explanations of poverty, this chapter will show the importance of structural and biological causes as being responsible for the precarious conditions of many people living below or around the poverty line.

Chapter 4 will argue not only that there is a lack of quantitative information over the extent of poverty, but that historians also have problems of selection and evaluation of the criteria according to which comparison about the extent of poverty in various countries can be made. The same problem exists in the prevalence of poverty over time. The sources present us with groups of people who have been labelled 'poor' according to criteria that are often vague and that always vary according to the society, the institution, the period and the place. Detailed enquiries into the numbers, living conditions and needs of the poor date back to many decades before the Reformation. Most of the historical data available seem to overlook the large and floating population, though they always include – alongside the able-bodied local beggars – aged or infirm individuals to whom some form of charity or alms were given. The distortions in recent estimates result from the different interpretations of the various categories of deprivation and poverty. The range of the criteria employed by modern historians implies that the data-sets and figures are not strictly comparable and can only be regarded as an approximation to reality. All scholars agree, however, on one issue, namely that there was a sharp difference between the city and the countryside.

The distinction between the worthy and the undeserving poor has attracted considerable literature because of its multiple implications, practical, ideological and symbolic. The second part of this book is devoted to this privileged group of the poor. In Chapter 5 we will look at the living conditions of the resident poor. Very few studies have concentrated so far on the mental attitudes of the local poor and on the miseries which they faced in everyday life. How did they experience their situation? This chapter attempts to reconstruct their material culture (nutrition, housing, clothing) and the mentality which it fostered.

'Charity begins at home' – this famous English proverb characterizes one of the most important though often neglected forms of coping with poverty. In order to survive people could seldom rely on charity or poor relief but had to activate social networks (family, neighbours, friends, employers) of which they were part. Others were forced to migrate (subsistence migration) in order to escape their present state of misery and deprivation. The happy few who received public poor relief had to adapt themselves to the standards of the institutions which granted alms and – in some cases – even provided existence allowances. We will trace these powerful strategies of survival in Chapter 6.

With the increase of pauperism, the poor constituted a menace to public order. New schemes of poor relief were introduced in order to deal with the new situation. Major institutional changes occurred in the early sixteenth century and were to continue in successive waves until the early nineteenth century. The chronology of these institutional changes differed across early modern Europe. The same applies to the forces (private, municipal, ecclesiastical, governmental) which motivated them. Chapter 7 attempts to give for the first time a typology of poor relief schemes in early modern western Europe based on structural, organizational and functional variables. Only within a general European framework can such early examples of a social welfare be evaluated and more subtly nuanced. For the sake of clarity it seems useful to introduce a rough bi-polar typology. The two ideal types could then be defined as a centralized form of poor relief on the one hand, and as a more decentralized one on the other. The latter seems to be typical for Catholic states while the first type was prevalent in Protestant communities.

The last part of this book deals with the 'undeserving' poor who were denied charity and relief because of their deviant behaviour. Idleness, petty theft, vagrancy and prostitution were the most common infractions of the law connected with poverty. The various forms of poverty-born deviance will be the subject of Chapter 8. As we will see, this problem is not unrelated to the rise of new attitudes towards the poor in general, yet it is not simply an offshoot of that development.

Poverty as such was not degrading. However, as early as the fifteenth century the distinction between the deserving and the undeserving poor became part of the discriminatory social policy towards beggars. The partition line between those who merited assistance and the unworthy was very often not clear. Nevertheless, governments were busy punishing offences brought forth by a new concept of collective crime which is usually summarized under the heading 'vagrancy'. This concept involved a variety of measures against rogues and 'sturdy' or able-bodied beggars. Such a discriminatory philosophy encouraged a social policy which encapsulated the three characteristics of marginalization: stigmatization, segregation and punishment. We will discuss these measures in Chapter 9.

Recent research provides new evidence that the literary portrayal of vagrancy and marginality should be taken seriously and not excluded without further ado as pure fantasy or fiction. Chapter 10 argues that the so-called 'literature of roguery' is a valuable source for the reconstruction of the subculture of poverty. The enforcement of social discipline and the penalization of begging and vagrancy met with resistance. Those who were accused by the authorities of being a threat to public morality and order adopted strategies of survival, which somebody from outside might view as ephemeral anti-societies consisting of outsiders, unified by their way of life and certain values. Some of the cases which we examine do indeed suggest that socially marginalized groups of people formed a kind of subculture. The reactions to repressive strategies of local and national government were, however, limited. The deviant poor had in most cases only three options: self-organization, rebellion and (e)migration.

Analysis of the resemblances as well as the differences in the nature of poverty and its treatment today and in the past we must reserve for the concluding chapter, which will serve to sum up and to bring into perspective what we have examined throughout the book.

Last but not least, the reader should be encouraged to look at and to make use of the chronological chart and the short biographies of eminent poor relief reformers, which have been added to the book to remind students that social history cannot do without the history of events and the actions of individual men. It was actually the eminent French historian Fernand Braudel, often considered a 'structuralist', who suggested we divide historical time into geographical time, social time and individual time.

Finally, a word on the footnotes and bibliography is in order. This book is meant for a wide readership. Since it contains information accumulated from many sources, books and articles over a period of years, it would be impractical to cite all the material used. So I have used notes sparingly, and, for the most part, only to locate a quotation from contemporary sources. At the end of the book, however, I have included a bibliography in which the reader may find the most important books and articles on the particular subjects discussed in the various chapters. Headings have been used to facilitate orientation. Although many of the studies could have been listed in several places, for reason of space I have double-listed these sources only in those cases where it is absolutely necessary. These include many of the more general titles, which students might find useful for further reading. In any case I do hope to have indicated in the bibliography those authors and works from which I have borrowed most.

2 Images of poverty

The language of poverty

Language can be a guide to social reality. But historians often have to be reminded that the study of language is more than an 'academic exercise in semantics' (Asa Briggs). This point can be amplified by reference to the kinship vocabulary which reflects the important kin relationships in a society. And it is not only kinship terms which may reflect the structure of society. The language of poverty, for example, reveals much about the differences between our modern society and the pre-industrial society under study here. Although there is always some dissonance between language and reality, the vocabulary used for describing various degrees of poverty and indigence, taken in conjunction with other facts, may be an important social indicator. As society is reflected in language this way, social change can produce a corresponding semantic change. If, for example, the structure of early modern society altered radically so that it came to resemble more closely a class society than a society of orders, we would expect the linguistic system to alter correspondingly. This has indeed happened. According to a recent study the changes that were taking place in the idea of poverty and the image of the poor during the late eighteenth century led to the increasing use of the 'language of class' (Gertrud Himmelfarb) to define poverty and to describe the poor. Class in the modern sense only came into existence, as Marxist historians have pointed out, at the historical moment when classes began to acquire consciousness of themselves as such. This consciousness expresses itself in language and ideas as well as behaviour. Late eighteenth-century and early nineteenth-century England was, however, not yet a fully developed class society. The fact that terms like 'workmen', 'people' and 'poor' still figured prominently in the public discourse shows that the language of class had not yet replaced the 'old' language of 'orders', 'ranks', 'sorts' and 'degrees', in which the terms 'rich' and 'poor' suggested the idea of godly, orderly, stable and organic society. Until the end of the *ancien régime* the vocabulary of poverty still carried with it medieval

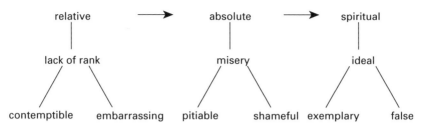

Figure 1 Components of meaning
Source: Roch, *Vocabulaire*, p. 285.

connotations of social relations, defined largely in terms of birth and mutual dependency. 'Thus we saie that the poor are made for the good of the ritche',[1] declares an anonymous English writer at the end of the sixteenth and the beginning of the seventeenth century, and he could be sure that many of his contemporaries still agreed with him, seeing the poor as an integral part of a Christian commonwealth and a necessary stimulus for the rich to practise virtue and to show humility. In pre-industrial Europe poverty was more than a certain lack of material goods or just a relation between means and ends, it was above all seen as a subordinating relation between people.

There has been a marked social and political change and this has been accompanied by a corresponding change in the meaning of the word 'poverty' and its equivalents in other European languages. Whereas 'poverty' has a rather narrow meaning today, it had in medieval and early modern times a much broader semantic scope and also more connotations (see Figure 1). In early modern English 'poverty' has, according to the Oxford English Dictionary, the following meanings: (1) the condition of having little or no wealth or material possession; (2) the deficiency in the proper or desired (social) status or quality; (3) dearth, scarcity; (4) poor condition of the body, feebleness resulting from insufficient nourishment. 'Poor', therefore, expresses more than just the opposite of 'rich' or 'wealthy'. It not only indicates the various degrees of poverty (absolute, relative and spiritual), but is basically evaluative, saying that a person is such, or so circumstanced, as to excite one's compassion or contempt. These evaluative meanings of 'rich' and 'poor' are logically distinct from other semantic polarities (e.g. young v. old, large v. small), because we cannot discuss their implications of truth value without distinguishing 'true for Mr X', 'true for Miss Y'. While contemporaries could and did make these subjective distinctions, the historian has to take these evaluative terms at face value. The sources present him with groups

[1] 'Of poore and rytche', *c.* 1600, British Libary, Harleian MS 1713:18, f. 129r.

1 MISERY	2 NECESSITY	3 NAKEDNESS	4 SUFFERING
(a) indigence	(a) want	(a) nudity	(a) exhaustion
(b) dearth	(b) need	(b) ruin	(b) pain
(c) suffrance	(c) extreme need	(c) solitude	(c) melancholy

Figure 2 Synonyms of 'poverty'
Source : Roch, *Vocabulaire*, pp. 286ff.

or individuals who have been labelled 'poor' according to criteria that are often vague and not always understandable. He must therefore keep in mind that the norm behind the polarity between 'rich' and 'poor' is subjective and speaker-related.

In order to understand what language reveals about the perception of the poor and the values associated with the poor in the period under study, we have to look not only for antonyms (words of opposite meaning) but for words with semantic relatedness. The following English terms, which have their equivalent in other European languages, are used throughout the late medieval and early modern period to describe various aspects of 'poverty' (see Figure 2).

Some of these synonyms refer to the relative nature of poverty. One is always poorer or better-off than someone else, and in a variety of ways, ranging for example, from states of wanting means to procure the comforts or necessaries of life to mental and physical conditions. This scheme brings out two other specific aspects of poverty in addition to deprivation, want and insecurity. The first is the anonymity or solitude that comes from helplessness or powerlessness, and the second the constant or temporary deficiency of some desirable quality or inferiority, which made people in the eyes of their contemporaries not only pitiable but sometimes also despicable. In the beginning of the early modern period a poor man might still be described as one who was 'ready to starve for want of bread' or as 'one that wants things needful to him'. Later on, in the seventeenth century, the term 'poor' referred not only to those in necessitous or humble circumstances but specifically to those dependent on charitable or parochial relief. And it was not until the end of the eighteenth century that a clear line was drawn between poverty on the one hand and indigence on the other, between the masses of the labouring poor and those being so destitute as to be dependent on gifts or allowances for subsistence.

How the poor and the various degrees or features of their poverty were seen, classified and described by contemporaries varied greatly according to the people, the institution, the period and obviously the place. From the standpoint of early modern administrators and social reformers, the poor most often seemed to fall into two categories: the deserving and the undeserving poor, depending on whether or not they were regarded as victims of circumstances or were held responsible for their present miserable condition. In the sixteenth and seventeenth centuries it was the 'language of order' and not the 'language of class' which governed the semantics of poverty. Seen as a group and not as individuals the poor were perceived in terms of a vertical society, with varying 'sorts' and 'degrees'. The vocabulary which can be found in chronicles, statutes, mandates and ordinances, and by which writers and administrators sought to define the poor and locate them in relation to the society in which they lived, reflects the fundamental social categories of orders, ranks, sorts, degrees and estates, which were largely defined in terms of birth but not rigidly or exclusively so. In his detailed description of poverty, the sixteenth-century English writer William Harrison[2] classifies the poor into three 'degrees' and subcategories ('sorts'):

1 The poor 'by impotency' comprise:
   1.1 'the fatherlesse child'
   1.2 'the aged, blind, and lame'
   1.3 'the diseased person that is iudged to be incurable'
2 The poor 'by casualty' comprise:
   2.1 'the wounded souldier'
   2.2 'the decaied householder'
   2.3 'the sicke persone visited with grieuous ... diseases'.

And whereas the poor of the first two 'degrees' were regarded by himself and also by poor relief administrators all over early modern Europe as the legitimate or 'deserving' poor, the following category was most certainly excluded from sympathy and aid:

3 The poor 'thriftless', comprising:
   3.1 'the riotour that hath consumed all'
   3.2 'the vagabund that will abide no where'
   3.3 'the rog[u]e and strumpet'.

Similar clear and explicit statements of contemporary and collective definitions of what constituted 'true' poverty can be found in other sources. Private wills as well as poor law legislation articulate the normally much less concrete qualities that contemporaries employed in evaluating the poor. From the sixteenth century onwards governments and magistrates directed public attention to the danger of the third category, the 'idle poor' (as can been seen in Table 1).

---

[2] Cf. William Harrison, *Description of England in Shakespeare's Youth* (1577/87), ed. F. J. Furnivall (London, 1877), p. 213.

Table 1. *Terms used in early modern France to define the begging poor* (*'pauvres mendiants'*)

	16th c.	1601–30	1631–68
pauvres, mendiants (paupers, mendicants)	11	11	8
vagabonds (vagabonds)	2	9	5
gens de néant (idlers)	2	1	1
fainéants (loafers)	–	1	2
gens sans aveu (masterless men)	–	3	1
débauchés (rakes, debauchees)	–	1	–
gueux (beggars, tramps)	–	1	2

Source: Alain Croix, *La Bretagne aux 16e et 17e siècles. La vie – la mort – la foi*, 2 vols. (Paris, 1981), I, p. 436, Table 61a.

The increase in those categories which most certainly had a pejorative meaning (*vagabonds*, *gens sans aveu*) indicates the fear and disgust which mounted in the early sixteenth century and continued throughout the following century. The same message was propounded in territorial and imperial police ordinances in Germany as well as in Tudor and Stuart proclamations. There the problem of poverty was invariably presented as that of the 'masterless man', the wandering beggar or vagabond. Pounded into people's heads by numerous tracts, statutes and proclamations, the distinction between the worthy and unworthy poor became a commonplace concept through which contemporaries organized their view of the social order. The change which took place in the seventeenth and early eighteenth centuries was that this distinction between 'pauper' and 'mendicus' was made less often. Increasingly, *all* the able-bodied poor were considered wilfully idle and unworthy of charity.

But how did the poor describe themselves? How does their language reflect their poor condition and their way of living? These questions are difficult to answer because of the lack of sources. The argot spoken by vagabonds, tricksters and thieves alike offers, however, invaluable evidence to the historian of popular culture and mentalities. The linguistic process, affecting the language of communication between the ruling and the dangerous classes, can be seen as operating in both directions.

On the one hand, it led to the fearful but compulsive curiosity of contemporaries (e.g. Mathias Hütlin, Martin Luther, Thomas Harman, John Awdeley, Ollivier Chereau) about the early modern underworld. And it does not come as a surprise that those investigators explained this counter-culture in 'sociological' terms of the Christian commonwealth in which they lived. John Awdeley, for example, called his book on the Elizabethan underworld *The Fraternity of Vagabonds both Ruffling and Beggarly* (1561).[3] The first chapter of *A Caveat for Common Cursitors, Vulgarly Called Vagabonds* (1566)[4] by the English Commissioner of the Peace Thomas Harman starts with a detailed description of the *ruffler* 'because he is first in degree of this odious order and is so called in a statute made for the punishment of vagabonds'. This specific nomenclature was a little later copied by William Harrison in his *Description of England*, in which he refers to the 'seuerall disorders and degrees amongst our idle vagabonds'.[5] Speaking of 'dis-orders' Harman alludes to the contemporary concept of 'orders' and 'estates' but makes clear that these various companies of vagabonds are the negative transfer of the hierarchy existing in the Christian commonwealth. The same concept or world view is manifest also in a later edition of the famous German representative of the so-called 'literature of roguery' (F. W. Chandler), the *Liber vagatorum* (first edition, c. 1509), which refers in its title to a 'bedler orden' (the order of beggars), while the Italian equivalent speaks of 'compagnie' (companies) in which beggars are organized, reflecting thus the social fabric upon which early modern urban society was based.

On the other hand, this linguistic process may be connected to the hypothesis that different languages (in this case: argot and vernacular) may express differences in perceptions of the world. It suggests that the wandering beggars or vagabonds habitually perceived their environment in a rather different way from the lower-, middle-, or upper-class speaker of colloquial English, German, French etc. A statistical survey of the vocabulary of some of these argots suggests that the 'secret' languages developed by these closed and highly corporate groups manifest the predominant concern about how to make a living. It is essential for the pauper person to be able to distinguish efficiently between different types of illicit begging and alms-giving. The vernacular, of course, is quite able to make the same distinctions: carrying a feigned licence, pretending to be a leper, and so on, but in argot this sort of distinction is usually lexicalized – made by means of individual words.

It is even more difficult to find an answer to the question of how the 'worthy' or 'shamefaced' poor defined themselves linguistically. An interesting attempt was recently made by an English historian who analysed an Italian source containing the self-description of the respectable poor qualifying for assistance according to various criteria, of which the possession of job-skills was one. The terms used by the

---

[3] Reprinted in Arthur F. Kinney (ed.), *Rogues, Vagabonds, and Sturdy Beggars: A New Gallery of Tudor and Early Stuart Rogue Literature* (Amherst, 1990), pp. 91–101.
[4] Reprinted in Kinney, *Rogues*, pp. 109–53.   [5] Harrison, *Description*, p. 218.

labouring poor to describe their economic activities and skills give us a glimpse of a language rich in variety of expression. And the wealth of nomenclatures point, according to Stuart Woolf, 'to an extremely close identification with the concrete, material experience of day-to-day work'.[6]

The visualization of the poor

Like the highly popular 'literature of roguery', visual images of the poor attest to the increasing interest of the public in poor relief during the early modern period. The viewer recognized the intention of these pictures, as they conveyed the same messages endorsed in many contemporary tracts, sermons and treatises on the poor, i.e. to distinguish between the deserving and the unworthy poor. Images of the poor have to be interpreted therefore as effective means of visual propaganda. Recent research on the use of images in the Reformation has shown that it is possible to interpret images in terms of certain codes: 1. the code of transmission (the medium of the visual arts); 2. the morphological code (the composition and structure of the image); 3. the linguistic code (use of explanatory texts and subtitles); 4. the gestural code (gestures and attributes signifying moods, character, states and roles).

The question of which medium the artist chooses to express his concept of poverty becomes particularly important, if one thinks of the potential customers of altar paintings, epitaphs and sculptures, who prided themselves on their benevolence. Another group consisted of buyers, viewers and readers of illustrated books, broadsheets and single-leaf woodcuts, who either wanted to satisfy their curiosity or wanted practical advice how to fulfil their Christian duty of charity. The variety of roles represented visually by beggars in the various media suggests a complex perception of beggars among their contemporaries. The morphological code helps us, for example, to understand a recurring type of composition: the poor as a social type or as an object of mercy. In the fifteenth century the pauper was often depicted as a cripple. In the sixteenth century he was no longer characterized by physical deformities but was designated by begging gesture and a pathetic condition. This change reflects a new attitude towards the poor. It was no longer a physical handicap that denoted a beggar, but something less concrete, less tangible: a gesture, a way of behaving, in short the physical and moral condition.

---

[6] Stuart Woolf, *The Poor in Western Europe in the Eighteenth and Nineteenth Centuries* (London and New York, 1986), p. 156.

The linguistic code provides us with additional information about the artist's concept of reality as can be seen, for instance, in the illustrated text of Petrarca's *Trostspiegel* (first German edition: Augsburg 1532), where one scene depicts the distribution of benefits out of the common chest. This woodcut bears the significant subtitle: 'The one who deserves our help most, is he who shows indigence and virtue.' Another striking example is found in the frontispieces of the various editions of the *Liber vagatorum* (1509ff). While the text describes various kinds of beggars as deceptive, the many title-page illustrations do not reflect the sceptical attitude of the author, but present beggars without visual comment, often expressing the genuine poverty and disability of many such figures. The contrast between text and image indicates the underlying contemporary clash of opinions ranging from suspicion to compassion. Around 1524, the Nuremberg artist, Barthel Behaim, published his broadsheet *The twelve vagrants* (see Plate 1). Its form, as broadsheet, and its verbal format, in verse, enabled it to reach less literate audiences with its particular message, namely that sometimes the poor are victims of both internal and external forces, but that the presence of poverty is a part of the divine order.

Decoding the gestural code makes it possible for us to recognize the deserving poor as those who are characterized by neatness and cheerful industriousness, whilst the non-deserving poor can easily be identified by their baseness of manners, expressions and dress. Gestures are certainly the most important elements of visual language. They reflect patterns of behaviour delineated and defined by social and political norms. The gestures of certain saints (St Francis, St Martin, St Elizabeth) distributing alms to the poor make visible a specific, Christ-imitating relationship between those heavenly intercessors and the poor who stand before them. St Elizabeth of Thuringia, in particular, resembles in her gestures the ideal attitude of the pious Christian to the destitute, so much that her figure often replaced the allegorical figure of 'Caritas' in German-speaking countries.

The pictorial evidence on the poor must also be interpreted in relation to the specific moral and political ideology of the artist about whom we often have very few biographical details. In any case, their works do not mirror the reality of poverty and welfare in early modern Europe, but they are more concerned to promote a certain image of the poor for the edification and education of rich and poor alike. The late medieval artist still presented the poor and acts of mercy in the context of the traditional Christian concept of sainthood, sanctification of poverty and charity, in which the poor were mostly passive agents of a pious spiritual action. Many sixteenth-century portrayals of the poor convey a different

Plate 1 Barthel Behaim, *The twelve vagrants*. Woodcut, *c.* 1524.

message. The pauper is often reduced to another stereotype, that of the sturdy beggar, unworthy of charity, on the one hand, and that of the cheerful, thankful, domestic and labouring poor on the other hand.

The attitude of artists to the poor or their 'sujet' has thus changed in the course of time. A picturesque image of poverty often indicates (as in the case of Jacques Callot's famous series of etchings known as *Les Gueux*) a mainly aesthetic interest in the object. It may be replaced by a kind of 'romantic' image of an almost pastoral quality, as, for example, in some engravings by Lucas van Leyden (1494–1533). In other representations of the poor the artist's criticism becomes more transparent, as for instance in Albrecht Dürer's illustration for the 1494 edition of the 'Ship of Fools' or in the famous engraving after a drawing by Hieronymus Bosch (1450?–1516) known as 'Diverse Examples of the Art of Begging'.

In order to make the poor easily recognizable, late medieval and early modern artists emphasized certain characteristics such as manners, expression and dress. Like their contemporaries they considered poverty to be a natural, everyday phenomenon, so that they could restrict themselves to the external manifestations of poverty. The most common features of the life of this pitiful mass engaged in almost daily struggle for subsistence were signs of malnutrition, sickness, age, disability, and the lack of a permanent home or abode. An outstanding example of this genre is an engraving after a drawing by Pieter Bruegel the Elder (1525?–69), which is entitled 'arm ghasterije' (meagre cuisine) and which will be discussed in more detail later on in this book. Another common theme is the conspicuous dress of the poor. In its raggedness and sometimes eccentricity it amplifies the outward distinction between the well-dressed rich in fashionable clothes and the tattered and torn outfits of those who could not afford anything better. The ragged clothes serve therefore as one of the main attributes of deprivation and indigence. At a deeper level of analysis we must see, however, the ragged dress in line with the iconographical tradition of the Middle Ages, where this *Demutskleid* (humble dress) served as symbol for man's sinfulness and his tainted soul.

Confining the poor as well as outsiders became, according to the French philosopher Michel Foucault, one of the major principles of an all-embracing social policy based on disciplinary measures. While the early forms of confinement (e.g. for lepers and madmen) can be found in engravings, etchings and woodcuts of the period 1450–1650, the 'Great Confinement' described by Foucault did not leave traces in images before the late seventeenth and early eighteenth century, when pictures of prisons, workhouses, general hospitals and their inmates became rather popular in European art. In the whole period under study we may distinguish three main locations for scenes either involving the poor alone or showing them together with their benefactors: the street, the countryside, and the inside of buildings (hospital, church, almshouse, workhouse, etc.). Each location has its significance and reveals the artist's conception of poverty. The emphasis may lie on social control, education, repression and punishment, or, alternatively, as far as the wandering beggar is concerned, the images manifest a certain admiration for the 'freedom' enjoyed by the beggar, having no abode and being able to move freely. In fact, it is hard to rid oneself of the impression that in these images, as in the Elizabethan and Stuart theatre, the poor and the vagrant are often introduced because of the eccentric, nonconformist traits associated with them and because they provide entertainment for viewers eager for visual stimulation. The pastoral element in this picture of poverty is nowhere more clearly discerned than in many landscape scenes, where the 'happy' poor gather in the field, in the woods or on the green, pretending that even if life was not completely free of need, it nonetheless offered personal freedom.

The poor, the legitimate as well as the non-deserving, are very often attached to groupings, and this is not merely for aesthetic considerations. Poverty and vagrancy are phenomena which contemporaries associated with groups rather than with individuals. The companion of the pauper could be a member of the various marginal groups (Jews, gypsies, etc.) or a representative of the established orders. The tableau itself often tells us a great deal about the social life of the poor. Sometimes we see the whole kaleidoscope of wayfaring life, reminiscent of the variety of outsiders depicted in literary texts of the early modern period. Another category, consisting of images which show the poor together with those who distributed alms or relief to them, represents the complex nature of Christian brotherly love, being self-cleansing and self-negating as well as magnanimous and subservient. This applies especially to those images which present various saints distributing alms. The visual representations of the Seven Works of Mercy, of which there are examples throughout the early modern period, did not have as their message that Christian humility which linked the saints to the object of their attention. Their implicit meaning is slightly different: not the objects of the acts of mercy but the act itself is of importance.

In delineating the lowest section of early modern society, it was possible for the artist to depict a wide range of social outcasts in various conditions and situations. His choice was, of course, determined by his interest in the picturesque quality of the subject matter, by aesthetic considerations or simply by iconographical conventions. But there can be no doubt that the grim reality of recurring subsistence crises provided sufficient illustrative material for the artist. What appears as the main theme in many picaresque novels (e.g. *Lazarillo de Tormes*), is also a common feature in the images of the poor: hunger and people's response to it, namely begging for a piece of bread. The majority of the visual representations show all those who are in need of food, drink, shelter, clothing or care. And the figure of the beggar seems to embody best four of the seven conditions for works of mercy. In contrast, one of the famous paintings by Pieter Bruegel the Elder ('The Combat of Carnival and Lent', 1559), illustrates how misery, sorrow and distress suddenly change into merry-making. Some early modern broadsheets and wood-cuts also present to us the 'cheerful' poor, the 'merry' beggar who for a moment forgets his indigence and prides himself on his imaginary 'freedom' from all social constraints. This tableau filled with merry beggars, which exists as a topos in contemporary literature as well, is complementary to the world of misery and destitution which we usually encounter in early modern visual representations of the poor.

Artists paid attention to the problems of poor relief, too, depicting paupers as either legitimate or undeserving recipients of public assistance or private charity. They showed concern not only for the support of the poor but also for the allied problems of social 'rehabilitation': the welfare of the interned beggar in a workhouse, the care of the impoverished sick in hospitals, and vocational training for young boys and girls. In many indoor and outdoor scenes displaying the distribution of alms the kind or even the amount of assistance is indicated. We also have visual representations of how those capable of earning their living were set to work, either in houses of correction or in public building projects. Many woodcuts, etchings, and engravings of the seventeenth and eighteenth centuries mirror the drastic change in social policy, with the emphasis changing from undiscriminating alms-giving to an enforcement of social discipline via poor relief. However, there is also some pictorial evidence which suggests that traditional concepts of charity and alms-giving survived at least until the end of the eighteenth century despite repeated legislation against wilful beggars and idle vagabonds and despite attempts by the authorities to reform poor relief so that alms would be distributed to the poor in a more rationalized way through a public institution. The traditional attitude towards charity is most striking in those scenes where the artist follows the iconographical convention of medieval represen-tation of sainthood, delineating the life and work of St Martin or St Elizabeth, to name only the most prominent saints connected with the poor. These images still convey the traditional message, the definition of Christian love given by Augustine – 'Caritas is that movement of the soul toward delight in God and in one's neighbour that originates in God himself.'[7] And even in those prints in which the central sign was not a

---

[7] 'Caritas est motum animi ad fruendum Deo propter seipsum: & se, atque proximo, propter Deum', quoted by Pietro Ridolfi, *Dictionarium pauperum* (Konstanz, 1600), p. 201.

gesture of brotherly love, there was at least a symbol or indication of those duties that Christians, Catholics and Protestants alike, take up in their faith. At least the visual tradition which was part of the mainstream socio-religious discourse continued to present images of a loving Christ, who cared for the poor and who sacrificed Himself for the sake of humanity.

3   The causes of poverty

Poverty had many faces in pre-industrial society. Several causes contributed to the problem of poverty and vagrancy, varying in importance, however, from country to country, from area to area and from decade to decade. The following list is not intended to be a comprehensive enumeration of the various causes of poverty. Its purpose is merely to indicate broadly the major forces which generated mass impoverishment before the nineteenth century. Poverty was experienced at many social levels, although the lower classes were prone to life-threatening deprivation. Not only day-labourers, smallholders and wage-earners but also artisans, middle-ranking peasants and even the lower nobility were at risk. Everyone could fall victim to ill fortune (illness, accident, premature death of the breadwinner, captivity, etc.) from which recovery in an age where social security was not guaranteed was more difficult and therefore could lead in many cases to impoverishment or even destitution.

Accidental causes

For centuries it has been recognized that poverty is often accompanied by illness or its social and economic consequences. Despite health insurance and welfare progammes, disease and its effects remain numerically important as a cause of poverty up to the twentieth century. The report of the English Poor Law Commission of 1909, for example, stated: 'Sickness is ... admittedly one of the chief causes of pauperism (dependency), and the more chronic its character and the longer its duration, the greater likelihood of its producing dependence .... We estimate that at least one-half of the total cost of pauperism is swallowed up in direct dealing with sickness .... '[1]

---

[1] Quoted in Antonio Ciocco and Dorothy Perrott, 'Statistics on sickness as cause of Poverty. An historical review of U.S. and English data', *Journal of the History of Medicine and Allied Sciences* 12 (1957), 57.

In an age which did not yet know a national health service or any other form of compulsory health insurance the effects of prolonged illness or sudden death during an epidemic were disastrous. It meant the bringing down of the formerly self-sufficient lower income groups to the ranks of the destitute. When the victim recovered, he emerged ensnared in debts incurred during his malady. Epidemic diseases incapacitated at least as many people as they killed, thus reducing income and assets as well as leaving orphans and widows in their wake. On a European scale it is impossible to impose any pattern on the appearance of epidemics such as plague, influenza, typhus, typhoid fever or smallpox, but even within national boundaries there was seldom a rigid pattern to the outbreaks. From the Black Death in 1348 until the beginning of the eighteenth century, outbreaks of the plague occurred every ten or fifteen years in the larger European towns, often killing between one-tenth and one-fifth of the urban population. For an analysis of the demographic, social and economic impact of the plague on a small community, we can take the town of Uelzen in northern Germany. Here the plague of 1566 killed 23 per cent of the population of 1,180. Another outbreak in 1597 carried off 33 per cent of a population numbering 1,540. The high death-rate for plague may be contrasted with a dysentery epidemic in the same town in 1599 which killed 'only' about 14 per cent of the population. Great urban centres were naturally the places where outbreaks of the plague occurred rather frequently and the death toll was very high during severe epidemics. Venice, for example, lost in 1575/6 more than 46,000 of its population of about 170,000, a proportion of 27 per cent. For Naples and Genoa we have estimates which indicate that both cities lost nearly half their population in the plague of 1656. Plague was most fatal in overcrowded suburbs of towns where the lower classes lived. Bills of mortality and eye witness reports show the epidemics taking their origin in the poorest suburbs. An analysis of the incidence of plague in some Europeans cities (London, Amiens, Augsburg) has shown that the plague broke out in some of the poorest quarters and than was spread to other areas of the town.

Why the poor were particularly prone to epidemic diseases is evident from a glance at the inadequacy of their diet and the unhygienic conditions in which they lived. Under such circumstances both the spreading of infection and the general low resistance to epidemic diseases are easily understandable. Figures available for some European cities suggest that it was the common people and not the rich who suffered principally when the plague struck. Not surprisingly, a frequent result of this linkage between plague and the poor was a marked increase in repressive measures directed not only against vagabonds but also against the native indigents. Italian city states pioneering in plague legislation and the management of public health were the first to ban marginal groups (among them also beggars and mendicants) for fear of plague. In fifteenth-century Sienna as well as in seventeenth-century Barcelona indigents and itinerants were suspected of being plague carriers and therefore made targets of preventive social control (e.g. expulsion, stigmatization).

Plague epidemics were not only a 'symptom of poverty' (Paul Slack) in early modern Europe but were also one of the major causes of indigence since they totally disrupted the urban economy. The ban on bringing in outside merchandise (e.g. raw materials) also had an impact on employment and marketing of goods. Especially in the important textile industries many people were thus out of work when an epidemic struck the city. This means that they were in most cases without money to buy food. More people than before were therefore in need of public or ecclesiastical poor relief. An epidemic in Salisbury in 1627, for example, left half the population of the town in need of relief. For early seventeenth-century Augsburg we have evidence that during the same outbreak of the plague 2,400 households (out of 10,000), numbering about 9,000 members (out of a total population of about 45,000) received a special relief (called *Brechhilfe*), providing indigent citizens not only with payments in kind (bread, flour, lard, firewood) but also with money for buying medicine. In most quarters of the city the majority of poor relief recipients were weavers. When the plague struck Toledo in the years 1598–9 the lower classes were less fortunate. There were frequent complaints about the poor 'who wander through the streets, begging and sick, because they find no relief and nowhere to sleep'.[2] It was only in April 1599 that the town council managed to find 400 ducats for poor relief, which, of course, was not enough for the many people in need.

Although the plague struck with an unusual ferocity, it was – like the other virulent epidemics – in quantitative terms a less important threat to the family economy than the daily burden caused by common diseases. A prolonged illness or a permanent physical debility could, more than anything else, push an individual or a family over the narrow boundary between poverty and indigence. For if someone in health had problems in making ends meet, the incapacity to work aggravated his already precarious financial situation and social dislocation was likely to ensue. It is therefore important to keep in mind that it was not primarily the cost of health care (help by non-professional healers was sometimes equally expensive!) which quickly used up the small savings or other financial

[2] Quoted in Linda Martz, *Poverty and Welfare in Habsburg, Spain* (Cambridge, 1983), p. 155.

and social resources of the population at the lower end of the economic scale. When the main earner was sick, it became more difficult for a family to raise money for the ordinary cost of living. And when the person died on his sickbed the dependants had to find a livelihood and were often forced to acquit debts incurred during previous episodes of illness. In eighteenth-century Lyon, for example, a master weaver, potentially capable of earning 40–50 sols per day and with capital assets of 600 livres, when struck by a fatal illness, left his widow with only a small fortune which was outweighed by his liabilities.

Although ecclesiastical and lay authorities often varied in their approaches to the problem of defining indigency, we always find acceptance of the role of sickness in poverty. This is manifest not only in the legislation which in one way or another provided more medical care to the indigent, but primarily in the basic tenet which was restated from time to time, to wit: that sickness and its consequences are distinctive features of the 'deserving' poor. Although the importance of sickness as a causative element of poverty had been indicated since the late Middle Ages, we do not find until the middle of the nineteenth century any real attempt to measure the extent to which sickness is responsible for poverty. However, from recent studies on poor relief we learn that between 10 and 25 per cent of persons relying on outdoor relief were sick; furthermore that old age or permanent disability was the cause of destitution in more than half of the persons described as ill. As shown in Table 2, which classifies specific illnesses cited in early modern sources on poor relief, the maladies which affected the poor were many and varied. Many of these physical disabilities reflect the impact of insufficient diet and insanitary living conditions on the health of the lower classes. Blindness, for example, could be caused by malnutrition (avitaminosis). Injuries incurred at work often maimed a man or woman for life. This partly explains the large number of people described as 'lame' by poor relief authorities. The same applies to indigents who suffered from paralysis or had difficulties in walking because of missing limbs. Among those poor and disabled persons were many soldiers who because of such afflictions could rarely find employment, and thus were forced to beg to survive. Only in the late seventeenth and early eighteenth century did various European governments try to redress this problem, either by establishing special public funds or by building hospitals for disabled soldiers. Unemployability also explains the rather large number of mentally handicapped who appear in many lists of poor relief recipients. These halfwits were often forced to wander from place to place, surviving on what little food and money they received by begging in the streets.

Table 2. *Physical disabilities of beggars and poor relief recipients in early modern Europe (sample)*

DISABILITY/ILLNESS	Toledo 1598		Lower Saxony 1651–1799		Aix-en-Provence 1724	
	n	%	n	%	n	%
Lame	28	15.0	192	24.1	41	24.8
Maimed (soldiers)	1	0.5	187	23.5	1	0.6
Sick (not specified)	14	7.5	103	12.9	7	4.2
Frail	16	8.5	96	12.1	1	0.6
Blind	14	7.5	71	8.9	24	14.5
Epileptic	2	1.1	44	5.5	3	1.8
Fractured/missing limbs	22	11.8	26	3.3	49	29.6
Insane	–	–	22	2.7	20	12.1
Deaf and/or dumb	–	–	19	2.4	1	0.6
Without tongue	10	5.3	12	1.5	–	–
Crippled	–	–	10	1.3	–	–
Cancer	–	–	6	0.8	–	–
Pocks	22	11.8	2	0.3	1	0.6
Other illnesses and illness not given	58	31.0	7	0.9	17	10.3
TOTAL	187	100.0	797	100.0	165	100.0

Sources: Calculated on Linda Martz, *Poverty and Welfare in Habsburg Spain* (Cambridge, 1983), p. 154; Ingeborg Titz-Matuszak, 'Mobilität der Armut – Das Almosenwesen im 17. und 18. Jahrhundert im südniedersächsischen Raum', *Plesse-Archiv* 24 (1988), 66ff.; Cissie C. Fairchilds, *Poverty and Charity in Aix-en-Provence 1640–1789* (Baltimore, 1976), p. 114.

However, one has to be careful not to generalize such scanty and sparse information on the disease conditions and physical disabilities of the poor. From these limited observations it should be clear that the study of the interrelationship of disease and poverty must take into account the pre-disease economic status of the individual and the nature of the disease itself. The impact of disease is not the same for everybody, not even for those who belong to the so-called 'lower classes'. But the difference depends also on the nature of the disease, as a future social history of epidemics will surely demonstrate.

Warfare was another major cause of poverty. The great wars which afflicted early modern Europe (the Great Peasants' War, the Huguenot Wars, the Thirty Years' War, the English Civil War, the War of the Palatinate 1688–97, the various Turkish Wars, the Seven Years' War, etc.) further increased the number of the destitute. The negative direct effects of warfare (loss of goods and chattels, death of the breadwinner, financial ruin by levies and taxes) were less significant than the indirect effects of war which include famine, the spread of disease and subsistence migration. A report on the impact of the *Fronde* on the area around Paris, drawn up in 1652, speaks of 'villages and hamlets deserted and bereft of clergy, streets infected by stinking carrion and dead bodies lying exposed, houses without doors or windows, everything reduced to cesspools and stables, and above all the sick and dying, with no bread, meat, medicine, fire, beds, linen or covering, and no priest, doctor, surgeon or anyone to comfort them'.[3] An English chronicler noted in 1587 that 'the dearth of corn yet remains ... and yet this country is further charged with ammunition and harness, expecting and providing for invasions and wars, which maketh the common sort to fall into poverty for want of trade, so that divers fall to robbing and stealing'.[4]

While there are some historical studies on early modern Europe which tell us exactly how war brought about a decline in wealth and economic status, we hardly have investigations providing basic data on the question of the extent to which war uprooted people and forced them to require assistance from the community. During the seventeenth and eighteenth centuries, to take one well-documented example, Germany on the whole and north Germany in particular was afflicted by many wars. In Lower Saxony, a region only moderately hit by wars, many people (1,726 out of a total of 9,418 foreigners asking for charity) received alms from various local agencies because they claimed that they had fled from the atrocities committed by the French army during the War of the Palatinate (1688–97). For 1,165 of these refugees or displaced persons we have data which allow us to differentiate between three major groups of indigents: 74 per cent of them were male, 46 per cent were female, and 7 per cent were children, in which case no gender was given. The evidence seems to be conclusive that the war effected not only men and women but whole families. It is therefore probable that a long series of exhausting wars resulted in growing pauperization. In certain circumstances wars could, however, also lead to a decrease in the number of poor persons.

Not only innocent civilians were pauperized when a fully fledged war ravaged towns and countryside. Often enough the numbers of the poor were increased by demobilized soldiers. Among the identifiable types of vagrants in sixteenth-century Württemberg, wandering soldiers seeking employment as mercenaries made up by far the most fearsome single group. Many contemporaries were aware of this perennial social problem, among them Sir Thomas More who in his most famous book *Utopia* (1516) pointed out that in inter-war periods demobilized soldiers and

[3] Quoted in Henry Kamen, *The Iron Century: Social Change in Europe 1550–1660* (London, 1976), p. 44.   [4] Quoted in Slack, *Poverty*, p. 51.

redundant retainers 'were thus destitute of service [that they] either starve for hunger, or manfully play the thieves'.[5] The problem of ex-servicemen was one which waxed and waned. In normal years it could be contained without too much difficulty. When it coincided with a subsistence crisis or an economic slump it became a real threat to the rural population and a nightmare for the enforcers of law and order.

Cyclical causes

The steadily rising population (cf. Figure 3) – a trend which was interrupted only by occasional incidents of one of the three scourges bewailed by the Litany ('a peste, fame et bello, libera nos Domine') – led to increasing pressure on limited resources that failed to grow as quickly and therefore brought about a steady rise in prices. It is interesting to juxtapose the inflation of the early modern period with the same economic phenomenon in the twentieth century. First it must be said that the causes of inflation were different. Today wage increases above productivity growth, increases in taxation, and rising prices of industrial raw products (e.g. oil) are more important than population trends. In our times inflation also has a different face. In early modern Europe the annual inflation rate was rather low (in England the annual increase between 1532 and 1660 was 0.86 per cent), but calculating the arithmetic mean is somewhat misleading because it mitigates frequent and catastrophic short-term leaps in the price-curve. Today many industrial countries have a much higher annual inflation rate but a subaverage price-increase as far as agricultural products are concerned.

Not only modern economic historians but also some contemporaries already surmised a link between a rising population and the scarcity of foodstuffs due to limited agricultural resources. An anonymous English pamphleteer writing in the second half of the sixteenth century stated that the main causes of scarcity and want were: 'A barren soyle. fear & commodities/Inhabitants abounding. Yet veary many ydell & poore/ Domesticall comodities not well estemed nor vented, at home nor abroad.'[6] The most popular explanation given by contemporary writers was, however, that the price rise resulted from European imports of American silver or high-handed decisions to debase the coinage by reducing the percentage of silver. From the second half of the sixteenth century England was almost the only major European country to have a currency that did not get heavily devalued. When the amount of silver in coins was greatly reduced under the reign of Philip III or in Poland

---

[5] Thomas More, *The Utopia of Sir Thomas More*, ed. J. H. Lupton (Oxford, 1895), book I.   [6] British Library, Lansdowne MS 55, f. 33r.

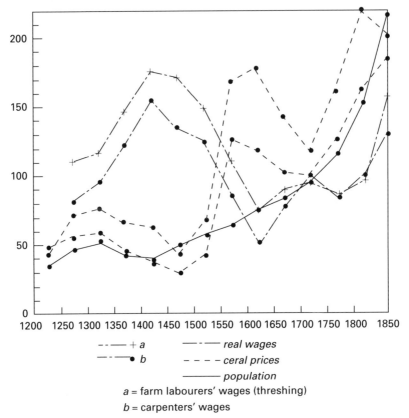

--·--+ a   —·— real wages

—·—• b   – – – – ceral prices

——— population

a = farm labourers' wages (threshing)

b = carpenters' wages

This graph is intended to give a diagrammatic picture, and therefore extreme variations are omitted

Figure 3 Indices of population and real wages, 1200–1851 (period 1771–45 = 100)
Source: Slicher van Bath, *Agrarian History of Western Europe AD 500–1850* (London, 1963), p. 103, Fig. 13.

between 1578 and 1650, wage-earners were the first to feel the pinch of poverty. Although monetary inflation emanating from America or home-made debasements and currency crises (*Kipper- und Wipperzeit* in Germany of the 1620s) may have played a part in the price rise, it was certainly not the main factor. The inflation was a selective one which means that the basic consumer goods in particular became more expensive. Food prices rose about twice as fast as those of other commodities. The so-called 'price-revolution' of the 'long' sixteenth century expressed itself in a sharp rise in agricultural prices and in a shift in the prices for foodstuffs as compared with the prices of manufactured products. There were, however, differences in the way individual agricultural prices worked out; the prices for cereals rose further than those for meat and animal products. It thus can be assumed that grain prices rose, and not just occasionally as a result of bad harvests, but quite generally and extending over many generations. This, taken by and large, was a new phenomenon, since earlier centuries, particularly the first hundred years after the Black Death, had seen a consistent fall in agricultural prices. But from the late fifteenth century onwards this downward trend was over and would remain so for generations to come.

Research into the history of prices in various European countries reveals three secular trends (cf. Figure 3), as far as the long-term movements of cereal prices are concerned:

1 an upward trend, which started in the thirteenth century and came to a sudden halt in the late Middle Ages,
2 another upsurge in the sixteenth century interrupted by the impact of the Thirty Years' War on Central Europe,
3 a third upward trend during the eighteenth century characterized by short-term and sometimes contrasting movements that come towards each other in the late nineteenth and early twentieth century.

Wages did not keep up with the rapid development of prices. At the beginning of the seventeenth century weavers and carpenters earned twice as much as at the beginning of the sixteenth century, while the price for food had almost tripled. Studies by Wilhelm Abel and other economic historians have made quite clear that the purchasing power of wages declined by almost 50 per cent on average in major German cities between 1500 and 1700. Only in the eighteenth century does there seem to be a small improvement in some cities at least, but even then the real wages did not reach again the level they had at the beginning of the early modern period.

What this bare statistic meant for the subsistence of an average household can be explained by the following example. In 1500 a building worker living in Augsburg could buy with his annual wage 1.5 times as many commodities as were actually needed by a household consisting of five members. At the beginning of the seventeenth century his income covered no more than 75 percent of his household expenses. If starvation was to be avoided this household had to find additional sources of income. Therefore it does not come as a surprise that in times of soaring food prices the lower-income groups often had no other choice than to supplement their wages by private charity or public poor relief. In the city of Trier, for instance, about 20 per cent of the recipients of outdoor poor relief only appear once in the account books of the *Almosenamt*, which indicates that in most of these cases poor relief must have been granted in a temporary situation of economic and financial distress. Modest improvements in real wages in the second half of the seventeenth century may have reduced the proportion of wage-earners seeking relief, although the total number of destitutes was still rather high. When allowance is made for differences in time and space, it remains true that from the sixteenth to the eighteenth century over most of Europe a drastic decline in living standards made the common man, both in town and countryside, feel the bitter taste of poverty. This is made plain by Figure 3, which illustrates that it is more important to look at a man's real wages rather than to refer to his nominal or money wages. In a less flexible (and only partially market-oriented) economy than ours is today, with large sections of the labouring classes subsisting on relatively fixed incomes, the impact of creeping inflation could be disastrous.

So far we have considered only the long-term trends of agricultural prices. Now we shall examine the short-run fluctuations caused by harvest failures. The Englishman Gregory King, writing in the seventeenth century, estimated that with a harvest 20 per cent below the normal or average level, grain prices rose 80 per cent. If the deficit was 50 per cent the increase was 450 per cent. In a normal crisis the consequence of high food prices was not starvation but general impoverishment. However, there were crisis years in the sixteenth and seventeenth centuries, when grain prices rose to a staggering height and contemporaries complained that poverty and hunger were mounting in quantity and intensity. The welfare administrator of the City of Strasbourg, Lucas Hackfurt, outlined in the memorandum which he directed to the town council the reason why suddenly so many people asked for relief in the city:

What drives the poor here in such numbers? The answer: the great need and the dearness of all things. And where does the dearness come from? From God. Why did he send it to us? Because of our disbelief and sins, our ingratitude and selfishness, from which develops great cruelty and unbrotherly hardship for our neighbours.[7]

Hackfurt identified the underlying cause of escalating prices due to scarcity. God wanted to punish mankind for its sins by troubling rich and poor alike with devastating harvest failures. Scarcity, however, must not be mistaken for famine. The Swiss theologian Ludwig Lavater explained in one of his sermons in 1571, when Zurich like many other European

---

[7] Quoted in Otto Winckelmann, *Das Fürsorgewesen der Stadt Strassburg vor und nach der Reformation bis zum Ausgang des sechzehnten Jahrhunderts* (Leipzig, 1922), pt II, p. 147 (English translation of this passage by M. U. Chrisman).

cities suffered from a severe subsistence crisis, that one had to differentiate:

Dearth means that anything, which people must have and have to live upon – be it food, beverages, clothes, firewood, accommodation – is available, but cannot be acquired at a moderate sum of money. If one wants to have it, one has to spend twice or three times as much money. Famine, however, is if one cannot buy food, drinks and other things even though one is willing to pay for it.[8]

A famine or subsistence crisis occurred when there were several bad harvests in a row, as for example, in 1527–34, 1565–7, 1571–4, 1594–7, 1624–5, 1637–9, 1659–62, 1691–3, 1739–41 and 1771–4. Three great famines – those of 1527–31, 1594–7 and 1659–62 – had a particularly disastrous impact on early modern Europe. In those years one can find many entries in burial registers mentioning that a 'poor hungerstarved beggar child' or a 'poor fellow' had died 'for want of food and maintenance'. Seventeenth-century Russian chronicles report that there was a great famine in all of Russia from 1650 to 1652 caused by excessive rains and floods and that people were forced to 'eat sawdust etc.' and that many people died despite the Tsar's permission of free grain imports. The possibility of starvation depended on a great number of independent factors and not on the weather alone. The major factors influencing food supply were: demand (size of population); degree of land exploitation (crop yields); ease of transport (customs barriers, access to food markets by land or by sea); presence of wars (boycott measures, devastations); weather (unsual heat or cold, heavy rainfall).

In cases where crop failures caused shortages the sequence of events was as follows.

1 A series of very bad years occurred in which harvests failed.
2 Stocks of grain diminished gradually as there was no further supply.
3 Food shortage which ensued caused a steep increase in grain prices.
4 To buy essential foodstuffs townspeople were forced to spend more on victuals. The demand for services and products of industry fell off.
5 Markets and trade stagnated. There was less demand for labourers. Wages remained low or sank still lower.
6 The lower classes did not have the money to buy food at the very high market prices and therefore had to be content with food in less quantity (likelihood of starvation) or of poorer quality (possibility of poisoning by ergot-infected grain).
7 The mortality rate rose. Death from hunger was rare, but susceptibility to disease may have increased by a low level of nourishment.

---

[8] Quoted in Wilhelm Abel, *Massenarmut und Hungerkrisen im vorindustriellen Europa: Versuch einer Synopsis* (Hamburg and Berlin, 1974), p. 38 (my translation).

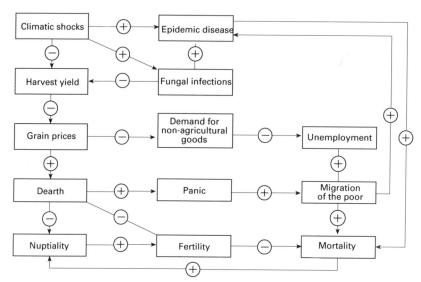

Figure 4 Model of demographic and subsistence crises
Source: Jacques Dupâquier, 'Demographic and subsistence crises in
France, 1650–1725', *Famine, Disease and the Social Order in Early
Modern Society*, ed. John Walter and Roger Schofield (Cambridge,
1989), p. 199.

8 The number of marriages also declined and resulted (about nine
   month later) in a slump of the birth rate.
9 As soon as better harvests were brought in, food supply was back to
   normal and the subsistence crisis and its concomitant, the demographic
   crisis, ended. An upward trend developed and continued until poor
   harvests plunged town and country into yet another crisis.

The theory of subsistence crises was first formulated by the French
economic historian Jean Meuvret in 1946. In the meantime supporters of
this theory have adopted a more flexible attitude, taking into account the
role of epidemic and fungal infections in explaining the conspicuous
variations in nuptiality, fertility and mortality. To make the complex
relationship between the various factors clearer they have been represented schematically in Figure 4. Previous research ignored, for example,
the problems of regional differences and the fact that we still do not know
exactly the proportion of the population who were dependent upon the
market for grain or employment.

Vulnerability to famine was both regional and socially specific. There
were many areas that were spared from the disastrous consequences of
famines resulting from poor harvests. Some towns had municipal grain

stores which people could turn to in times of scarcity. Even whole regions succeeded in getting rid of the constant threat of a food crisis, as, for instance, England which had slipped the shadow of famine by the mid seventeenth century, in sharp contrast to most other west European countries, because of the well-established improvement in the productivity of English agriculture (increase in the cultivated area and adoption of improved agricultural techniques, e.g. a mix between spring- and winter-sown crops which helped to mitigate the impacts of harvest failures).

There is another variable, however, which is particularly relevant to pauperization: the state of the European economy generally. A division of this period into three reflects more or less the decisive breaks in European economic history between 1450 and 1850, although this period was full of ups and downs, and these were partly the effect, partly the cause, of disproportionate situations in the particular economic sectors, notably in town and countryside.

The first period, from 1450 to 1630, might be characterized as one of economic expansion. Growing demand went hand in hand with qualitative transformations of proto-industrial and agrarian production. Agrarian changes brought a shift from personal to economic dependence and led in the long run to rural depopulation, deforestation, agrarian stagnation and consequently an absolute impoverishment of the rural masses. The rising demand also gave a boost to most labour-intensive industries. Despite the growth of mass production in the 'long' sixteenth century no decisive step was undertaken in the direction of a new division of labour (putting-out system, manufactures) or technological improvements (mechanization). Centralized production could be found – to a certain extent – in a few branches of industry, such as shipbuilding, mining and metal-working. If there was a 'rise of capitalism' (Richard Tawney) it was essentially commercial capitalism which prospered most. Only a few entrepreneurs and merchants may be considered beneficiaries of these changes. Contemporaries were aware of the fact that industrial growth was no synonym for prosperity. The German *Meistersinger* Hans Sachs, in his dialogue on avarice, blamed the merchant entrepreneurs for paying their workers so little that their wives and children lived in poverty. The town secretary of the city of Leiden, Jan van Houtte, accused in 1577 the rich textile merchants of exploiting their workers, stating that 'the poor workers – better call them slaves – after having worked a whole week, are compelled to beg on Sundays to supplement their wages'.[9] In short, the rise of commercial capitalism implied the

---

[9] Jan van Houtte quoted in Catharina Lis and Hugo Soly, *Poverty and Capitalism in Pre-industrial Europe* (Hassocks, Sussex, 1979), p. 69.

polarization of society and the impoverishment of innumerable artisans, journeymen, apprentices and day-labourers in the four most labour-intensive industries: textiles, construction, mining and metallurgy.

The second period, from 1630 to 1750, was one of depression and changing economic patterns. The impoverishment processes which had reached such enormous proportions in the sixteenth century remained at work in the seventeenth and early eighteenth century. The crisis of agrarian productivity which most European countries (with the exception of England) experienced in this period had catastrophic results for the rural population. With agricultural reorganization ruled out by the policies of absolutist rulers, maximum exploitation of the peasantry was achieved through sharecropping tenures (e.g. in Spain and in France) or the revival of feudal obligations (e.g. in Brandenburg and in Prussia). In England the development of agrarian capitalism accelerated the impoverishment process in the countryside. By the end of the seventeenth century about 40 per cent of the English rural population were forced to abandon the land, giving them a choice of three alternatives: wage labour, industry or migration.

The industrial areas of seventeenth-century Europe also witnessed major socio-economic changes and shifts in production. The Italian cloth industry suffered a heavy blow and nearly disappeared from the European export market, as the textile industry in Holland and England entered a phase of spetacular growth. Wool-weavers in Venice, Milan, Como and other Italian cities could no longer compete with the new draperies in England which had a decisive advantage because of the low price which the latter paid for raw materials and labour and the government support which they received. The number of wool-weavers in the major Italian export centres for textiles dropped in this period to almost 5 per cent of their sixteenth-century total. While thousands of craftsmen and workers lost their livelihoods in some industrial centres, in northern Italy and France in particular, more jobs were created in other areas of Europe (e.g. in Holland and England).

Another important change which occurred during the second period was the displacement of industry to the countryside. The textile industry moved gradually from town to countryside. By the beginning of the eighteenth century the bulk of all wool, linen, cotton and cloth in Europe was produced in the more rural districts of England, France, Germany, the Netherlands and Switzerland. This development undermined the already precarious socio-economic position of the vast majority of town-dwellers. In many urban centres with an important textile industry (e.g. Augsburg, Beauvais, Florence, Leiden) the vast majority of those receiving poor relief consisted of textile workers (among them small craftsmen as well as journeymen and casual workers). The 'industrial restructuring of Europe', as Catharina Lis and Hugo Soly called it, ultimately led to the proliferation of an agrarian and urban proletariat.

The third period, from 1750 to 1850, was one of agricultural progress and the breakthrough of industrial capitalism. Economic growth continued and coincided with a rapidly rising demand for manufactured goods. The booming international trade spurred on merchants and entrepreneurs to make use of the growing mass of poor cottars and rural paupers as an industrial workforce. The availability of a large and cheap labour force was a precondition for the expansion of the cottage industry – a process which is nowadays known as 'proto-industrialization'. After 1750 England was the first European state which experienced the transition from home industry, based on the family economy, to the factory system characterized by concentration of labour and mechanization of production. The expansion of urban and rural industries led to the disintegration of the guild system and the proletarianization of most artisans. Only drastically reduced wages enabled the smaller entrepreneurs and craftsmen to survive. As the possibilities of employment declined, the margins of subsistence grew narrower for significant sectors of the urban population. In late eighteenth-century Bruges, for example, more than 70 per cent of the master fustian weavers received poor relief. At the end of the eighteenth century the chairmen of the Antwerp cloth dressers' guild summarized the consequences of the breakthrough of industrial capitalism in their own city: 'The factories of this town accomplish nothing than enrichment of a few and impoverishment of innumerable widows and children.'[10]

The impoverishment of broad sections of the urban population, however, cannot be understood in isolation from developments in the countryside. There the gradual dissolution of the traditional peasant economy was important, too. A growing number of cottars were forced to search for new resources. In late eighteenth- and early nineteenth-century Piedmont, for example, over 20,000 peasants left their mountain villages each year for periods of six to nine months in search of employment elsewhere in Italy or France. During the first half of the nineteenth century the surplus population of many European towns consisted therefore of two largely distinct groups: on the one hand a pool of impoverished textile workers and on the other a reserve army of poor immigrants from rural areas who were prepared to accept the most badly paid jobs, especially casual labour. The final crisis of traditional peasant economy, fluctuations of urban commerce and overseas trade, and the

[10] Quoted in Lis and Soly, *Poverty*, pp. 169f.

acceleration in the development of industrial capitalism went thus hand in hand with massive impoverishment. In some regions and towns the rise of industrial capitalism signalled a basic decline while in others rapid industrialization and commercialization provided new employment opportunities. The switch from cottage industry to the factory system brought about economic growth in some areas and underdevelopment in others. A comparison between various European regions proves that pauperization in the first half of the nineteenth century cannot be related to the absence or presence of industrialization or modernization but have to be explained by pointing out the ambivalent effects of a new international division of labour which brought about a different spatial distribution of economic activities.

This periodization is undoubtedly rather schematic, but it serves to set the scene for the next section which deals with structural dependence. It suggests that from the late Middle Ages until the early stages of industrialization the waves of pauperism can be measured againsts the rhythms and crises of the early modern agrarian, trade and manufacturing economies.

Structural causes

Although the dimensions and extent of pauperism varied according to short-term business cycles and long-term transformations of the pre-industrial economy, the causes of poverty at the individual or family level display a remarkable continuity across the centuries. The fact that impoverishment had something to do with economic fluctuations and technological changes has for a long time directed historical attention towards the causes rather than the condition of poverty. Social historians are more and more aware of the fact that some economic and demographic phenomena can be better explained in terms of the life-cycle.

A graph (Figure 5) marks out the critical points in the life-cycle where public relief or private charity was likely to become necessary for the impoverished family or individual. The first phase of poverty starts in childhood. Children, especially the very young, were a major cause of pauperism because they put a great strain on a family's economic resources. The course of relief payments to such a household with young children can prove the changing costs of keeping children. Francis Smyth, a pauper living in Hedenham (Norfolk), was in receipt of parish poor relief after his wife had died in 1672 and had left him with four young children, aged twelve, eight and six, and a two-month-old baby daughter. There were peaks in the monthly amount he received, followed by a steady dropping over the years as the children got older. Payments

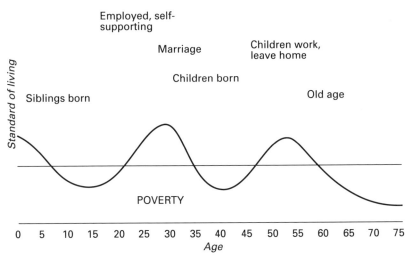

Figure 5 The life-cycle of impoverishment
Source : Robert Schwartz, *Policing the Poor in Eighteenth-Century France* (Chapel Hill, 1988), p. 106.

became steady when his second-youngest daughter became fifteen and ceased altogether when his youngest son reached the age of seventeen. This single case makes it already quite clear that children of either sex caused a 'deficit' in the family budget of the lower classes until about the age of fifteen when they became for the first time contributors rather than consumers within the family economy (see Plate 2). It is a reflection of the difficulties facing more or less 'complete' families (in a demographic sense) at this level of society. The breakdown of families by death or desertion of one parent was also in many cases the immediate cause of hardship among pauper children and juveniles in their early teens. This is brought to light by the hospital registers extant in many European municipal archives. Of 210 children under the age of fifteen confined to a hospital in eighteenth-century Bayeux (France), only 11 per cent came from complete families, and 38 per cent were orphans whose parents had died. The greater importance of the loss of the male head of the household is clear from the rest: 42 per cent of these children had lost their fathers, while only 6 per cent had been deprived of their mothers by an untimely death. Censuses for the poor in sixteenth- and seventeenth-century England depict almost the same pattern. As many as one-fifth of the destitute children in Norwich (1570) compared with one third in Salisbury (1635) were in effect orphans because the father either had died, or run away, or – in a few cases – he was in gaol.

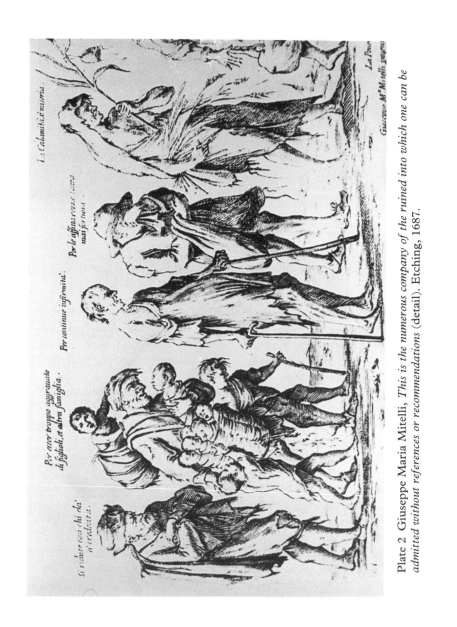

Plate 2 Giuseppe Maria Mitelli, *This is the numerous company of the ruined into which one can be admitted without references or recommendations* (detail). Etching, 1687.

Contemporary writers and observers were well aware of the high proportion of children among the poor eligible for relief. John Howes, for example, tells us that the survey made throughout London in the early 1550s showed a total of 2,160 persons in need of relief, of which 300 were 'fatherless children' and 350 'poore men overburdened with theire children'.[11] Children up to the age of fifteen constantly dominate lists of beggars. Of the beggars registered in Aix-en-Provence in 1724, 42 per cent were under the age of twenty. It is with these young people that the problem of unemployability comes to the fore. Youth and lack of training and skills often made it difficult for children who were forced to leave home very early to find employment. In 1532 Lucas Hackfurt mentions in his memorandum written for the Magistrate of the City of Strasbourg that

the citizens complain that young boys and girls go up and down the streets begging so that no one can eat in peace .... Even if they should find a job, they do not have the clothes they would need – and what citizen's wife (assuming they were given a servant's position) would let herself be followed by such a rag-a-muffin ... ? Nor is there any craftsman who would teach such a lad for no pay.[12]

Alarmed by the great and increasing number of begging children in the streets, many European cities developed schemes for coping with the problem of destitute children. In London, Christ's Hospital was designed 'to take oute all the streates all the fatherless children, and other poor mens children, that were not able to kepe them'.[13] In an eighteenth-century French city (Aix-en-Provence), as in many other early modern towns of this size, considerable range of charitable care was available for poor children. The Hôtel-Dieu would nurse the younger children, while the Charité would take care of the older ones. On reaching maturity they might receive a dowry or an apprenticeship from one of many charitable funds in the city. The beginning of the active working life of the labouring poor was a matter subject to different definitions and assumptions. Contemporary sources make different and at times conflicting judgments on the question of when the young should become self-supporting. By using the age seventeen, fifteen or even twelve as a guideline, poor law officials in various European cities attempted to take into account the dependency and employment difficulties of boys and girls. The poor themselves were often forced to draw the line at the age of twelve or even earlier. Boys were more likely to earn money outside the home and found themselves detached from family at an earlier age than

---

[11] John Howes, MS (1582), ed. W. Lempriere (London, 1904), p. 21.
[12] Quoted in Winckelmann, *Strassburg*, pt 2, pp. 157ff. (translation of this passage by M. U. Chrisman).   [13] John Howes, MS (1582), ed. W. Lempriere, p. 11.

girls who instead could be employed in the home industry, at least until they reached the age of marriage.

The only extended period of relief from economic pressures was in late adolescence and early adulthood (age group 15–35), when the fortunes of a youth could improve for a time, as efforts to seek a living on his or her own met with some success and he or she – still unmarried – was not yet burdened with costly offspring.

The second phase of poverty occurred roughly from ages thirty-five to fifty and involved those persons who had married in their late twenties or later, depending on whether and when they were establishing a household, and had children living at home. With the marriage and the birth of children the family's fortune began to decline. Another structural feature of poverty in this age group is the rather high proportion of widows left with their offspring or single households with children. Recipients of poor relief in early modern European towns differed in their household structure from that of the overall urban population. Poor households were usually very small and rarely made up of complete nuclear families with a married couple at their head. More than half of the households consisted of single persons, usually widows, and some of the rest were also headed by women. This also accounts for the sex ratio among recipients of poor relief (see Table 3).

Provided the family unit remained unshattered, the lower classes might look forward to a brief interlude of meagre comfort when the parents were in their late forties and early fifties. By then the departure of elder children had relieved economic strain associated with a large family household.

The third stage was old age. Censuses of the poor and lists of poor relief recipients from all over Europe show that the ages of the poor differ from the age distribution of the total or normal population and that the very old and the very young were over-represented among the poor. The Norwich census of 1570, for example, underlines the degrading impotence of the aged. Those regarded as totally unable to work were nearly all elderly. In late eighteenth-century Grenoble more than half of the bread recipients were sixty-one and older.

Although a closer look at the life-cycle of impoverishment reveals the underlying structure of extreme hardship, this impression cannot be regarded as a complete picture of the main causes of poverty in early modern Europe. On the one hand, families often had to cope with more than one disadvantage, on the other hand it is obvious that the relative importance of different 'structural' causes of poverty varied from place to place. The most common misfortunes and the proportion of families affected by them (shown in Figure 6) tell us something about the various

Table 3. *Sex ratio of poor relief recipients in selected European communities, sixteenth to eighteenth centuries (percentage)*

	Strasbourg 1523	Toledo 1573	North Walsham 1706/7	Grenoble 1771/4	Würzburg 1791
male	31	37	28	33	18
female	69	63	62	67	82

Sources: Thomas Fischer, *Städtische Armut und Armenfürsorge im 15. und 16. Jahrhundert* (Göttingen, 1979), pp. 128ff.; Martz, *Spain*, pp. 204ff.; Tim Wales, 'Poverty, poor relief and the life-cycle: some evidence from seventeenth-century Norfolk', *Land, Kinship and Life-cycle*, ed. R. M. Smith (Cambridge, 1985), Table 11.3; Kathryn Norberg, *Rich and Poor in Grenoble 1600–1814* (Berkeley, 1985), p. 186; Hans-Christoph Rublack, *Gescheiterte Reformation* (Stuttgart, 1978), p. 153.

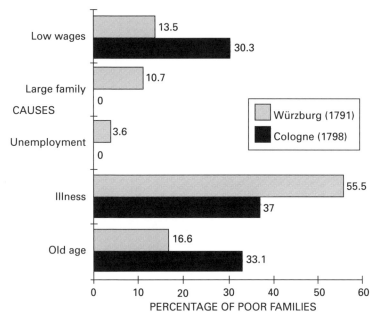

Figure 6 The causes of poverty in some selected European towns
Sources: Hans-Christoph Rublack, *Gescheiterte Reformation* (Stuttgart, 1978), p. 153; Norbert Finzsch, *Obrigkeit und Unterschichten* (Stuttgart, 1990), p. 304.

Table 4. *Occupational classification of the recipients of poor relief in selected European towns, sixteenth to eighteenth centuries (percentage distribution)*

	Trier 1591–1650	Augsburg 1622	Antwerp 1780
Textile and clothing crafts	17.7	44.6	57.0
Leather and fur crafts	6.1	13.8	—
Construction	12.2	5.0	6.3
Metal ware	5.8	1.7	0.8
Food and drink trades	10.1	3.8	—
Commerce and retailing	14.6	3.0	3.8
Others	33.5	28.1	32.1

Source : Maria Ackels, 'Das Trierer städtische Almosenamt im 16. und 17. Jahrhundert: Ein Beitrag zur Analyse sozialer Unterschichten', *Kurtrierisches Jahrbuch* 4 (1984), 95; Bernd Roeck, *Eine Stadt in Krieg und Frieden: Studien zur Geschichte der Reichsstadt Augsburg zwischen Kalenderstreit und Parität* (Göttingen, 1989), p. 525; Catharina Lis, *Social Change and the Labouring Poor, Antwerp 1770–1860* (New Haven and London, 1986), p. 187.

incidences and causes of impoverishment in some selected European towns.

To turn from size of the household and its age structure to the relationship between low-income professions and poverty allows us to identify more precisely the differences and relative weaknesses of the family structures. Within the pre-industrial economy, the distribution of earnings was markedly splayed, reflecting not only the sexual division of labour and the life-cycle of the individuals but also the unequal distribution of wealth among occupational groups. No weaver in seventeenth-century Augsburg, for example, could earn as much as a butcher or taverner. And we have studies on the hierarchy of earnings between different skills in late eighteenth- and early nineteenth-century Florence and Antwerp which prove that no silk-reeder, for example, could earn as much as a tailor.

The distribution of occupational groups among poor relief recipients displays in almost 'classic' fashion the profile of a pre-industrial urban economy (shown in Table 4). One has, however, to keep in mind that even within the same trade, standards of living diverged widely because wage rates varied greatly according to craft status, age, local conditions and sex. Some of the most extreme differences in wage rates existed, for example, in the textile industry. In most cases individual occupations were highly stratified, but there were some occupations which almost invariably implied a certain wealth level – obviously merchants were almost all near the top, and weavers and textile workers almost always near the bottom. In other early modern towns the rural sector was still important. Agricultural labourers were notoriously impoverished as we know from studies on the distribution of wealth in French and German towns. Especially bad was the situation of the simple day-labourer who worked in the vineyards and fields in the precincts of the city. Only a few were hired by the year; the rest had to stand in the hiring corner of the marketplace, hoping to be engaged for a few days or weeks at a time. And when they found a job their wages were rather low: 16–18 *Heller* per day was the rule (female workers only 10 *Heller*) in Frankfurt am Main in the middle of the sixteenth century. At the end of the century a male vineyard worker could buy for his daily wage 5.7 litres of grain (his female counterpart only 3.4 litres) which is much less than, for example, the daily wage of a building-worker who earned the equivalent of 8 litres of grain per day on average. Another occupational group which contributed a disproportionately large number to those who depended on charity were the petty artisans, in particular those trades which suffered from overcrowding (most often weavers and shoemakers but also some building trades).

The list of occupations declared by those arrested for mendicancy or vagrancy in this period shows a similar picture. The pattern for men confirms the precarious position of wage-earners in notoriously poor trades. Agricultural workers, casual labourers and textile artisans, and soldiers, sailors and servants and apprentices were predominant among the wayfaring poor of early modern Europe. Beyond that, the pattern varied according to the economic profile of each city and its hinterland. In sixteenth-century England, for example, most vagrants had worked in lowly positions before they took to the road. About a third were engaged in the production of food, leather goods, cloth and metal wares, and in mining or building; at least a quarter were servants, apprentices, journeymen, labourers and harvest workers; almost a fifth were petty chapmen, makers and sellers of 'small wares', entertainers and tinkers; and a tenth soldiers and mariners. The remainder included a variety of professionals – healers, students, clerics and even gentlemen. In the seventeenth century this pattern began to change slightly. There was, however, according to the study of A. L. Beier, no major shift from one industry to another but rather a drift away from traditional industries due to the crisis in the cloth trade.

The contribution of the female partner to the setting-up of a household was obviously no less important although the relative invisibility of women's work indicates the nature of their working lives. Women had no access to most recognized trades and crafts, and when they were married and had small children they had to see to the care of the household as well as their own work which was still necessary in order to keep the family economy going. Unfortunately, poor law officials rarely recorded the occupations of women. The most common experience for women living in early modern Europe was to work in a wide variety of poorly paid jobs. In the rural areas a young girl or a housewife who could not afford to renounce or shift her employ upon marriage assumed various responsibilities, either in badly paid jobs in domestic industry or in husbandry for which there was often no monetary remuneration but payment in kind. In the town the occupational choice for girls and women was different. Many of them, as long as they were unmarried, became household servants, enjoying at least some kind of protection by the employer (in the more affluent households at least). They received in most cases an adequate amount of food, clothing and even small amenities (e.g. gifts) on a regular basis. Other female workers were not so well off; they had difficulties remaining employed because of economic slumps and had to be content with low wages. The daily pay of people hired to fold draperies in Caen (France) at the beginning of the eighteenth century provides a striking example of this disadvantage inflicted on women: two or three *sous* for children, five *sous* for women, and twelve *sous* for men. According to figures we have for eighteenth-century Antwerp, a large proportion of adult women registered as paupers were lace-makers (51 per cent). The second-largest group of female poor relief recipients (17 per cent) had various jobs in the textile industry (cleaning and sorting of wool, pressing and folding of cloth, sewing, spinning). Almost the same number of women had no occupation. The near absence of female servants from the list of recipients confirms what we have said about the relative job security in this sector of the urban labour market.

4   The extent of poverty

Poverty is a rather relative and variable concept because its definition is governed by the patterns of needs and values which exist in a given society. It is interesting to apply contemporary standards of need to the more recent past. When 1990 standards are applied to western Europe of the 1950s, for example, it appears that more people four decades ago were poor than were considered to be poor at the time. And if we were to use the standards of forty years ago and project them forward to today, we would find that 'poverty' had decidedly dwindled. Modern standards of need tend therefore to be unrealistic and lack a consistent historical perspective.

Measuring poverty

In the twentieth century precise conceptions of poverty may be worked out by social scientists and accepted by government. As far as the past is concerned, the historian has no choice but to adopt the criteria and definitions he comes across in the documents. Since the nature of these sources is so varied, most studies on the history of poverty have produced more impressionistic generalizations than systematic and comprehensive research on the prevalence of poverty in the 'world we have lost' (Peter Laslett). There are various problems in producing such studies. First, basic information – the still rather small welfare bureaucracy of early modern towns did not produce essential statistics – is just not available for most European countries before the nineteenth century. Censuses of the poor took place in some pre-industrial European cities but were not very common. When statistics do exist, they are often unreliable or estimates, as, for example, Gregory King's famous 'Scheme of the income and expense of the several families of England calculated for the year 1688', which lists 400,000 families of cottagers and paupers as well as 849,000 vagrants (among the gypsies, thieves and beggars).[1]

[1] Cf. Peter Laslett, *The World We Have Lost – Further Explored* (London, 1971), Table 1, pp. 32–3.

As well as the lack of quantitative information over the extent of poverty there is, second, the problem of selecting and evaluating the criteria according to which comparisons between towns and rural communities as well as between countries can be made. The same problem exists with regard to variations in the prevalence of poverty over time. The sources, as we already pointed out, refer to individuals or groups who have been labelled 'poor' according to criteria which often remain vague and vary according to the author of the document, the institution which stood behind him, and last but not least the period and the place which have inevitably left their mark on the observations by contemporaries.

The view put forward by most historians is therefore that the description, analysis and measuring of poverty in the past must proceed within the context of contemporary sources and not within a general theory of basic needs or social stratification. But this is easier said than done. Three groups of studies upon which a great deal of attention has recently been concentrated are more or less related. These are (a) studies of the form of social stratification within countries which are based on tax surveys; (b) studies of the number of poor relief recipients mentioned in records of early modern welfare institutions; and (c) studies of the scale and nature of poverty relying on data produced by early modern censuses of the poor. I will start by looking at the so-called 'fiscal poor' and consider the problems of using tax records as a basis for comparative analysis. I will then endeavour to show how the arbitrary or rather subjective distinction imposed by the selective and often inconsistent hand of poor relief agents can be used as a guideline for any attempt at quantification. This theme will be followed up by a discussion of the kind of problems presented to modern historians by contemporary censuses of the poor. Finally, I shall shed light on the topographical distribution of poverty within the municipal area.

Fiscal poor

Among the sources which define and count the poor are fiscal records. Tax assessments are often used used by historians as an approximation for the 'poverty line'. However, one should be aware that most taxation records from the early modern period register differences in wealth rather than income inequalities. It is therefore clear that nil or minimum assessments should not automatically be equated with destitution. Fiscal records do not provide us with an exact measure of the economic condition of the poor because they often include quite a range of wealth

Table 5. *'Fiscal poor' in early modern taxation records*

Place	Year	Total no. of taxed households/persons	exempt/have-nots No.	%
Urban communities				
Cologne	1582	4,062	189	4.7
Augsburg	1618	8,738	4240	48.5
Augsburg	1646	4,218	1570	37.2
Grenoble	1735	2,163	808	37.3
Lille	1740	15,710	7077	45.0
York	17th c.			20.0
Norwich	17th c.			62.0
Verona	1635	?	?	77.0
S. Gimignano	1670	?	?	75.0
Rural communities				
Warwickshire	1669–70	?	?	36.0
Hertfordshire	1662–90	?	?	39.0
Essex	1662–90	?	?	38.0
Flanders	1544	?	?	40.5
Brabant	1750	?	?	41.5
Westphalia (one village)	1536	44	10	22.7

Source : see Bibliography s.v. 'fiscal poor'.

within their exempt categories. And there is another problem in using taxation records as an indicator for the the extent of poverty. Tax assessments indicate geographical variations in the distribution of poverty more effectively than alterations over time because of changing criteria for exemption. Taxation records are therefore dogged by problems of representativeness and interpretation. However, in the absence of anything approaching a local or nationwide census of the poor, historians are forced to make use of these listings of wealth to recover the profile of poverty for pre-statistical societies.

Data and figures produced for the poor from studies based on taxation records are available for many towns and rural areas of early modern Europe (see Table 5). Recent studies suggest the need for a downward revision of levels of urban and rural poverty derived from fiscal records. It has been shown that even for the same place the criteria might have changed over a short period of time. And it is doubtful whether the local authorities who determined the level of tax allowance and exemption used the same method later on. There were, for example, numerous uncertainties about the precise methods of assessing personal property. The principles governing the assessment of real property are not so difficult to trace for most of our period. In only a few cities did the tax formula remain unchanged throughout the sixteenth and seventeenth centuries. In the German Imperial City of Nördlingen, for example, each year each citizen had to pay $\frac{1}{2}$ per cent of the assessed value of his and his wife's real and personal property. In any given year only a few citizens would be listed as having made no tax payments (i.e. paupers). But most citizens, even the very poor, were required to pay a minimum amount. At the end of the sixteenth century this minimum was $\frac{1}{8}$ florin. By the beginning of the Thirty Years' War this minimum had increased to $\frac{1}{5}$ gulden or florin. In fifteenth- and sixteenth-century Flanders and Brabant the recipients of poor relief appear as a separate group in the hearth tax list because this group presumably did not pay taxes. In Artois, Hainaut and Luxemburg, on the other hand, the poor were in most cases included in the list of taxpayers and taxed with them. Where such a taxation system was in use, no one, not even the poorest person, theoretically fell through the fiscal net. But even in those places where the poor were included in the overall list a fiscal limit of poverty had to be set up. The official demarcation line lay between the needy of no fixed abode who do not appear in the tax records and the recipients of poor relief who were taxed. In some Artoisean villages, for instance, the annual quota for the poor varies between 1 and 4 *patars* – the daily wage of a very humble workman. In some German towns this minimum tax was called *Habnit-Steuer*. Although the poor relief recipients were assessed by the same standards as all other inhabitants, they enjoyed a considerable remission. In practice, however, a number of them were unable to pay, and the local authorities had to grant them exemption. When in the year 1582 the town council of the city of Cologne agreed upon a special levy (chimney tax), about 5 per cent of the owners and tenants of houses which had at least one chimney were listed as paupers and did not pay the tax.

Where detailed local sources have permitted a closer look at the taxation system or even have made possible a comparison with other records indicating social stratification, it becomes clear that hearth tax and property tax listings involve serious problems in translating levels of exemption into levels of poverty. And there is a further caveat in using such records for comparative studies. Stripping fiscal records from their socio-economic, as well as their administrative, context, can be deceptive. The poverty of the urban exempts was probably different from that of their rural counterparts. And within the same type of society differences in what some English historians have called 'local ecologies' drew further distinctions. We need therefore more detailed local and regional studies which provide us with the context in which to assess the social meaning of tax exemption. It is clear that such studies have to use record linkage in order to translate the categories imposed by tax authorities into reliable indicators of the extent of poverty in a given society.

Despite the obvious need to re-assess the meaning and the validity of the commonly accepted and widely quoted figures derived from fiscal records, these sources can give us at least a rough idea about the increase or decrease of poverty in town and countryside in the early modern period. In Memmingen, a major centre of linen production in Upper Swabia, the number of 'have-nots' rose from 31 per cent at the end of the fifteenth century to 55 per cent in 1521. In Augsburg, one of the financial metropolises of sixteenth-century Germany, the number of those paupers who paid only the minimum tax (*Habnits*) dropped from 48.5 per cent in 1618 down to 37.2 per cent shortly before the end of the Thirty Years' War (1646). The latter figure, however, does not mean that the distribution of wealth had considerably improved during the war. On the contrary. For the middling citizens, predominantly craftsmen, the effect of the war aggravated by ceaseless financial exactions had been constantly to swallow up their earnings. Although all groups suffered financial losses during the war, in relative terms the burden of military taxation and economic hardship must have fallen much more heavily on the middle classes than on the 'bottom' group or on the rich. In the larger cities of Brabant, the number of poor hearths leapt from 14 per cent in 1480 to 19 per cent in 1526. This comparatively modest rise was obviously caused not only by the further impoverishment of urban artisans (often working in the textile industries), but also by the influx of rural poor.

The effects of the restructuring of agriculture and industry in seventeenth- and eighteenth-century Europe led to the proliferation of an agrarian and urban proletariat. In France, for example, the high number of paupers mentioned in the tax records of the eighteenth century is indicative of the structural character of poverty. Regional studies confirm the grim verdicts and estimates by contemporary writers. In Brittany, for example, 20 to 90 per cent of inhabitants of the twenty-three towns included in the sample were exempted from capitation. The towns which had fewer than 50 per cent fiscal paupers were in most cases either political, administrative or commercial centres. In those towns which were in a precarious socio-economic position because they depended largely on export industries (especially the cloth industry), the number of craftsmen, wage labourers and poor who were not able to pay taxes exceeded more than half of the urban population. There were thus many different social and economic histories behind regional variations which are to be found in rates of exemption from capitation or hearth taxes in early modern Europe. Not only in France, but also in England, Italy and Germany, industrial towns produced some of the highest proportions of exempt householders. The proportion was also high in parts of rural Europe which were prone to harvest failures and because of changes in the structure of landholding depended on rural textile industry (e.g. Cumbria in England, and Electoral Saxony in Germany). The proportion was markedly below average only in towns which had adjusted to the decline of staple industries and diversified their economies, such as York (20 per cent) or Frankfurt am Main (10 per cent), in areas of industrial growth (e.g. Sheffield), and in all farming regions close to centres of consumption. In the northern parts of Essex, for example, 53 per cent were exempt from the later Stuart hearth taxes while in the south, in the neighbourhood of London, only 23 per cent were not required to pay taxes. If we bear this local diversity in mind, we have to give up the idea of trying to estimate the national extent of poverty. Nevertheless one has to admit that tax assessments are still one of the most promising sources of information on the distribution of wealth and poverty in early modern Europe, provided one takes into account the methodological limits which have already been pointed out.

Poor relief recipients

The eminent German sociologist Georg Simmel (1858–1918), who was a contemporary of Max Weber, held the opinion that the poor as a distinctive social group exist not because they are suffering from a certain degree of deprivation but because they are either receiving charity or are eligible for poor relief according to the prevalent social norms in a given society.[2] This approach avoids the problem that the terms 'poor' and 'indigent' changed their meaning significantly over the centuries. In the period under study here contemporary writers ever more frequently used the term 'poor' to describe someone who owned only his labour, and by the end of the eighteenth century this term had acquired primarily economic connotations to describe the labouring classes. The question of whether the number of needy registered by the poor law administration and charity institutions corresponds to the number of poor depends therefore on the definition of poverty. The answer must be 'yes', if a person is labelled poor because he or she had to rely on alms or poor relief in order to cover even the most essential daily needs. One has to answer in the negative, if one applies the concept to all who owned nothing more than their labour and were therefore often called the 'labouring poor'. The latter would imply that the poor represented more or less two-thirds of the population in many early modern European towns. Using the narrower definition one comes to the level of the so-called 'structural

---

[2] Georg Simmel, *Soziologie: Untersuchungen über die Formen der Vergesellschaftung* (Leipzig, 1908), p. 490.

poor' who were recognized as recipients of permanent relief, among them people unable to earn a living because of physical disability as well as the aged, orphans or impoverished widows. Their number is, of course, much smaller, although for a number of reasons it is difficult to give an average figure. On the one hand, most of the data available for early modern European towns are as incomplete as they are inaccurate. Inmates of hospitals or local poorhouses were not counted, while those who petitioned two or three times a year for support were probably registered more than once. And what we also do not know in the present state of research is the extent to which private or ecclesiastical charitable institutions cared for indigent people not registered at the municipal poor law administration. Another problem is that a large number of those receiving outdoor relief were householders and not single persons. The actual number of the supported needy may thus perhaps be doubled.

To illustrate the lacunae of those records let us take, for example, a city for which a thorough case-study is available. Cissie Fairchilds[3] estimated that in eighteenth-century Aix-en-Provence roughly 20 per cent of the population, that is about 5,000 people, received some sort of charity. This calculation is, however, at most an approximation because for only one of Aix's larger charity institutions were complete records of entries preserved. The archives of the other organizations of poor relief show astonishing gaps. One of the town's most important charities, the Miséricorde, left no lists at all of recipients of public assistance. In a special ceremony it burned its records at every year's end, in order to protect the identities of the people it helped, most of them being *pauvres honteux*, shame-faced poor who did not want to be known as recipients of alms. Only by taking all the bits and pieces of information available is it possible to calculate the number of people aided by each of the city's charitable organizations. There are, however, estimates for similar towns in France and elsewhere during either the sixteenth or the seventeenth century, for which the difficulties involved in such calculations are not so formidable. The city of Toledo, for example, kept records of the number of people in need during a subsistence crisis. The first list was compiled in 1556, when grain became scarce. In December 1556 the magistrate counted 10,608 needy people. In 'normal' years, however, when the town was not afflicted with grain shortage or epidemic diseases, no such list was compiled. In these years relief was left to the numerous confraternities, hospitals and charitable endowments whose record books either did not survive or do not contain information on the number of people they assisted. A town in which such lists do not lack consistency because they were kept on a regular basis is sixteenth-century Augsburg.

[3] Cissie C. Fairchilds, *Poverty and Charity in Aix-en-Provence 1640–1789* (Baltimore, 1976), pp. 75ff.

The municipal poor relief agency (*Almosenamt*) recorded the number of people it assisted each year and in 1575 it even published a survey of how many poor householders and individuals had been supported during the past twenty-five years. That such a disclosure of facts and figures was quite unusual even in the eighteenth century can be illustrated by an example of the city of Amsterdam where the city treasurers enquired in 1793 why the number of people receiving poor relief was not stated. The answer by the trustees of the *huiszittenhuis* (one of Amsterdam's poor relief centres) was that this 'has never been the practice or ever demanded'.[4]

The documentation is, as we have pointed out, nowhere perfect. Therefore one has to select towns which happen to provide better and more consistent records than other, mostly small communities. But before we turn to such case-studies there are some further problems to be addressed. Even for those towns for which we have account books, records of payments are partial. Overseers of the poor in early modern England or similar officers in other European countries usually recorded the number of pensioners or recipients of regular payments but often did not bother to specify the *ad hoc* payments to the poor in the course of a year. Accidentally recorded 'extraordinary' or 'casual' payments therefore inhibit an accurate calculation of the total number of poor supported from public funds. Another problem is that even if a quantitative study based on a variety of sources comes near to the 'real' number of people who received some sort of aid this number will normally alter from year to year or in some cases from month to month. These sudden jumps are often caused by temporary crises such as bad harvests, epidemic diseases and commercial slumps. Even if the numbers of the poor relief recipients remain more or less constant, this does not mean that the depth of the problem did not change. On the contrary, the stable number of persons on poor relief can indicate that the quality and extent of assistance were drastically restricted in order to avoid an excess of expenditure. It will therefore be necessary to distinguish between long-term levels of poverty and the levels reached during crises, which might be three to four times as high. The two have been called 'structural' and 'cyclical' poverty by some French and Anglo-American historians while the English historian Paul Slack prefers to refer to the same phenomenon as 'background level' and 'crisis level' of poverty.[5] Crisis levels fluctuate much more

---

[4] Quoted in Peter Jansen, 'Poverty in Amsterdam at the close of the eighteenth century', *Acta Historiae Neerlandicae* 10 (1978), 106.
[5] Jean-Pierre Gutton, *La Société et les pauvres. L'Exemple de la généralité de Lyon 1534–1789* (Paris, 1971), p. 53; Fairchilds, *Aix-en-Provence*, p. 73; Martz, *Spain*, p. 119; Slack, *Poverty*, p. 39.

than the background level which only alters in the medium to longer term. This is, surely, the reason why the data and figures produced for poor relief recipients from studies covering a very wide area and a long period of time are in effect so varied and, indeed, often confusing. This issue of different levels is worth considering if the figures for one community or area are to be compared with those of other towns in early modern Europe such as Toledo, Lyons, Verona, Augsburg, Amsterdam and Norwich where historians have estimated the level of the 'cyclical' poor at between 20 and 30 per cent and the 'structural' poor at between 5 to 10 per cent (see Table 6).

Given the present state of research on poverty and poor relief in rural areas of early modern Europe, it is almost impossible to tell whether there was an equally large proportion of the population on the dole. The few studies we have indicate that their number amounted to no less than 5 per cent of the householders. We have, for example, figures for the hinterland of early eighteenth-century Nuremberg which show that between 5 and 10 per cent of the parish population were recognized recipients of temporary or permanent support. Few such estimates exist for other rural areas. Perhaps the most comprehensive of these is Ingomar Bog's calculation that at the end of the sixteenth century in the rural territory belonging to the city of Zurich at least 4.5 per cent were supported by the 'common chest'.

Problematic as the evidence is, we are nevertheless able to arrive at conclusions which are not only valid for the local studies on poor relief but which are also indicative of broader, national and European developments. But after what has been said so far about the obstacles inhibiting an accurate calculation of the number of poor supported by charitable and poor relief institutions, we should also bear in mind that even the most correct estimate of the number of those receiving poor relief provides only an approximation of the 'real' extent of poverty in early modern Europe. What we usually do not know is the number of persons who applied for alms or grants of charity but did not get them. Luckily, we have some recent studies which deal with this problem. As far as late eighteenth-century Amsterdam is concerned we know that in 1799 about 37,500 children and adults received poor relief but a much higher number (81,080) had wished to be considered for a share of the money raised through a special collection. A study of early nineteenth-century Florence shows that less than half of requests to an important charitable institution (the Congregation of San Giovanni Battista, founded in 1701 as a Florentine variant of a late seventeenth-century Jesuit model of charity imported from France) were accepted by the deputies, over a third were rejected, and the remainder were modified. In

Table 6. *Poor relief recipients as percentage of total population in early modern rural and urban communities*

Place	Year	No. of recipient/ supported households	% of population
Urban communities			
Frankfurt am Main	1539	400	3.6
Trier	1623	324	24.8
Cologne	1799	3,132	8.2
Berlin	1665	280	2.0
Berlin	1799	11,125	7.2
Vitré	1597	949	11.0
Amiens	1625	1,149	3.8
Aix-en-Provence	1760	5,000	20.0
Norwich	1578–9	381	5.1
Exeter	1691	482	7.2
Salisbury	1725	180	5.1
Venice	1740	?	14.0
Toledo (1 parish)	1573	518	15.6
Antwerp	1773	?	11.0
Brussels	1755	?	7.0
Malines	1794	?	13.0
Rural communities			
Nuremberg district	1700–10	?	10.0
Zurich district	1590	3,459	4.5
Solothurn district	1768	156	22.5
Kenilworth	1663–4	31	23.0

Source : see Bibliography s.v. 'poor relief recipients'.

eighteenth-century Turin not even the very old and feeble persons who applied for relief could be sure that old age or decrepitude alone would be accepted as sufficient reason in itself. Of 154 single old people who requested help from the Ospedale di Carità in 1783 thirty (about 20 per cent) were refused admittance.

Censuses of the poor

Taking a census of the poor was not a common practice in European towns before the eighteenth century. The only exception to the rule is England where by 1601 there was even a printed guide (see Figure 7) available which showed the 'overseers of the poor' how the statistical

1	2	3	4	5	6	7	8	9	10	11	12
Wardes	Names and families	Years	Defects	Usuall workes	Weekley gettings	Of whom they have worke	Who want worke	Such as be fit for apprentices and service	Such as keepe orphans and others	Weekly allowance	Beggers licensed in the parish
East	Father Got, his wife, Ioane, Richard	71 69 19 15	palsie ideot	knitte	VIII.d	W. True	Iohn Gott			X.d	Rich. Got
West	Mother Ter, Marie Iohn Alice	67 20 15 9	lame deafe	spinne	X.d	John Mert		Alice Terre	Mother Terre keepeth W. Ren Io. Ren base	II. s	
North	Widow Fit William Richard Iohn Henrie	51 16 1 8 6	diseased dumme	weaveth	XII.d	H.Till	R. Fitt H.Fitt	Richard Fitt		VIII.d	John Fit
South	Thomas Fig Susan Raph Leonard Rose Henrie Thomas	43 34 14 9 5 3 2	bedred blinde lame	labourer	II s	of divers men			Thomas Fig-ge keepeth Ro.Segge Th. Segge Hen. Tod (orphans)	III.s	Rose Fig.
	Persons		Diseased	Workers			Idle	Apprentice	Orphans and other	Allow.	Beggers

Figure 7 'A readie forme for a speedie inspection of the poor' (1601)
Source : An Ease for Overseers of the Poor (Cambridge, 1601), p. 4.

Table 7. *Censuses of the poor*

Place	Year	No. of poor	Poor households	Percentage of total population
Strasbourg	1523	649	252	?
Worcester	1557	777	321	18.0
Norwich	1570	2359	790	22.0
Huddersfield	1622	700	155	20–25.0
Valladolid	1561	?	?	9.5
Segovia	1561	?	?	15.7
Toledo	1558	11,105	?	19.7
France (on average)	1770	?	?	10.0

Source : see Bibliography s.v. 'censuses'.

survey should be carried out, describing, for example, the number of columns which should be used in the documents, and the information, from ages to occupations and earnings, they should contain. These censuses tended to be drawn up at moments of crisis and could be easily influenced by changing definitions of indigence. There can be no doubt that the men who compiled those lists had different concepts of poverty in mind and that they usually found what they were looking for. When attention was restricted to the absolutely dependent poor who received relief, as was the case in seventeenth-century Salisbury, the poor comprised no more than 5 per cent of the population. Where the definition of poverty was broader, as for example in Worcester (1557), the household size as well as the overall number of the poor was larger than in other cities.

Detailed statistical enquiries into the numbers, living conditions and needs of the poor date back to the early sixteenth century and culminated in the vast and often nationwide surveys of the eighteenth century (see Table 7). Unfortunately, not all surveys which were undertaken by poor relief agencies or local government survived. One of the earliest censuses of the poor we know of is the Strasbourg survey of 1523, which recorded the name, address, marital status, number of children, citizenship, needy members of the household and circumstances (e.g. ability to work, state of health) of 649 poor people. The poverty line was broadly defined to take in families burdened with many children, widows or wives abandoned by their husbands, the blind, the lame, the impotent, the sick and the old. The first English census of the poor dates back to 1557. The Worcester survey resembles the one in Strasbourg. The proportion of the population contained in the Worcester census of 1557 was, however, larger, but it was not surveyed in similar detail. Only the names of heads of households, their wives, and the number of their children were generally given. One of the best known early modern censuses of the poor is the Norwich survey of 1570. It lists 22 per cent of the local population (ignoring thus the large community of foreign refugees living within the city walls) and gives a detailed description of their households. It included many who were not receiving poor relief as well as those who were. This implies a kind of general recognition of the much greater potential extent of poverty. The Norwich census and similar listings enable us therefore to come to the conclusion that while about 5 per cent of the population of a town were poor relief recipients, another 20 per cent at least had a legitimate claim to charitable aid (even if they were not granted it at the moment).

One of the most comprehensive and vast censuses of the poor undertaken during the *ancien régime* is that by the French Comité de Mendicité in 1790–1.[6] But even this great and apparently thorough inquiry was not really concerned with counting the poor. The Comité was – as is quite understandable – only interested in discovering the number of 'individuals who were in need of relief' to whom it hoped to provide sufficient help, namely work for the unemployed, hospitalization for the infirm, and a subsidy for the children of poor wage-earners until they were fourteen years old. The global figures for France show that about a tenth of its population fell into these three categories. The figures compiled by the Comité have therefore to be considered a gross underestimation of the real extent of poverty. And it is also revealing that the global figures of the Comité are not those returned by the districts but are an addition of the numbers in the various categories (children, sick, aged and unemployed). The only convincing explanation is that it disregarded the calculations made by the districts on the grounds that those had a vested interest in swelling the number of the poor in need of assistance. The information requested from the districts obviously left room for considerable ambiguity.

It is certainly not justifiable to deduce from the significant discrepancy which exists between the local returns and the final list in many statistical inquiries of the Revolutionary and Napoleonic years, that the figures are without value or cannot be relied on. Despite the variety of criteria employed by local officials and 'cosmetic' manipulations on overall numbers by those who ordered such surveys, these comprehensive censuses offer some indications of the degree of poverty in different areas

[6] For the various lists drawn up by this committee, see Olwen H. Hufton, *The Poor of Eighteenth-Century France, 1750–1789* (Oxford, 1974), pp. 5ff.

of the countryside and show clearly the concentration of poverty within the major cities. We can, however, learn much more from those censuses than simply the numbers of the poor. The value of this unique source lies in the light it throws on the social features and distinctive patterns of poverty in early modern towns. The range of characters and circumstances revealed in these documents is usually rather wide. We learn, for example, about the high proportion of children and old people among the poor and we can also evaluate such factors or variables as household size, marital status and life-cyle. The early modern censuses of the poor tell us something about the origins of poverty in computable terms. They represent therefore a favourite starting point for much historical investigation of social problems in pre-industrial Europe.

In quantitative terms alone these numbers must have been disturbing for the municipal authorities and poor relief administrators who had some information about the numbers, living conditions and needs of the poor and who also knew about limited financial sources set aside for the assistance of the needy. Apart from the growing desire expressed by magistrates and poor relief officials alike to accumulate as much 'useful' information as possible, it was essential not only to acquire precise figures about the deserving poor, as well as about the able-bodied beggars, but also to keep such vital information secret. As in many other spheres of political activity and municipal administration during the *ancien régime*, there was general consent that decisions and figures should be for the eyes of the sworn town council members or local government officials only (for this very reason the minutes of the town council meetings were also kept secret). The threat of an escalating number of paupers was thus sharply perceived by the magistrate but not by the citizens who could have only a vague notion of the overall number of paupers and beggars in the city. But the inhabitants could not overlook or ignore the 10 or 20 per cent of the population who hovered around the poverty line in their own little world, the parish. The same pressures were felt earlier or differently in some local communities than in others. Especially in the parish, if not in the town, the poor were more than an anonymous mass which could at best be statistically measured, they were by and large familiar figures. It is therefore necessary to say also a few things about the residential distribution of poverty in early modern towns.

Topography of poverty

Most historians agree that there was no rigid social zoning in early modern towns, although there can be no doubt that there was a kind of suburban concentration of poverty in some cities. In every larger

European town mansions were fewer and poor tenements much more common on the periphery, just inside the town walls, or outside the main gates. In Grenoble, for example, the lodgings of the poor had been fairly evenly distributed by the beginning of the eighteenth century. By 1770 the impoverished and needy were already pushed to the margins of the city, into the populous suburbs south of the town. At the same time, quarters of wealth had emerged both in the centre of the city and along the rue Neuve (see Figure 8). This slowly emerging residential pattern points already to the separation of rich and poor that would characterize most nineteenth-century industrial cities. Grenoble was not singular in this respect. All major European towns had at least one suburb where the number of paupers was higher than elsewhere in the city, where plague and harvest crises had their worst demographic effects, where alehouses and places of public entertainment were common, where new immigrants and beggars found temporary or permanent lodging. In St Giles parish (Cambridge), in Green Dragon Yard (situated in the London suburb of St Saviour), along the rue Royale and the Cour à l'eau (Lille), in the faubourgs of eighteenth-century Paris (Saint-Denis, Saint-Antoine, Roule) in the parishes of San Isidoro and Santiago del Arrabal (the northern outskirts of Toledo), in the suburb of St Katharina (Schwä-bisch-Gmünd), and in the suburban parishes of Augsburg (especially Frauenvorstadt, Lechviertel and Jakober Vorstadt), there was a vicious circle of poverty, high death rates, immigration, makeshift economies and deviance. The impression of 'ghettoization' at the periphery is, however, not reinforced by a study on eighteenth-century Paris combining the information on lodging with data on the places where beggars were arrested for mendicancy. For obvious reasons the numerous poor who lived on alms which they begged in the streets flocked into the city centre and squatted in the most crowded places, the hubs of commerce (e.g. marketplaces) and social activities (e.g. in front of churches). The poor were therefore not only visible in their living quarters, often located far away from the more or less homogeneous residential areas of the more affluent classes, but were easily recognized in every part of the city, causing eloquent laments by contemporaries about the unpleasant concomitances of poverty, as for example, that by an Englishmen called Henry Arthington about the 'great multitude of poor people... in this city [Oxford] and suburbs, wandering, walking and going idly up and down the streets and other places, begging and often pilfering, filching and breaking of shops and houses'.[7] The unequal distribution of poverty among the residential districts was greatest and more conspicuous, of

[7] Henry Arthington, *Provision for the Poore, Now in Penurie Out of the Store-House of God's Plentie* (London, 1597), sig. C2v.

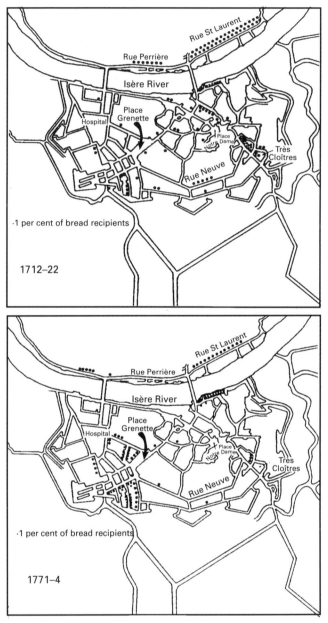

Figure 8 Homes of the poor according to the bread distribution in eighteenth-century Grenoble
Source: K. Norberg, *Rich and Poor in Grenoble, 1600–1814* (Berkeley, 1985), pp. 184–5.

course, in the big cities. But even here there was – at least in the sixteenth century – no rigid social segregation. The social topography of a London suburb (St Saviour), for example, was marked by some social mixing and the existence of gradations within alleys and yards which in most cases only contained a small number of high-quality tenements. But one should also not forget that despite the 'social intermingling' observed in early seventeenth-century London and late eighteenth-century Paris, the big cities were notorious for a phenomenon known in French as *paupérisme vertical*. Studies on housing and living conditions in some French towns (Lyons, Bordeaux, Paris) suggest that there were not only fine gradations in backstreet housing but also distinctive features as far as the vertical distribution of lodging is concerned. It is very likely that the principle 'the higher the floor, the lower the class' applied in nearly all districts of the French capital, but it is important to find whether this pattern of accommodation was also widespread in other French cities. Evidence from eighteenth-century Lille suggests that this was not always the case. By the middle of the century 72 per cent of the city's poor population lived in deplorable lodgings: 38 per cent in courtyards, 24 per cent in small chambers, and 10.7 per cent in cellars. These findings are confirmed by studies on other early modern European towns (e.g. London and Bremen) which show that the poor often dwelt in cellars underground.

An analysis of the numerical and spatial distribution of poverty has revealed several patterns of the extent of this social problem which evolved differently in various communities and countries but were in some ways comparable. These differences depended largely on economic factors, but at the same time political forces, social conflicts and mentalities had a great significance, for both the quantitative and the qualitative aspects of poverty.

5   Standards of living among the poor

Domestic environment

The dwellings of the poor had a bad reputation: they were the outward and often most conspicuous sign of misery. John Stow, in his *Survey of London* of 1958, showed his disgust when he referred to the 'filthy cottages, and other ... purpressors, inclosures, and laystalls ... no small blemish to so famous a city',[1] which could be found just outside Aldgate. Sébastien Mercier (1740–1814), was obviously such a fascinated observer of everyday life in eighteenth-century Paris that he even looked into such lodgings. His report conveys the repulsion the élite must have felt when confronted with the abominable housing conditions in the urban slum of the early modern period:

A whole family occupies a single room, with four bare walls, wretched beds without curtains, and kitchen utensils rolling around with the chamberpots. All the furniture together is not worthy twenty *écus*, and every three months the inhabitants change their hole, because they are chased out for failing to pay the rent.[2]

Overcrowding and unhealthy housing conditions were not a peculiar urban experience. In the country the poor also dwelt huddled together. The Englishman Arthur Young, who travelled extensively through eighteenth-century France, thought that the Breton and Languedoc peasantry were the worst housed. A century before, in the last years of Louis XIV, the French parish priest of Sennely (Sologne) described the ramshackle cottages of the poorer sort of his parishioners as 'dark and more fit to serve as dungeon for felons then lodgings for free human beings'.[3] In Italy travellers and contemporary observers were also struck

---

[1] John Stow, *A Survey of London* (Everyman edition, London, 1956), p. 376.
[2] L.-S. Mercier, *Le Tableau de Paris* (Paris, 1781), vol. I, pp. 255ff., English translation in Daniel Roche, *The People of Paris: An Essay in Popular Culture in the Eighteenth Century* (Leamington Spa, 1987), p. 97.
[3] G. Bouchard, *Le Village immobile: Sennely-en-Sologne aux XVIIIe siècle* (Paris, 1972), p. 94 n. 32.

by the horrible sight of rural and urban slums, showing the same characteristics everywhere: narrow, badly built and overcrowded houses, lack of light and ventilation and often unhealthy proximity to livestock.

To find out about the housing conditions of the poor, such impressionistic and often heavily biased sketches by travellers and contemporary writers (e.g. medical topographers, hygienists) can be helpful if they are confirmed by other sources. Two sorts of evidence are particularly valuable: papers such as rent agreements and rent recipients teach us about the cost of the cheapest possible tenements which lay in the financial grasp of the labouring poor; and the descriptions by notaries and assessors in probate inventories which enable us to reconstruct piece by piece a concrete picture of the domestic environment in which the lower classes lived. As far as the study of the housing conditions and lodgings of the poor is concerned, the geography of the information is important in order to know for which towns or regions such investigations have been undertaken. Six areas stand out: early modern Oxfordshire, Worcestershire, Württemberg, Westphalia, Bordeaux and Paris. While each of these regions or towns had its unique characteristics, they have one thing in common: records which reflect the living conditions and the consumption habits not only of the élite households but also of the popular classes. In the following paragraphs rent agreements and probate inventories will be used to investigate the way poor people lived in early modern Europe: first examining the types of accommodation in relation to the money the poor could spend on rent; next describing the use and organization of limited space; finally, drawing attention to the distribution of basic household items and the domestic 'tactics' (Michel de Certeau) of those who bought or owned such more or less valuable objects.

A sharp contrast between the more affluent classes and the working poor appears when we consider the status of accommodation. For the many single or multiple households with limited financial resources there were only a few possibilities: boarding houses, free accommodation with the employer (only in the case of journeymen and servants), renting and sub-renting. There was, of course, also the hospital, which in the early modern period still offered permanent or temporary shelter to a wide variety of social types. Those who could stay in such charitable institutions for a limited period were, for example, pilgrims, travelling clerics, itinerant workers, travellers and migrants. The chronically ill, the aged, abandoned or orphaned ill, in short all those who had for some reason fallen between the meshes of the social networks (kinship, family), were normally considered as longer-term cases. In those multi-functional hospitals the inmates were often crowded together pell-mell into a single-chamber, room or hall, which was the typical architectural feature of the medieval hospital. The only real spatial differentiation within these hospital institutions was the accommodation of the sacred alongside the profane. Even the larger hospitals with more than one hall or chamber were usually based on the plan of a church, emphasized by placing an altar at the head of the nave or, in the case of a cruciform design, at the meeting point of the four arms of the cross. This was to have both a practical and spiritual purpose, in order that the staff could easily supervise the inmates and that the latter, especially the bedridden poor, would always be able to see Mass being celebrated. There were only a few larger hospitals with more than one hundred inmates. In sixteenth-century Brittany most hospitals did not contain more than twenty beds. Even in 1789, a quarter of France's hospitals contained fewer than ten beds. Only in a few early modern European hospitals did inmates not share a bed. In a sixteenth-century Florence hospital (San Paolo), for example, there were at least forty-one instances of doubling up two patients in one bed for periods lasting from one to eighteen days, and interestingly enough no clear correlation between number of inmates, length of stay and availability of bed space is to be found. There can be no doubt that despite endless efforts to maintain cleanliness, hygienic conditions were pretty grim in many early modern European hospitals providing institutional care for the resident paupers and indigent aliens alike. In spite of shortcomings – and these occurred mostly during periods of fiscal difficulties – inmates of such charitable institutions were considerably better off in the hospital than in their own dilapidated quarters.

The question is, however, how many indigent people could hope to find such privileged accommodation. Although many early modern cities were described by contemporaries as being copiously provided with hospitals which are, of course, all beautiful, sufficient and suitable (e.g. Florence in 1464, and Cologne in 1582), we must doubt that by the end of the *ancien régime* many cities were able to provide considerably more accommodation than in the later Middle Ages. In fifteenth-century Florence, for instance, the ratio of beds to inhabitants of the city was twenty-five per thousand. In seventeenth-century Brunswick the capita/bed ratio was of the same order (23/1000). A systematic investigation of the relation between population size and number of hospital beds in various French departments at the end of the *ancien régime* brings to light pockets of real poverty with respect to hospital capacity. The massive availability of hospital beds in large population centres is in sharp contrast with the situation in the smaller communities. Without Reims (21·49 beds per 1000 inhabitants), for example, the ratio in the department of Marne would have been 2·77 rather than 4·84. Despite the very limited availability of hospital accommodation in almost every early modern town those paupers who were either too sick or too old to earn their living tried to enter the hospital and almshouses, for the alternatives were neither numerous nor pleasant. Not all of them could be admitted, for reasons already mentioned. Of those individuals who in the eighteenth century petitioned to be taken into the Hospital General of the city of Grenoble, 74 per cent received a flat denial. At that time it cost the welfare authorities about 200 livres annually to house an inmate in the hospital. Therefore some 13 per cent of the petitioners in Grenoble were admitted only in return for cash payment. This practice was common in many charitable institutions of early modern Europe. However, the admission fees differed according to the financial means of the applicant. In sixteenth-century Germany, for example, a person who was well-off and looked for a secure place where someone took care of him in old age was charged between 100 and 200 florins for lifetime care. Those who had only small assets to offer to the hospital administration paid up to 50 florins for shelter and life-long maintenance in a hospital, which was indeed a bargain price if one considers the subsequent costs for room and full board in such institutions. Despite the many advantages of being cared for in hospitals or alms-houses, the poor in general must have preferred home relief to confinement but they were also intelligent enough to adapt the local hospital system within a collective subsistence strategy that changed according to the vulnerable moments in the life-cycle of any lower-class family.

For the floating proletariat and for many immigrants flocking into early modern cities, not hospitals and boarding houses, but alehouses or furnished rooms were the only alternative when they were looking for a place which could give them shelter. Even non-resident beggars could not risk being picked up by the watch for sleeping in the streets. And it is characteristic of the clientele of alehouses, especially in the countryside, that this type of accommodation was considered almost as primitive and disgusting as the homes of the poor. The rent for a furnished room was often high but still within one's means. In 1520, when Thomas Platter, the famous Swiss physician, was a poor student looking for accommodation in Zurich he was willing to pay 1 shilling per week (which amounts to an annual rent of 1·3 florins) for a shabby and poorly furnished room in a house also frequented by prostitutes. The borderline between such lodgings, inns and hotels is not always easy to trace. Sébastien Mercier and many other contemporary writers agreed that furnished rooms (often attics or basements) which cost in eighteenth-century Paris between 48 and 72 livres a year were often dirty, overcrowded, infected by filth and pests, and, above all, let at exorbitant prices by greedy landlords who often did not care to report arrivals and departures of aliens to the authorities. Although all social levels and all professions could be found in the registers of landlords, a considerable number of their tenants were poor migrants looking for work, from the journeyman on his professional tour to the miserable day-labourer of uncertain means. Of those caught in eighteenth-century Paris for stealing food 54 per cent lived in rooms hired by the night or in innkeepers' rooms. There can be no doubt that many of these petty criminals were living on the poverty line although only 12 per cent of the offenders admitted being unemployed. Those who lived in the cheapest, most insalubrious hovels paid 2 to 4 sous a day. According to research by Daniel Roche, a rent of 37 to 40 livres per person per year represented the borderline of misery in Paris around 1750. In sixteenth- and early seventeenth-century Bordeaux the lower classes could afford a lodging which cost them between 12 and 60 livres a year. Although this wretched temporary accommodation had a bad reputation, it often offered the only possible solution to the housing problems of a shifting urban population who were mostly poor and without a social network. And it does not surprise that many of those committed to the precarious life of furnished flats often changed their abode secretly to avoid paying debts and arrears of rent.

Evidence from eighteenth-century Paris and Lyons suggests that less than 10 to 15 per cent of the new immigrants and temporary residents were living in furnished rooms. Many shared a flat with members of their family. Some were taken charge of by their masters, but only few of them could afford to rent a small dwelling in one of the suburban slums or the backyards and blind alleys of the city center. And even the vast majority of the labouring poor who had achieved the status of denizens did not own a dwelling but had to rent it. In eighteenth-century Paris 90 per cent of the wage-earners were tenants. Local studies on some sixteenth-century German towns reveal, for example, that between 29 (Schaff-hausen, 1502) and 63 (Vienna, 1563) per cent of the taxed inhabitants lived in rented rooms. As far as these two types of accommodation (renting and ownership) are concerned, it is clear that they confirm not only the contrast between the lower or popular classes on the one hand, and the urban middle class and élite on the other, but also the unequal distribution of wealth among occupational groups. Records such as inventories of rents due and account books of charitable institutions paying rent allowances give an idea of average costs. In seventeenth-century Bordeaux the average rent paid by poor relief recipients was 33 livres for a room suited for one person and 55·5 livres for a lodging which could put up more than three persons. In Paris the average rent paid by wage earners was 41 livres at the beginning of the eighteenth century, 95 livres at the end. In seventeenth-century England, £1 a year was the common rent for one room, and sometimes the tenants had to take in pauper children in order to get parish funds with which to pay it. In sixteenth-century Germany the urban lower class had to pay an annual rent up to 1·5 florins. The rather low rent (1 florin a year) paid by poor families living in the privately financed and rather spacious flats of the almshouse quarter in Augsburg known as Fuggerei was, of course, subsidized by funds from the famous German merchant and banker dynasty. In eighteenth-century Amsterdam the lower classes had to spend about 17 per cent of their real income on rent which was still a rather favourable financial situation compared to what happened in the first half of the nineteenth century, when commercial expansion and large-scale immigration led to an increase in weekly rent (expressed in kilograms of rye bread), by 87 per cent for a one-person household (compared to the proportion paid in 1780). From the records of the welfare administration kept in many municipal archives it can be seen that the weekly or annual payment of rent was one of the most acute problems faced by the poor in early modern Europe. Numerous complaints by landlords show that moving due to sudden increases in rent was frequent and that tenants often left rent arrears behind when they changed their abode secretly. Sébastien Mercier confirms this common practice: 'In the suburbs [of Paris] there are three or four thousand families who do not pay their quarterly dues, and every three months they drag from one garret to another furniture which is not worth twenty-four francs in all.'[4] The question of rent is, however, only one important aspect of housing. The organization of space is another indicator for the difference in life-style between the comfortably off and the impoverished.

In many fast-growing early modern towns there was, as we have already mentioned, some evidence of vertical stratification. This trend certainly began earlier in the big cities than in provincial towns. The poverty-stricken popular classes lived either in cellars or quite often on the upper floors of small buildings, starting from the second, where rent was cheaper but where one paid in fact more, as Sébastien Mercier noted, because one had 'to have wood and water brought up'. In other cities a kind of horizontal stratification can be noticed. Instead of raising the height and reorganizing the storeys of houses, landlords exploited the space to the maximum by back-to-back building. Land facing the street

---

[4] Mercier, *Tableau de Paris*, vol. X, p. 358, English translation by Roche, *People*, p. 107.

was the most expensive and the owner of houses with one or two bays at the front could charge more rent for such lodgings than for dwellings built on the narrow parcels of back gardens and inner courtyards. These cheaper dwellings, connected with the street via narrow, dark alleys and often closed off by a small door, existed, for example, in eighteenth-century Amsterdam and were also quite common in north Germany (e.g. Lübeck and Hamburg) where those blind alleys – on each side of which single-room dwellings were built – have been known until today as *Gänge* (passages).

The number and type of rooms occupied by the labouring poor is also significant. In eighteenth-century Paris being poor meant living in a single room. Fifty-seven per cent of the working-class had to be content with one-room lodgings compared to 41 per cent of the servants. An investigation of living space available to lower-class families in early modern Bordeaux shows that the majority (75 per cent) did not occupy more than one room. As in Lyons, where 30 square yards (one room) was the living and working space of a whole family of wretched silk workers, this phenomenon was a sign of the poor cutting back on space in order to economize on rent and heating. The degree of crowding in these lodgings is difficult to estimate, for we do not always know the exact number of inmates. In early eighteenth-century Paris there were 2·3 occupants per room in wage-earner households. Unfortunately, we do not have sufficiently detailed sources before the nineteenth century to enable us to calculate the number of square metres per person in houses occupied by poor relief recipients. However, we can assume that almost the same degree of crowding as in Amsterdam in the 1830s (in more than half of the dwellings of the poor less than 6 square metres were available per person) was the general rule for most of the poor in early modern Europe.

Overcrowding was not a peculiarly urban experience. In rural France it was common for two or three families to share premises of under 20 square yards. In the Auvergne up to ten people shared a single-room cottage. Sharing a small house or cottage was the norm amongst the poor in rural Beauvais. However, there were regional differences. In sixteenth-century Oxfordshire, for example, poor and middling sorts of rural households (wealth categories 1–20, and 21–100 pound sterling) had a mean of 3·6 rooms, indicating a first attempt to achieve some individual privacy. The fact that so many people dwelt huddled together was often a direct result of inheritance customs where the principal heir (in most cases the eldest son) was unable to compensate his brothers by providing them with enough money to buy or rent separate premises. The cottages in which the day-labourers, cottagers and paupers lived were usually single-roomed, with an earth floor, mud walls, a thatched roof, a hole in the wall for a window and another for smoke to escape from the open hearth. In some areas, where stone was readily found, as in the Alps or in Scotland and Wales, this more solid building material was used for such hovels. Any specialization of space was a luxury. If a single room was divided by partitions for living and sleeping areas, it was accomplished by setting up, for example, a draught screen beside the front door or placing a piece of furniture in such a manner that it sub-divided the room into small, partitioned units. The poorest rural houses were single storey; only a few had an attic in which grain could be stored or a cellar in which animals (e.g. pigs) might be kept. For all the rural poor it can be said that life in such cottages must have been crowded, uncomfortable, dirty, insalubrious (because of the unhealthy proximity to livestock) and lacking in privacy.

As appalling as their lack of privacy was the meagreness of material comforts in these households. Furniture and other consumer goods were confined to the basic necessities and often of poor quality. The estate left in 1700 by a widow living in the small Westphalian village of Altenhüffen is perhaps typical for the rural poor: bad black linen clothes, one cow which died soon after her death, two spinning wheels, one reel, a small kettle, a small old oven, an old chest and a bad bedstead. Robert Holland, a day-labourer of Hampton Poyle, Oxfordshire, who died in 1568, had besides a cow, a heifer and a sheep, only three kettles, one little pot of brass, one bedstead, one coffer, a sack, four platters and a saucer, two pairs of sheets, one bolster and one twill cloth. The whole value of his personal estate was not more than 19s. A French linen weaver left his widow when he died in 1776 a wooden table, five spoons and eight lead forks, six bottles, two dishes and four plates, two beds and four pairs of sheets, and a chest containing wretched clothes. The whole estate was valued at 140 livres. One can readily multiply this sort of inventory and establish a rule wherein a bed, a chest, a few cooking pots or pans for the hearth, and mostly patched and worn clothes constituted the entire assets of a poor family.

In regard to furnishings, the few other inventories of poor households which have survived until today definitely underline the importance of beds and bed-clothes. The bed was important for its value as well as its function. According to recent studies on early modern French probate inventories the bed represented a considerable part of the legacy: in eighteenth-century Paris, for example, 15 per cent of the total and on average 25 per cent of the value of furniture and furnishings for the lower classes. However, households where each member of the family had a bed were a rare exception. Two persons to a bed was the average, and at the worst three generations shared the same bed. In sixteenth-century

Bordeaux one fifth of the households did not even own a single bed and people had to sleep on the floor on pallets. Only at the end of the seventeenth century almost every inventory mentions at least one bedstead per household. A poor day-labourer was willing (and obviously also able) to spend 20 to 30 livres on his bed. The poorest of the poor had to be content with crude palliasses stuffed with straw and thin, patched woollen blankets as bed-covers. It is interesting, however, to note that the labouring poor invested more in bedding than in any other household item. The average value of bed linen in early modern Bordelaise inventories was as high as lowest annual rent for a modest dwelling.

In an early modern household the fireplace performed multiple functions: cooking, heating and lighting. In all accommodation occupied by the popular classes in eighteenth-century Paris there was at least one fireplace. Only the very poor did not own a hearth. The connection between the lack of heating facilities and poverty was already known to sixteenth-century tax authorities. The English hearth tax legislation of 1664, for example, allowed exemptions only to those with two hearths or less ('No person ... inhabiting any dwelling house ... which hath ... in it more than two chimneys ... shall be exempted from payment of the duties thereon imposed'[5]). A similar tax on chimneys was known already in sixteenth-century Cologne. Fifty-six per cent of all households in this German city had at that time only one chimney, the rest of the citizens paid taxes for more than two fireplaces. We can assume that almost everybody was included in this hearth tax, even the very poorest (4·7 per cent of the total tax payers). Frequent entries of 'poor' or 'pauper' suggest, however, that the poorest inhabitants were listed but not taxed. To have a fireplace was one thing to have it heated another. From the sixteenth century onwards firewood became more and more expensive and it was difficult to find cheap substitute energy for it. Stealing wood was therefore a common practice among the poor, even before the nineteenth century when Karl Marx wrote his socio-critical essay on the theft of wood.

Linked with the hearth and the preparation of meals are cooking utensils. For reasons which have to do with the type of information gathered from probate inventories it is difficult to offer precise figures or generalizations about these consumer goods. The poor certainly owned fewer kitchen-utensils than the more affluent classes. An overall average of 13·4 cooking devices and dishes was inventoried per household in early seventeenth-century Brunswick while the lowest wealth category possessed only 10·3 items on average. In the sixteenth century the vast

[5] Statutes of the Realm, 16 Charles II c. 3.

majority of rural inventories listed at least a large cooking pot (74 per cent) and a kettle (85 per cent). And even where such household items were owned by the lower classes, the existing economic hierarchy implied – as far as the material sphere is concerned – a shift from good-looking, solid, expensive kitchen-ware to ordinary, cheap and breakable cooking and dining utensils.

The catalogue of furnishings likely to be found in a poor man's household is not a long one. More important – at least in numerical terms – than the wardrobe was the wooden chest. Equipped with a solid lock, it was the quintessential mobile piece of furniture in every man's home. Its use was not only dictated by the lack of means for buying more expensive furniture. It also suited the mobility and instability which characterized the life-style of the poor. One of its many advantages was that the few wretched belongings in a poor man's home could be quickly grabbed and stuffed into those chests without fear of breakage or great expense in moving. Household and bed linen, in which the poor invested a considerable portion of their meagre savings, were kept in them most of the time. Expenditure on other furniture was negligible and consisted of tables, benches or collapsible arrangements like planks and trestles. In sixteenth-century Bordeaux, for example, one third of all inventories studied did not mention furniture required for social intercourse among family and friends. People obviously had to sit on chests, kneading-troughs or similar multi-functional items.

Studies on inventories from early modern Oxfordshire and Worcester-shire have analysed the frequency with which commodities turned up as the most heavily invested-in consumer item for various wealth groups. In Tudor times, the poorest wealth category (up to £20) had fewer inventories with bedding as their most expensive good (44·6 per cent). Instead the most simple and crude furniture was registered as the most valuable item in those households. In Stuart England the same wealth group became the one which had the most descendants with beds as the most expensive category, while the middling sorts of households, with bedding needs already satisfied, invested in other things – wearing apparel and furniture, for example. The significant trend observable in poorer households since the sixteenth century is therefore the practice of devoting over half of investment in consumer goods to bedding and linen. The lower classes thus followed a pattern that had been established by the affluent members of society in the later Middle Ages and had filtered down to the labouring poor by the sixteenth and seventeenth centuries. Declining prices for some manufactured goods and inheritance made such a change in consumer strategies among the lower classes possible.

Nutrition

In 1563 the Flemish artist Pieter Bruegel the Elder finished the copper engravings which are known as *vette cuecken* (fat cuisine) and *arm ghasterije* (a poor man's banquet). No other picture of the early modern period illustrates better the fact that for the poor the question of how one lived was, above all, a question of how to survive on a diet which was minimal in both quality and cost. The engraving which offers some penetrating comments on the disastrous effects of an insufficient diet on health shows a room filled with lean and pallid people, some of them stretching out their hands towards the frugal meal on the table, consisting of a loaf of bread, turnips and cockles. A man is sitting at the open fireplace, cooking a watery soup in a cauldron handing above the fire. A child with scrawny arms tilts a pot, licking up the left-overs. An emaciated mother feeds a sickly child sitting on her lap with some kind of liquid, most likely watery milk, as her dried up breasts clearly lack any milk of her own. Further signs of poverty and deprivation help to create an atmosphere of utmost misery. What a contrast to the rich man's banquet depicted in the other engraving! His table is loaded with all kinds of good and expensive food, roast chicken, a crispy porkling, and many other delicacies.

The general character of the poor countryman's food seems to have changed steadily for the worse during the early modern period. From the early sixteenth century, changes in the structure of landholding led in many European countries to a polarization between proportionately fewer subsistence farms and more landless people selling their labour to large-scale farming units. A growing proportion of the rural population was thus forced onto the market especially in years of harvest failures. Their earnings, although in some cases supplemented by payments in kind, failed to keep pace with galloping food prices. Wheat was always the most expensive grain, followed usually by rye, barley and oats. Rising grain prices forced the poor to switch away from wheat and to look for cheaper grain alternatives. Their diet deteriorated, if not in terms of quantity then at least from the standpoint of preference. Sixteenth-century writers were already aware of this phenomenon. 'As for wheaten bread', wrote William Harrison in 1577, 'they eat it when they can reach unto the price of it. Contenting themselves in the meane time with bread made of otes and barlaie: a poore estate God wot!'[6] Another contemporary writer, Sebastian Franck, described the German peasants' diet in his chronicle (1545) as follows: 'Their nourishment is black bread

---

[6] Quoted in John Burnett, *A History of the Cost of Living* (Harmondsworth, 1969), p. 125.

made of rye, oatmeal porridge and boiled peas and lentils; water and whey their only beverage'.[7] In eighteenth-century rural France up to 95 per cent of a poor countryman's diet was cereal in its various forms (bread, broth, gruel). There was, however, regional variance in choosing cheaper grain alternatives. The Bretons preferred buckwheat porridge, the Burgundians ate bread made of rye and oatmeal, supplemented by a porridge (*bouillie*) of maize. In the Auvergne the peasant farmers had to live for several months of the year mainly on boiled chestnuts. The usual accompaniment was vegetables (cabbages, turnips, onions, carrots, etc.) made into soup which could be thickened with old bread or pearl barley. Up to the end of the eighteenth century potatoes had not yet made a triumphal entry into the diet of the poor, either in France or elsewhere in Europe. The Charity Bureau in the City of Antwerp noted in 1805 'that if the potato has not yet replaced bread, at least it has become here a matter of prime necessity'.[8] Peas and beans were an important supplemental food for the poor although people often resisted eating them because they were normally fed only to animals. In Sir Hugh Platt's treatise entitled *Sundrie new and Artificiall remedies against Famine ... written vppon thoccasion of this present Dearth in 1596* the poor who were short of corn were advised to 'boile your beanes, pease, beechmast, &c. in faire water ... then you muste drie them ... and make bread thereof'. In eighteenth-century France parish priests of the diocese of Rodez reported to the authorities that the normal diet of their parishioners consisted in winter of rye and oats and was increasingly supplemented by chestnuts and vegetables as their own grain reserve gradually dwindled and the lean summer months arrived. This was in normal times. When a wet spring had caused the grain to rot while still green the poor Breton farmers ate a mixture of bread made of bran and cabbages. In some cases harvest failures forced the peasants to eat grain which had mildewed in the damp or which was contaminated by weevil, or by ergot, a fungus infecting cereals and causing serious food poisoning, characterized by lameness and necrosis of the extremities.

Small quantities of milk, occasionally an egg, a little bit of cheese, lard, a slice of fat pork, all sorts of cheap fish (in coastal areas), were the only protein food the poor peasant ever saw, in sharp contrast, for example, to the farm-workers in sixteenth-century Poland, who received at least 1·5 per cent (the nobleman in charge of the manor got 10 per cent) of the caloric value of their daily food in the form of fish or meat. According to

---

[7] Quoted in Robert Jütte, 'Diets in welfare institutions and in outdoor poor relief in early modern Western Europe', *Ethnologia Europaea* 16 (1988), 121.

[8] Quoted in Catharina Lis, *Social Change and the Labouring Poor, Antwerp 1770–1860* (New Haven and London, 1986), p. 92.

Reverend Richard Baxter, poor tenants living in late seventeenth-century England were glad of a piece of hanged bacon once a week, 'enough to trie the stomach of an ostriged'.[9] Another Englishman, Jonas Hanaway, wrote some eighty years later: 'The food of the poor is good bread, cheese, peases, turnips in winter, with a little pork or other meat when they can afford it; but from the high price of meat, it has not lately been within their reach. As to milk, they have hardly sufficient for their use.'[10] Throughout the whole period under study here the rural poor appear to have spent their meagre income on the cheaper bread grains and not on meat.

In times of a severe subsistence crisis starvation could be the lot of many poor. A much more common problem was, however, permanent undernourishment. Even if the poor managed somehow to appease their hunger, the supply of proteins and vitamins was certainly inadequate. Various deficiency diseases (e.g. rickets and scurvy), some of them already endemic in early modern Europe, can be attributed to a lack of certain vitamins in the regular diet. In some parts of France (Velay, Vivarais), one could come across entire villages where the inhabitants were crippled or in some other way physically distorted. The rural poor and all the landless farm-workers who depended to a large extent on the market for grain often had no other choice than to reduce their food costs by eating larger quantities of rye, rice and other alternative grains – foods with the highest caloric yield for the money. Carried to the extreme – the consumption of grain only – a family budget could be trimmed by as much as 50 per cent. Such a strategy would, however, have been detrimental to one's health in the long run.

Almost the same dietary deterioration occurred in the towns and cities, where a much larger proportion of the population engaged in crafts and services was dependent on the market for food. Not only did town-dwellers have fewer opportunities of growing their own food, but their specialized occupations demanded more of their time and precluded the degree of self-sufficiency that was still achieved by many country people. There can be little doubt that the group which suffered most from the great price-rise was the town-worker whose purchasing power fell by over half and even more during the early modern period. In English towns of the early modern period there were many labourers and craftsmen who could not afford meat, normally at 3d to 6d a pound, more than once a week and the poor among them scarcely tasted it from one month to another. James Lackington, who did not belong to the better-off town dwellers, reports in his *Memoirs* (1792) that he and his wife

[9] Quoted in Burnett, *Cost of Living*, p. 126.
[10] Quoted in Burnett, *Cost of Living*, p. 167.

existed on 4s 6d a week. The little meat they could afford was made into broth; they could not afford beer, but made substitute tea from toasted bread and coffee from fried wheat. Already in the sixteenth century, especially in times of high grain prices, artisans and poor urban workers were forced, as William Harrison (1534–93) noted in his famous *Description of England*, to live on 'horse corn, I mean beans, peason, oats, tares, and lentils'.[11] The customary labourers' diet was coarse and monotonous (see Plate 3). Vegetables and fruit were scarce and it is likely that the urban poor ate fewer dairy products than the poor farm-workers and cottagers who often had a cow or some sheep which they could graze on the village common.

Even if the diet of the poorer townsman was monotonous and not very healthy, he had one advantage over the poor countryman. The cities had charities and welfare institutions which could mitigate the terrible effects of harvest failures. During the famine which struck Nuremberg in 1491 the magistrate provided the local poor with bread, butter, salt, meat, fish, vegetables and wine. Not every early modern European town could obviously afford such a generous outdoor poor relief, especially when later on, in the course of the sixteenth century, the price of food products increased considerably. Except for some private charities poor relief in the form of food supplies meant the distribution of one commodity: either bread or grain. Nevertheless it is difficult to reduce the variety and differences in quantity of outdoor poor relief, provided, of course, that alms were still given in kind, to a common denominator. Rich laymen's charities, e.g. the one established by the Tucher family in Nuremberg at the end of the fifteenth century, provided an opulent and nutritious meal for the 'happy few' among the local poor, whereas the regular food allowance for resident paupers in another German town (Konstanz) consisted only of staple food like bread, gruel and lard. As financial difficulties grew, anything other than bread was excluded from outdoor poor relief and thereafter even the bread ration itself could be diminished owing to a sudden rise in the number of poor in need of immediate help. In the early sixteenth century the Heilig-Geist-Spital in Cologne still distributed food portions made up of herring, rye and wheaten bread. Later on the payments were no longer in kind but rather modest amounts of money for which the poor could buy less and less on the market because of soaring food prices. In eighteenth-century Aix-en-Provence the hospital general called La Charité distributed approximately 4,000 loaves of bread to an average of 410 people every week. The bread distributed was 'of wheat and good quality'. A single person received

---

[11] William Harrison, *Description of England in Shakespeare's Youth (1577/87)*, ed. F. J. Furnivall (London, 1877), p. 133.

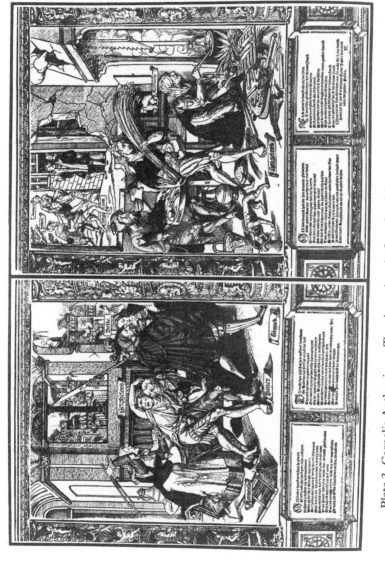

Plate 3. Cornelis Anthoniszon Teunissen (attr.), *Sorgeloos [Careless]. Woodcut*, 1541.

seven one-pound loaves as a weekly ration. In late sixteenth-century Augsburg the poor relief recipients were somewhat better-off because they received on average not only a four-pound loaf per person but also spelt for gruel (0·56 litres) and lard (183 g) on a weekly basis. There can be no doubt that the bread-distribution by private charities or by the local government provided a major supplement to the diet of the many labouring poor who simply did not earn enough to support their families.

Some idea of what it was considered the poor ought to eat can be gathered from the records of diets provided by charitable institutions (hospitals, workhouses, orphanages, etc.). The regime provided by St Bartholomew's Hospital in London in 1687 included ten different items in the week's menu. The inmate received 10 oz (283·5 g) wheaten bread, three pints of beer, and two pints of soup, broth or milk potage every day. Meat (170·1 g) was served on Mondays, Tuesdays, Thursdays and Sundays. Cheese and butter were the substitute for meat on the other days of the week. In the Heilig-Kreuz-Spital in Cologne the twelve pensioners or prebendaries received in 1543 almost the same variety of foodstuffs every day: butter (48·1 g), cheese (27·9 g), bacon (155·8 g), meat (10·4 g), eggs (3) and bread (187 g). The diets provided in most charitable institutions in the sixteenth and seventeenth centuries were all of the meat, salt, fish, cheese, beer or wine and bread variety.

With workhouses and prison diets the dietary regimes become less homogeneous. The daily allowance for inmates in the House of Correction in Copenhagen (1627) is surprisingly high, even if one takes into account the fact that the prisoners had to work hard. The monthly food portions include 1 lb pork, 7 lb beef, 3 lb butter, 3 lb cheese, 20 lb bread, 20 lb herring, 3 lb dried fish, $\frac{3}{4}$ bushel (about 13 litres) gruel, and approximately 70 litres beer. The forced labourers (*Schellenwerker*) in seventeenth-century Berne had to be content with a rather frugal diet in comparison to their fellow sufferers in Copenhagen. Their daily meals were made up only of bread (1,137 g) and gruel (2,171 g). A greater variety of food is displayed in the diet sheet of the House of Correction in Bury St Edmunds, Suffolk. In this institution bread (453 g), porridge (1·136 kg), meat (227 g) and beer (1·136 l) figure on 'flesh days' and cheese (302 g) or herring (about 400 g) instead of meat on 'fish days'.

According to various studies on poorhouse diets in the period 1500 to 1800 it seems that the amount of calories supplied by those diets extended over a considerable range (1,700 to 5,000 calories per capita). The majority of the hospital and workhouse inmates, however, had an intake close to 3,000 calories per day. Nutritionists consider that a twentieth-century man of average physical activity needs between 2,900 and 3,200 calories each day. Men in pre-industrial Europe needed somewhat fewer calories because of their slightly smaller structure. It would therefore be misleading to imply that all those inmates of hospitals, almshouses and workhouses were somehow in the same boat as the needy who lived outside the hospital walls and who, only if they were lucky, had the chance to be on the bread lists of charitable institutions providing outdoor poor relief.

Clothing

The everyday clothes of the working poor would be made of coarse wool or linen, even of canvas, in the case of the very poor. Apart from what the paupers could produce themselves by spinning and weaving, the lower classes, in particular the urban poor, had to rely on receiving the cast-off garments of others (often family members, employer), or, in the case of servants, on clothes provided as part of the wage. Clothes were also bought second-hand at a 'slop-shop', but even then a family of seven or eight living in eighteenth-century England might easily spend up to £5 a year on dress. In 1560 the Strasbourg poor law administration estimated that the expenses for clothing a poor student would amount to 3 florins a year. In the early sixteenth century the Magistrate of Basel paid for a poor youth who had to be put up in one of the city's monasteries on average 3·9 florins every year for clothes. The various late medieval and early modern budgets collected by a German social historian indicate that food and drink, fuel and rent, were, of course, the principal recurrent expenses of the labouring poor, but that clothes and shoes came into either the fourth or fifth place. In late fifteenth-century Strasbourg the municipal orphanage spent 48·5 per cent of its annual budget for board and accommodation on food and drink, 16·1 per cent on fuel, and the same amount on clothes for the pauper children. A slightly lower proportion of expenditure on clothing we find in the budget of the common chest in Augsburg in the second half of the sixteenth century. The Gemeine Almosen devoted 10·7 per cent of its expenditure for outdoor poor relief to cloth, each recipient getting about 5 ells of cloth a year. For those living above the poverty line in sixteenth-century Germany 10 ells of cloth per year was the average amount of woollen or mostly linen fabrics considered to be sufficient for tailoring a proper dress or attire.

Even allowing for the fact that the few poor people's inventories that have survived cannot be regarded as representative of the garments owned by the labouring poor in general, they indicate a pitifully low level of clothing. Many of these inventories are not complete because some garments were worth too little to merit valuation or because the deceased

was buried in the few clothes he owned. Where popular dress is more or
less fully specified in English notarial documents, it generally ranges in
value from a couple of shillings to about a pound. The clothes owned by
a poor woman who died in Toledo in 1593 included two small headdresses
(worth 68 maravedis or 2 reales), an old shirt (85 mrs), an old brown
mantilla (68 mrs), some pieces of an old blanket (no price given), some
old rags (16 mrs) and an old brown mantilla that was given to another
poor person. In those years the salary for a woman nursing foundling
children was between 3 and 6 reales a month. A poor woman who died in
a hospital in the German city of Lindau in 1506 and whose stock of
clothes was assessed as above average bequeathed only two coarse coats
(a long and a short one), and three pieces of women's underwear. When
a beggar died in Basel in 1518 one found in his rented room a charity
gown (*Luxrock*, a garment made of a piece of cloth distributed among
indigent inhabitants of the city of Basel by a charitable institution), a grey
coat, a grey jacket, a breast fur, two shirts, and two table-cloths.
Headdresses and shoes are missing from this inventory of a resident
pauper. This impressionistic picture is in accordance with the average
levels found in probate inventories of the lower classes which have
survived, for example, in Basel, Bordeaux and Paris. Clothing and linen
represented a small but significant part (3 per cent) of the total fortune of
wage-earners in early eighteenth-century Paris. According to Daniel
Roche's study around 1700–15 most wage-earners in the French capital
owned a mediocre wardrobe, valued on average at 17 livres for men and
15 livres for women. Complete men's clothing consisting of a cloak (27
per cent), a jacket (65 per cent), breeches (80 per cent) and jerkin (95 per
cent) is rarely found in the inventories of the labouring poor. The female
popular dress consisted of five main garments: the skirt, which appears in
89 per cent of the inventories, petticoat (53 per cent), mantle (87 per
cent), apron (88 per cent), bodice and corset (41 per cent). Contrasts
between men and women did exist. While dark colours (black, greys and
browns), at least in the sixteenth century, dominated female garments,
men's clothing, apart from the cloak, was becoming more varied and
colourful even among the lower classes. Elegance and style, however,
were something for the rich. The poor, men and women, had a few simple
garments of rustic quality. The plainness and uniformity of the whole
was accentuated by the predominance in the inventories of expressions
like 'mean', 'old' and 'torn', giving us the impression that the poorest
among the labouring poor were dressed in worn, stained, patched
clothes.

Those poor who wandered from one place to another were forced to
wear their whole wardrobe. For any one who lived in a furnished room,

slept in barns, or found temporary shelter in a hospice or dormitory, it was impossible to store his most valuable belongings (e.g. clothes). If some beggars were wearing several jackets on top of each other, it was not necessarily a matter of keeping warm, but of having their meagre riches always on themselves all the time. For many beggars and vagrants clothing was reduced to essentials. Criminal and legal records attest this 'ragged' appearance of the itinerant paupers. The minimal wardrobe of the ragtag and bobtail, labelled *malvestus* in French sources, bore witness to their extreme poverty. And it was easy for contemporaries to identify by their clothes vagrants and other 'masterless men'. Wretched, incomplete, shabby, torn clothes signified their utter destitution as well as their immoral conduct. Jacques Callots' famous series of etchings known as *Les Gueux* (1622–3) illustrate both the dominant 'style' of clothing among wandering beggars and their miserable condition. There were, however, also beggars who deceived municipal gate-keepers by entering the city disguised as properly dressed artisans or petty traders so it took some time before these unwanted paupers were detected by vigilant poor law officials and banished from the city. Faced with rags and tatters or even with nudity, the symbol of extreme poverty in Christian theology, the citizens often felt pity and gave alms more quickly while welfare officers and magistrates expressed their aversion and revealed their fears of the badly dressed, filthy beggars and vagrants. In his most popular work *The Fraternity of Vagabonds* (1561), the English writer and book printer John Awdeley, for example, describes certain types of knaves, among them the so-called 'Green Winchard' who 'when his hose is broken and hang out his shoes he will put them into his shoes again with a stick, but he will not amend them', and he expresses at the same time his disgust for such a 'slothful knave, that had liefer go like a beggar than cleanly'.[12]

There is, however, a sharp division between those wretched beggars with their rags and their shabby clothing and the criminal underworld of urban or vagrant elements whose casual and rakish outfit symbolized toughness and unsubmissiveness. Their conspicuous outward signs (colourful coats, flamboyant headdress, etc.) often became part of a folk legend, and if not, they feature as prominent marks of identification in warrants of arrest for sturdy beggars and vagabonds. These documents which are a valuable source for the costume of the rather loose group called the 'non-conformist poor' (Eric Hobsbawm) survived in many European municipal and county archives but have not yet been studied systematically by social historians.

---

[12] Reprinted in *Rogues, Vagabonds, and Sturdy Beggars. A New Gallery of Tudor and Early Stuart Rogue Literature*, ed. A. F. Kinney (Amherst, 1990), p. 99.

Beggars or poorly dressed, it was all one to charitable institutions guided by the biblical image in the New Testament (Matthew 25:34–6) of God as hungry, thirsty, naked and homeless pauper, ushering the blessed to his right for having been generous, and damning misers and unmerciful folk to his left. Not only in the Middle Ages but also during the early modern period, confraternities, hospitals, parishes and even municipal poor relief bureaux distributed clothing to the needy. In sixteenth-century Spain, for example, the members of the confraternity Santa Maria y San Julian in Zamora arranged a ritual dole of clothing to the needy, in which the furriers of the confraternity gave to each recipient a cape of coarse goat's hair, a fur robe, and shoes. A Protestant community, like the one in seventeenth-century Bordeaux, did not concoct such imaginative or impressive rituals for the distribution of clothes but nevertheless also 'clothed the naked' by giving special grants to those who were in need of a new dress or proper outfit. Providing the poor with clothes was for the Protestant Church not primarily an act of mercy but a welfare contribution. Educating the poor and setting them to work was only possible if their female and male wardrobes did not frighten away potential employers or masters. We only have to remember what such an experienced welfare administrator as Lucas Hackfurt said in his letter to the Magistrate of the city of Strasbourg (1532), complaining about the idle young boys and girls who had difficulties in finding a job because they did not have the clothes they would need for becoming a servant or an apprentice. Occasionally, the local government, most likely a magistrate, would ask a welfare administrator or the parish priest to officiate and distribute money rather than the more traditional cloth or garments.

Bequests to clothe the poor were also popular among rural and urban testators, especially in Catholic communities. They commanded their heirs to clothe a certain number of paupers and often these gifts were loosely connected to funeral practices. It seems that towards the end of the sixteenth and the beginning of the seventeenth century donations of clothing and shoes tended to become detached from funeral processions not only in France but also elsewhere in Europe. Post-Tridentine spirituality fostered a taste for simple funerals and the large number of paupers and priests and crosses that formerly had manifested the wealth and generosity of the benefactor slowly disappeared.

The clothing of the poor was also the object of another kind of charitable institution. The inmates of hospitals, orphanages, almshouses and other welfare institutions were regularly supplied with clothes. In Troyes, Marseilles and Montpellier the local hospitals had the right to march the entire group of paupers round their city in their uniforms in order to illustrate the extent of the needs of the institution and at the same time to organize a massive collection. In sixteenth-century Nuremberg the one hundred poor men who received alms from the Pfinzing-Foundation marched through the streets wearing their new outfits consisting of coat, hat, stockings and shoes – all in white except for the footwear. The paupers confined in hospitals and almshouses were often obliged to wear institutional clothing which was made from coarse cloths, linen and hemp. Colours were normally dark and uniform and not many people wore warm or light colours (e.g. white). The female inmates of Montpellier's House of Correction had to wear grey linen uniforms which at least ensured that the women were warmly dressed. More touches of colour were to be found among the young boys and girls living in orphanages. In seventeenth-century Lübeck, the orphan boys wore white stockings, a blue jacket with a red cross on it, a white collar, and black shoes; the orphan girls' dress consisted of a red skirt and a red jerkin with puffed sleeves decorated with a blue cross, a white collar, a white apron, and a red cap. Figured cloths were mostly striped. The inmates of the Zucht- und Waisenhaus in Pforzheim, for example, were required to wear a striped black and white uniform which resembled modern prison clothing. And some of the detainees had to wear this dress even after their discharge from the workhouse. All in all, inmates of charitable institutions seemed better and more warmly dressed than the 'shamefaced' poor, since they got a proper dress when they entered the institution and they no longer had to worry about their minimal wardrobe.

6   The poor helping themselves

The importance of social networks

In 1859 the English newspaper editor and physician Samuel Smiles
(1812–1904) published a much acclaimed book entitled *Self Help with
Illustrations of Conduct and Perseverance*. This vision of a world of self-
help secured by local and neighbourhood action was very much shaped
by Victorian values as well as by his own personal experience. What he
had to say to his contemporaries was, however, far from being original,
but he can be credited with the fact that giving his book the title 'self
help' he coined and propagated a new term which was often used and
abused during the next 150 years.

Only recently historians have remarked upon the extent of self-help
and mutual aid among the labouring poor. There can be no doubt that in
times of dearth, emergency, unemployment, sickness and childbirth, it
was the poor who first tried to help themselves before asking for alms or
support by charitable institutions. As far as the labouring poor are
concerned self-help means 'the ability of individuals to endure a period
of poverty distress beyond the short-time logic of the market economy
without asking for assistance'.[1] This definition excludes other forms of
individual self-help such as begging and petty theft but includes formal
types of mutual aid offered by fraternities and similar corporations.

Self-help functions best in a framework of social relations with a rather
low degree of specificity. This means that an employer–employee
relationship, for example, can be as effective or helpful as personal
relations (e.g. friendship). Neighbourhood ties, on the other hand, are as
valuable as kinship in times of economic distress. Such types of
relationship can either be substituted by each other or combined with
other formal or informal social ties. Sociologists and social anthropologists call this complex field of relationship a social network. A major

---

[1] Martin Dinges, 'Self-help, assistance, and the poor in early modern France', paper
prepared for International Perspectives on Self-Help Conference (Lancaster, 2–4 July
1991), p. 3.

function of such networks is to help people to cope with various problems which occur in everyday life (e.g. poverty, illness). The social contacts that an individual makes with any number of persons (not necessarily intimates or status equals) with the result that help and advice is provided in case of a particular problem or crisis have been described by some sociologists as 'problem-anchored helping networks' (Donald Warren). These problem-oriented networks are heterogeneous in composition and can overlap with other networks. In contrast to other informal social ties problem-anchored networks do not require that specific persons provide the basis of networking. From one time to another the problem-experiencing individual may use a different neighbour (co-worker etc.) or the same one, but he turns to the same type of helper. For any given problem one can visualize a pool of potential helpers whose capacity to form a network depends on the single individual who seeks aid in this social context. In Figure 9 we have depicted the social bonds which played a pivotal role in pre-industrial problem-anchored networks. The fabric of networks among the labouring poor is thus closely interwoven with patterns of traditional institutions such as the family, kinship, friendship and neighbourhood.

In a social network each dyadic (one-to-one) relationship is normally based on the principle of reciprocal exchange. The intensity of this exchange depends on at least four factors: (1) social distance, (2) physical distance, (3) economic distance, (4) age distance. According to modern anthropological studies one finds certain degrees of reciprocity for each relationship: between brothers, friends, acquaintances, and so on. In kinship relations, for example, the reciprocal exchange is often camouflaged, but here reciprocity is nevertheless implied, too, even if it is not immediately satisfied. Peasants and cottagers in early modern Piedmont who sold tiny plots of land to their kin for higher prices than to their neighbours or to strangers knew very well that this exchange of goods for money often took into account past favours or help. Social closeness, such as consanguinity, was, however, not enough to safeguard reciprocal exchange. The daily interaction between close neighbours often generated more intense relations than between kin who lived far away from each other. The exchange tends to become asymmetrical when the helper is in a much more powerful economic position (e.g. landlord, employer) and the relationship turns then into one between patron and client. In general the social network of the labouring poor seems to be characterized by a balance of resources and wants. The fourth factor implies an automatically deferred reciprocity arrangement. While exchanges with more remote kin and with neighbours are more specific and short term, the reciprocity between parents and children is long-term and without

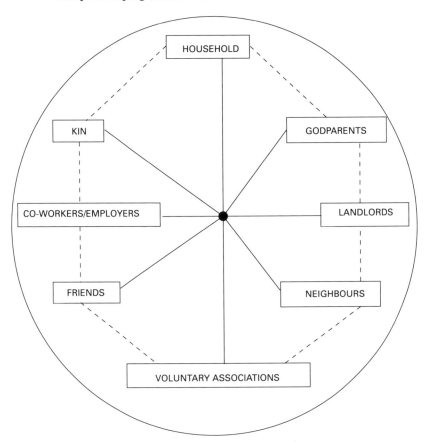

Figure 9 The structure of problem-anchored helping networks in
early modern Europe

conscious thought of return. In early modern Europe, old people could
in general expect help from their children based on the sustenance and
protection provided by parents during the childhood period. Thus active
participation in such a problem-anchored network fluctuates in time
according to the various stages of the life-cycle.

One of the primary aims for the labouring poor is to maintain
independence and to avoid becoming a burden on others by accumulating
enough 'social capital' (Martin Dinges) which could be exchanged for
instrumental help or advice on a day-to-day basis. A person's support
network and the larger social network of which it forms a part is to a
certain degree also a question of chance as much depends on the marriage
and fertility of earlier generations. While these biological factors are

ultimately beyond individual control, a person can alter the effects of biology by his or her own geographical mobility. A third factor affecting the formation of a broad support network has to do with the fact that some people are more gregarious or sociable than others. The types of helpers identified in the lives of the labouring poor of the early modern period are, therefore, the result of biological events, migration patterns and individual temperament.

Self-help, mutual aid and the poor

A key focus of the analysis of helping is the role of the co-residential unit usually referred to by historians as 'household'. To a certain degree, the household as a helping system is not identical to the family as a system of mutual suppport. At its core is, of course, the familial group. The myth about the large, extended, kin-enfolding, multi-generational, welfare- and support-providing household in the 'world we have lost' was successfully debunked by the founder of the Cambridge Group for the History of Population and Social Structure, Peter Laslett. Further research has shown that a family household, especially among the labouring poor, could be a very different thing from decade to decade or even from year to year, although it changed its size rather than its kinship composition. Parents died, women and men remarried, children were born, died early or left home when they were considered to be grown up. Lodgers, visitors, boarders, servants, apprentices and more distant kin were added to this core either by pure economic necessity or for some other reason. Evidence from early modern English poor censuses suggest that many poorer families took in lodgers who could contribute something to the family economy either by paying rent or by joining the labour force. Such lodgers were, for example, present in twenty households which appeared in the Norwich census of the poor from 1570. A few were unmarried labourers, others were undoubtedly paupers themselves, as, for example, the family of four, in which the mother was sick, that had taken in a woman deserted by her husband and who perhaps helped with the children. Another clear example involving disablement instead of illness, was a couple called Hales, both in their eighties and both 'not able to worke', who had with them a 'mayd' of eighteen who spun and looked after them. The fact that there were also households of the elderly poor which include fatherless children helps to explain the apparent anomaly of so-called 'servants' being present even in poor households. Where poor households included strangers, it is very likely that a mutually beneficial arrangement had been made between them. And this was often done on an exchange basis. Margaret Cully of

Table 8. *Household composition in Ardleigh, Essex, 1796*

Relationship to household head	Poor relief recipients	Others
Household head	1.00	1.00
Spouse	0.89	0.77
Child	3.41	2.10
Kin	0.21	0.26
Servant	0.05	0.91
Lodger	0.13	0.24
Total (= mean household size)	5.69	5.28

Source : Thomas Sokoll, 'The pauper households small and simple? The evidence from listings of inhabitants and pauper lists of early modern England reassessed', *Ethnologia Europaea* 17 (1987), 34, Table 3.

Norfolk, a blind and aged widow, made over her estate of £40 in exchange for a guarantee of being 'kept' for the rest of her life. The beneficiary, a certain Timothy Cully, was apparently unrelated to her.

Studies on the household composition based on listings of inhabitants and pauper lists of eighteenth-century England indicate that pauper households were different from others because they contained more children and fewer servants. The proportions of households with kin and with lodgers were more or less the same (cf. Table 8), but there were slight differences in the structure of the household. The proportion of complex households, that is extended family and multiple family households, was slightly higher for poor relief recipients than for the rest of the population. This was mainly due to the presence of elderly widows in the households of their married children. This flatly contradicts the widespread belief that solitary households were particularly prominent among the poorer classes in early modern Europe and that the kinship system and its rules of household formation gave rise to 'hardships' – brought on by the death of a spouse, old age, sickness or unemployment – such that many households found it difficult to be economically self-sufficient. On the other hand, finding quite a number of lodgers in the pauper household shows that family and household were not only a kin group but a 'collectivity' (Peter Laslett) consisting of household labourers who must not be necessarily related to each other. In other words, rather than relying on neighbours, and community-organized groups such as guilds and fraternities, the poor preferred extended kinship solidarity and the cushioning of life-cycle risks within more complex households which were not exclusively kin groups.

Demographic historians point out that the egocentrism of nuclear households often worked against kin solidarity in early modern European towns and villages. It is therefore interesting to look at the way in which the poor treated their kin and particularly their elderly parents. Legally, even relatives living outside the nuclear family were obliged to support one another. The English Poor Relief Act of 1601 stipulated that 'the children of every poor, old, blind, lame and impotent person... shall at their own charges relieve and maintain every such poor person'.[2] Magistrates could therefore, for example, compel grandparents to take in grandchildren or were entitled to force children to contribute weekly pensions to their aged parents. The parish of Myddle, located a few miles from Shrewsbury, entered a court battle with a neighbouring parish on the question whether grandparents-in-law or sons-in-law also 'though they bee not named in the Statute yet by the equity of the Statute... are obliged'[3] to maintain their needy relatives. That local kin could play an integral part in the system of parish poor relief is made clear in a letter from a Roger Cotton's daughter who wrote to the Churchwardens that she and her husband Nicholas Willis, a shoemaker, had 'great charges and expenses... by providing things necessary' for her deceased father who had lived in one of London's many local almshouses. Not by law but as a matter of fact and for simple economic necessity German poor relief administrators also placed an obligation to support 'impotent' poor on grandparents, parents and children. When in 1543, for example, the widow Elsa Bender applied for a place in Frankfurt's municipal hospital, the town council objected and referred the applicant to her children, 'who should take care of their mother and support her'.[4] But in some cases overseers and magistrates found it as important to prevent the fulfilment of kinship obligations as to insist upon them. The fundamental distinctions would seem to be those based on wealth and means, as Barbara Ziegler from Bächlingen in southwest Germany explained when finally admitted to the local *Spital* in the 1620s: 'I stayed with my son for four years, but the food was bad and [he] supported me only with great effort'.[5] Poor households which took in impoverished relatives coming from elsewhere were sometimes admonished by the poor law authorities

---

[2] 43 Eliz. c. 2, vii. The liability of parents to support their children, imposed already by the Poor Law Act of 1597, was extended to grandparents: see W. Newman Brown, 'The receipt of poor relief and family situation: Aldenham, Hertfordshire 1630–90', in Richard M. Smith (ed.), *Land Kinship and Life-Cycle* (Cambridge, 1984), p. 406.

[3] Richard Gough, *The History of Myddle*, ed. by David Hey (Harmondsworth, 1981), p. 254.

[4] Quoted in Robert Jütte, *Obrigkeitliche Armenfürsorge in deutschen Reichsstädten der Frühen Neuzeit* (Cologne and Vienna 1984), p. 333.

[5] Quoted in Thomas Robisheaux, *Rural Society and the Search for Order in Early Modern Germany* (Cambridge, 1989), p. 162.

to 'quietly put them away'[6] in order to avoid additional burdens on the parish. Even in those cases where family obligation was tied up with the future exchange of land and other forms of wealth the readiness of family members to care for each other was not self-evident or free from ambiguities. Whenever an aged parent or long-ill relative (brother, sister, uncle) was supported and nursed for any length of time, the relatives providing such help kept careful book. In a south German village (Neckarhausen), for example, the two daughters of Martin Bosch agreed in 1778 to share the costs of taking care of him in order to share future inheritances. Here we see again the exchange system at work, even if the evidence suggests that it was not simply based on cold calculation and devoid of parental or sisterly love. Family disputes over rather modest inheritances illustrate to what extent property and personal assets were part of a general set of exchanges and responsibilities.

Yet as far as the poor were concerned, family obligations did not run very far. Children were required to support their indigent parents according to their own means but could not be expected to take them in, since they very often had dependent children of their own with whom they had to share their overcrowded dwelling. The group which was most clearly closest to each other was composed of parents, children and siblings. Only very rarely support and help extended to step-relations and to uncles, aunts, nieces and nephews. Benjamin Shaw's (1772–1841) autobiographical account illustrates that when he was forced to cease work because of a sudden lameness the family survived on combinations of savings, put-out work, aid from a sister and poor relief. William Stout (1665–1752) frequently mentions in his autobiography his and his family's duty to sort out his nephews' debts when they went broke. And evidence from Hermann Weinsberg's famous diary, written in the second half of the sixteenth century, suggests that those family members who were better off took on the obligation to care also for more distant relatives while others shirked their responsibilities for economic reasons. The values of self-help and mutuality presented or implied in these autobiographical texts become apparent at all social levels.

The interplay of 'emotion and material interest' (David Sabean) and the complexity of obligations between kin have been the subject of a number of recent historical studies. Among the characteristics of the western family considered over time is the small proportion of housholds with resident kin. Figures given by historical demographers vary from region to region and according to socio-economic status. In seventeenth-century London, for example, wealthy areas were more likely to contain

[6] Quoted in Slack, *Poverty*, p. 84.

kin. In poorer suburbs (e.g. Boroughside) the small number of co-resident kin (3.1 per cent) is very similar to the proportion found in poor areas of other English pre-industrial towns and cities. In the suburbs of early modern Canterbury, for example, only 2.3 per cent of the households contained resident kin. The conspicuous absence of kin residents in the households of the labouring poor gives us, however, a distorted view of the social reality. Kinship did not stop at the front door. There is evidence from many early modern European towns and villages that the presence of kin living nearby was an important source of social and financial assistance for some poorer households. While fairly extensive local kinship networks can be reconstructed for wealthier households, especially where wills and other sources exist, the meagre data available for some pre-modern urban and rural communities suggest that the majority of kin networks involved only two households. A comparison of a London suburb with the Essex village of Terling suggests that the differences in kinship ties were more of degree than of kind. Owing to different patterns of mobility and population increase the kinship network in Terling was somewhat more 'dense' than that of London's Boroughside community. Between 37 and 52 per cent of all its housholds were linked to at least one other in 1670 compared to perhaps 18 per cent of those in that part of the capital.

Information as to the degree to which locally based kin networks actually provided substantial social and financial support for each other is rarely provided by the sources. Recent studies on early modern French, Italian and English cities indicate that kin could be of considerable importance in the 'economy of makeshifts' (O. Hufton), by providing, for example, temporary lodgings or financial aid to recent immigrants. It also seems probable that certain features of life in an urban community favoured the maintenance of ties of kinship, especially among newcomers who could not yet rely on neighbourly contacts. For many poor families kinship provided the chief institution for mutual support and betterment, but other urban householders, in the absence of local kin, tended to rely more on neighbours, employers, friends and other local networks than their counterparts did in rural areas.

Studies on early modern Italy, France, England and Spain indicate that the institution of godparenthood, although it fell into some discredit on the eve of the Counter-Reformation, still played an important role in a society where kinship was a dominant principle of organization. Sociologists and anthropologists as well historians have recently stressed the importance of such spiritual kinship, pointing out how significant such links may be not only in the acquisition of prestige and power but also in the establishment of problem-anchored networks. There is some

Table 9. *The social strategy in choosing godparents in an early modern German town (Oppenheim, 1568–1798)*

Godparent's occupation	Father: day-labourer	Office holder
clergyman	2.4	10.0
noble	4.9	2.2
office holder	31.7	61.7
soldier	–	1.0
merchant/alehouse keeper	7.3	9.5
artisan with a workshop	20.7	12.2
artisan without a workshop	17.1	2.0
day-labourer	9.8	0.2
farmer/farm worker	6.1	1.2
total (absolute)	82	402
total (percentage)	100	100

Source: Peter Zschuncke, *Konfession und Alltag in Oppenheim* (Wiesbaden, 1984), p. 160, Table 18.

evidence that the godfather had special significance for the lower classes because godparents were often chosen from people of higher status than natural parents. A sixteenth-century parish register from Bilton near York shows that at about a quarter of baptisms one of the three recorded godparents was a member of the gentry, more usually female than male, and that the child was quite often named after him or her. In the early eighteenth-century register of an English Catholic community (Lytham in Lancashire) the proportion was extremely low (2.7 per cent) and the children in question were invariably those of present or former domestic servants. This trend towards an essentially egalitarian character of the relation between child and spiritual kin is already visible in Florence at the end of the fifteenth and the beginning of the sixteenth century. On the other hand one can conclude from figures available for an early modern German town with a mixed religious community that through the whole period the social value of this relationship was esteemed higher by contemporaries than the spiritual or religious one. And there can be no doubt that the lower and middle classes in this small German town continued to choose godparents with a higher social status (cf. Table 9) in order to safeguard the future of a child whose chances of becoming an orphan stood at that time very high. However, social historians are presented with severe problems when they have to evaluate the socio-economic functions of these 'spiritual kin' for the lower classes. For example, how effective and strong was the relationship? Did better-off godparents often leave property to their godchildren? Did they feel any obligation to care for them in the event of the parents' death? All these questions are difficult to answer. One can conclude from the incidental references to the subject in the sources that many godparents understood *compaternitas* as a relation not only of formal amity but also of mutual trust and obligatory assistance. An analysis of bequests in the Essex village of Boreham over the period 1503–1620 shows that in nine out of seventy-eight wills godparents left a small gift (on average 12d) to their godchildren.

Despite such strong social ties as family, kinship and godparenthood people's jobs were also of some importance in making them part of the local community or excluding them. In one of the major occupational groups, the corporate trades, occupational ties, over a distance of several streets, were at least as important as those with the immediate neighbours. The small master craftsman in particular tended, however, to be closer to his workers and to have less contact with other masters of the same trade. In such cases a journeyman was more likely to be integrated into the master's family life, and might in that way form a problem-anchored helping network in times of prolonged illness or some other economic hardship. The biography of a seventeen-year-old French apprentice to a mason from a village in the Massif Central shows the importance of such ties. Very early in his life he became an orphan. An uncle pretending to be his godfather deprived him of his inheritance, maltreated him and finally evicted him from his household. The boy was forced to beg and moved to Bordeaux. There he had luck and became an apprentice. He lived in the house of the master craftsman. His employer looked after the boy and took care of him when he fell ill before he could even start work. The boy was so grateful to his master that he made him his sole heir and bequeathed to his own relatives only the legal minimum (5 sous).[7]

In another important occupational group, the street, port and market trades, the master–journeyman relationship was absent, because most tradespeople were self-employed. This created a different set of social relationships. Cooperation and solidarity existed nevertheless and was often reinforced both by proximity and by common geographical origin.

The third major occupational group in an early modern town was the domestic servants. Evidence from eighteenth-century Paris suggests that many servants had strong ties with other groups in the city. While those who were working in rich and larger households lived in relative social isolation, those who worked for humbler employers were less cut off. They were at least potentially able to form closer ties with their master,

[7] Cf. Dinges, 'Self-help', p. 8.

and this could facilitate their integration into the local community. But examples of close relationships between employer and employee are also common enough among affluent households. Of course, there were others who did not fit into the model which according to the late eighteenth-century French author Sébastien Mercier had existed in the good old days of the *ancien régime*:

Servants were in those days part of the family; they were treated less politely, but with greater affection; they perceived this, and were grateful. The employer was better served, and could count on a loyalty which today is quite rare. They were protected both from poverty and vice; and in return for obedience they received benevolence and protection... Once their lives were laborious, hard and frugal; but they counted for something, and the servant died of old age alongside his master.[8]

That in many cases the relationship between servant and master involved indeed a lasting commitment on both sides is reflected in promises of inheritances and pensions. In Sienna, for example, the relative share of gifts to servants increased from 3.7 per cent to 9.1 per cent of all pious bequests between 1401 and 1800. By the middle of the seventeenth century they had already overtaken all other charitable gifts to the poor, whether in form of handouts, dowry funds, or endowments. For testators their servants were in a sense the most respectable of all the needy. The 'loyalty–affection' model was, however, restricted to rather affluent households. It could be of vital importance for a humble employer's own survival to dismiss a servant who became ill or superfluous after the children were old enough to contribute to the family economy. Owing to the economic conditions in which most artisans and tradespeople had to live, relations between masters and servants were always brittle. Neither side expected any great commitment. Nevertheless one finds examples of less affluent households which looked after the servant who fell ill or became too old to work. Instances of solidarity and financial support the other way are rarer, reflecting the difference in the economic position between master and servant. A maidservant and a foreman in Plymouth, for instance, gave small amounts of cash towards the relief of plague-infected members of their master's family.

It is clear that certain trades and work structures facilitated the formation of problem-anchored network in urban communities. But what about the great number of labouring poor who lived and worked in the countryside? Evidence from English and French sources shows that rural labourers could obtain their grain through purchase from their

---

[8] L.-S. Mercier, *Le Tableau de Paris*, new edition (Amsterdam 1782–8), vol. I, pp. 171–2; English translation by David Garrioch, *Neighbourhood and Community in Paris, 1740–1790* (Cambridge, 1986), p. 134.

employers at lower farm-gate prices. Being able to buy food at a concessionary rate from their employer was one of the few privileges enjoyed by farm labourers. A report of the marketing of corn in Norfolk, drawn up in 1631 in response to the previous year's dearth, referred to 'labourers that buy it at an under price of them with whom they work'.[9] Another advantage was that rural labourers who had no cash were able to pay for their grain with the promise of future work. The already mentioned report from Norfolk pointed to the practice whereby the rural labourer 'hath now corn at home upon trust, or by agreement for work'. And according to evidence from eighteenth-century France even the seasonal migrants employed by farmers could borrow with the speculative profits of this temporary work as their surety. The same applied to day-labourers who could not do without advance payment to feed their families and to meet their obligations. While debts entered into within a local community and within horizontal relationships (kin, neighbours) may neither have carried interest nor have had a fixed term for repayment, credit given by employers could contribute to the increased pauperization of the debtor. But one should not forget that despite the fact that there were perhaps other institutions and relationships through which credit was available to the poor, loans and advance payment by employers offered vital protection against the short-term threat of starvation.

Living on a small family income that often did not cover the expenses for food the labouring poor automatically fell behind in the rent. Low as rentals of flats and rooms undoubtedly were in lower-class neighbourhoods, they nevertheless placed a real strain on the economy of the urban poor. Often paid quarterly rather than weekly or monthly, they required the accumulation of a relatively large sum of money. Indebtedness to the landlord was therefore another manifestation of accumulating 'social capital' within a city. Especially hospitals and other charitable institutions which owned a number of houses and flats had difficulties in getting in their rents. In some French hospitals in any one year up to a tenth of their revenues from this source could be in arrears. The decision of the corporation at Winchester to remit poorer tenants their rent arrears provides another example of sources of urban credit to ease economic difficulties. It was not only institutions that were apparently prepared to acknowledge the fact that the urban lower classes often fell behind in the rent; private landlords were also willing to allow their tenants to be on the credit side for a considerable period of time. An eighteenth-century French glazier, for example, permitted a lavender-seller to fall twelve

[9] Quoted in John Walter, 'The social economy of dearth in early modern England', in John Walter and Roger Schofiel (eds.), *Famine, Disease and the Social Order in Early Modern Society* (Cambridge, 1989), p. 101.

months in arrears before he finally summoned the bailiffs. Some landlords or keepers of lodging houses were even willing to lend money for the payment of doctors' bills and other expenses during any personal or general crisis.

Just as it was possible for the urban wage-earner to be in debt to the landlord, the rural labourer could hope to take out loans from the owner of his allotment. Two kinds of peasants were particularly liable to contract debt: the share-croppers (*metayers*), normally farmers with little or no personal capital, and smallholders or cottagers, who depended upon additional income from seasonal labour to make a living. The former, in the event of harvest failures, could contract debts to their landlords throughout the term of the lease (three, five, seven years); the latter could sell their property to their creditor and receive it back against an annual rent, in some cases on very advantageous terms. Many of these loans were based on informal agreements and therefore go largely unrecorded in a formal sense. Despite the many risks of getting into debt, if years of reduced harvest followed in succession, the smallholders and cottagers could acquire breathing-space from their landlords as well as from their feudal overlords at least until the next time difficulty arose. In the southwest German county of Hohenlohe, for example, the princes and their patrimonial state assumed the lion's share of smallholders' debts. There were, of course, also less charitable creditors, who imposed much harsher terms, in the long run pushing a peasant family over the narrow boundary between poverty and indigence.

Friendship was also important in both urban and rural contexts. The Norwich and Ipswich censuses of the poor record examples of paupers supported by their friends. One of them was Margaret Lamas, aged fifty-six, 'a wedow, a lame woman & worketh not but stylleth aqua vitae, & now lyv upon hyr fryndes, & hath dwelt here 16 yeris'.[10] When help was needed either in sickness or financial difficulties in many cases it was to be found amongst 'friends and neighbours'. Although the sources often mention both groups simultaneously, contemporaries were aware of the implicit distinction. For Ralph Josselin, the vicar of Earls Colne in Essex, neighbours were those with whom he had daily contact through co-residence, but friends were special. They were carefully chosen. Relations by marriage were also often collectively termed 'friends'. They were, according to the many examples given in autobiographies and diaries from the early modern period (e.g. Josselin's diary, Hermann Weinsberg's chronicle, and the famous Florentine *ricordanze*), not as close as blood kin, but were closer than neighbours. Among the rich and

---

[10] J. F. Pound (ed.), *The Norwich Census of the Poor 1570* (Norwich, 1971), p. 29.

powerful as well as among the poor and destitute friendship was of considerable emotional and financial importance in difficult and good times. Friends offered credits, took care of somebody when he fell ill, helped each other with the authorities, sending, for example, as a sign of friendship a petition to the town council on behalf of a poor man or woman applying for a place in the hospital. In late eighteenth-century Cologne, for example, more than half of the required certificates of poverty (751 out 1406) carried signatures from citizens who were apparently neither related to the applicant nor office-holders (parish priests, town officials, physicians, etc.). Although 656 (87 per cent) of them could be identified as neigbhours the others must have been either friends or acquaintances. A beggar arrested in 1592 in Cologne claimed that he had lived for a long time on what 'good people gave to him'.[11] He was even willing to pass on their names to the authorities. The four citizens whom he named during the investigation obviously formed a social network, although it is in this case difficult for us to make a clear distinction between friends and acquaintances.

Studying social relationships in early modern Europe, some historians recently shed light on the importance of the immediate neighbourhood as a source of social and economic support. The choice of overseers and witnesses to wills or the choice of bondsmen can be used to analyse the extent of neighbourly interaction. But such numerical calculations can only indicate a small proportion of the total number of possible neighbourly functions. Informal poor relief and mutual help among neighbours, which remains for the most part invisible and is therefore still under-researched, played an important role in urban as well as in rural communities. The available evidence suggests that, for the labouring poor, their neighbours, rather than kin or outsiders, were the single most important source of help in times of family hardship. Contacts with neighbours were of many kinds. The support was emotional as well as practical. Neighbours borrowed from each other, were hospitable to each other or they were called in when someone was sick. Neighbours assisted at funerals, acted as midwives, petitioners and bondsmen. They also exchanged small gifts and they made wills that took account of neighbourhood recognition and contacts. A London widow and sometime nurse made a general bequest to 'her very loving neighbours' in 1626. Another Londoner, John Simonds, son of Samuel the baker, made ten specific charitable bequests to poor widows living in the neighbourhood. Personal acquaintance based on residential prox-imity was often helpful when people applied for a place in a hospital or

---

[11] Historisches Archiv der Stadt Köln, Verfassung und Verwaltung G 228, fol. 75r-76v (1592 November 7).

requested to be put on the dole. In 1798 Godfried Schaben, a citizen of Cologne, signed at least seven certificates of poverty for petitioners who lived in the same house next to him. And in other early modern towns there were also many citizens who were said to 'help neighbours at need'. For the labouring poor the ties of neighbourhood and friendship were often more important defences against indigence than kinship. Yet they too were often found wanting during an epidemic. Luther, for example, composed an influential tract, *Whether one may flee from a deadly plague* (1527), in which he mentioned among other obligations that neighbours should not desert neighbours unless there were others to take their place. But it would certainly be wrong to conclude from the incidental references to people who behaved 'in a very unneighbourly, malicious and abusive manner'[12] that instances of neighbourly charity did not exist during an epidemic. The latter are less numerous than the former simply because the sources concentrate on negative examples. Like modern newspapers, they do not mention the ordinary acts of support and help which kept people alive in critical times.

In pre-industrial European confraternities and professional guilds, with their workaday ethos of mutual aid, we can see many features which were reproduced later on in more secular and complex forms in trade unions, cooperatives and friendly societies. In every early modern town there were a number of such organizations, which often functioned as mutual-aid societies or employment agencies, and were involved in alleviating financial hardship of their members. Let us first discuss the important role of the professional guilds which brought together workers from the same trade. We know, for example, that some German guilds stored grain to be sold to the poorer members at low prices. In Lüneburg, a journeyman who wanted to become a master craftsman in the pewterers' guild had to pay 10 marks for *Roggengeld* (i.e. the grain fund). Other guilds made similar provisions, allowing their members in times of dearth to buy grain below market prices. More direct help was offered to those members who were no longer able to earn a living because of prolonged illness or old age. In such cases some guilds payed a regular pension to their indigent members. The company of dyers in Lübeck, for example, paid an impoverished master a minimal sum of money (4 schillings) every week. The most important help offered to needy members was, however, in the form of loans which had favourable terms of repayment. There is also evidence of firm solidarity among journeymen of many trades, for example, in cases of illness and permanent

---

[12] Complaint made to the Hampshire sessions against a vicar who had not shut up his house when there was plague in it, quoted in Paul Slack, *The Impact of Plague in Tudor and Stuart England* (Oxford, 1985), p. 292.

impoverishment. Journeymen belonging to the coppersmiths' guild of Brandenburg were entitled to get a loan from their common fund when they were in need. The statutes of the company of joiners and coopers in the north German town of Lünen, dating back to 1736, mention already a special *Gesellen-Armen-Kasse* (i.e. a mutual poor relief fund for journeymen).

In Catholic countries confraternities which enrolled men and, in some cases, also women from different occupations, also offered mutual aid and spiritual welfare to their members. As far as early modern Spain is concerned, there can be no doubt about the supremacy of confraternities over guilds. Entry fees of the non-exclusive confraternities were generally small enough to permit the more humble craftsmen to join, and persons too poor to meet any financial demand could be exempted from membership fees. Much of the income of these corporations was used to finance religious ceremonies (masses, processions) and social festivities (banquets). But at least some money went into welfare services either for members or for worthy poor of the neighbourhood. Among the various charitable activities, paying for a decent and proper funeral was high on the list of corporate expenses. In Zamora (Spain) a considerable sum of money (300 maravedis) was distributed among the members of the Cofradi de San Nicolàs for attending funerals. And a wealthy member of a confraternity with the name Nuestra Señora del Rosario allocated 3 reales to the confraternity's priest for saying mass and ringing the bell at his funeral, one real to the poor who were present, and six reales to attending *confrades*. The social functioning of these voluntary groups depended on the existence of good relations and mutual interests among the members. In all confraternities which existed in early modern Europe friendship and the ideal of mutuality was formally cultivated and tested on various occasions in a ritualized manner.

Underlying this chapter on problem-anchored networks in early modern Europe and the extent of self-help is a concern to illustrate the functioning of social relations, both horizontally and vertically. Research has concentrated so far on the uses of family and kin as forms of solidarity but not on other groups assuming collective responsibilities. A theme that would merit further studies, precisely because it offers another way of exploring the unwritten norms, mechanisms and structures that conditioned and set the parameters for individuals and families, is the function of charity in the subsistence strategies and employment opportunities of the labouring poor. The direction of this research has to be twofold: on the one hand, to enquire about domestic strategies adopted by families to ensure subsistence (e.g. marriage strategies, transmission of skills, migration); on the other hand, to analyse what people expected from charitable institutions, and even more important, to find out at what particular moments of the life-cycle (childhood, old age) or under which circumstances (differences in availability of charitable institutions in town and countryside) they could no longer rely on self-help and mutual aid but had recourse to poor-relief.

7   The reorganization of poor relief

Common features

A change of perspective has occurred in the historiography of poverty
and poor relief in early modern Europe. Till the beginning of the
twentieth century theologians, historians and students of social policy
believed that the Protestant Reformation brought about a reorganization
of poor relief, pointing out the 'fundamental' differences in the ways in
which Catholics and Protestants treated their poor. These scholars
argued that the new Protestant theology, denying that 'good works'
(alms-giving included) were a direct means of securing salvation,
encouraged a secularization of the agencies of relief. The assumption of
responsibility for the relief of the poor by the civil authorities in
Protestant countries was seen as a direct result of Reformation theology.
Hence the Protestant Church was credited with new methods of dealing
with poverty and begging. Late nineteenth- and early twentieth-century
Catholic historians such as Franz Ehrle and Carl R. Steinbicker did not
really confute this controversial thesis. They wanted to prove that the
secularization (not rationalization) of poor relief in the sixteenth century
was an evil thing and that the Catholic Church was able to establish and
to manage charitable institutions which not only benefited the alms-giver
and the poor but also served the common weal.

More recent historical writing has emphasized the fact that the actual
welfare policy of European cities and states cut across religious
boundaries. There seems now be little doubt that Catholic and Protestant
rulers and communities showed an almost equally strong tendency to
discriminate between 'deserving' and 'undeserving' paupers. Historians now tell us that even Catholic theologians demanded that the
government intervene in assisting and disciplining the poorer members
of society, though with slight differences as far as the ways to achieve
this goal are concerned. Only very few clerical voices were raised in
Catholic Europe to protest against national and municipal legislation to
control mendicity, to employ the able-bodied poor and to improve

+ Humanists and secular writers
* Catholic theologians
^ Protestant theologians

(date of publication)

ALMS

Discriminating alms-giving

^ Luther (1519/20)
^ Karlstadt (1522)
^ Linck (1523)
^ Bugenhagen (1526)
* Vives (1526)
+ Cellarius (1530)
* Vauzelles (1531)
* Loyola (1535)
+ Forrest (1548)
^ Bucer (1557)
+ Wijts (1562)
^ Hyperius (1570)
+ van Hout (1577)
* Giginta (1579)
+ Coornhert (1587)
+ Arthington (1597)
+ Perez de Herrera (1598)
+ Medina (1606)

Indiscriminate alms-giving

* de Soto (1545)
* Villavicentio (1564)
* Drant (1572)
* Fulcus (1585)

BEGGING

Prohibition

^ Luther (1519)
^ Karlstadt (1522)
^ Linck (1523)
* Vives (1526)
+ Cellarius (1530)
* Loyola (1535)
+ Forrest (1548)
^ Bucer (1557)
+ Wijts (1562)
+ Vowell (1575?)
+ van Hout (1577)
+ Coornhert (1587)

Certain limitations

* de Soto (1545)
* Giginta (1579)
* Benincasius (1584)
+ Perez de Herrera (1598)

Figure 10 Controversial issues in the sixteenth-century debate on charity and poor relief

institutional care and and outdoor relief for the needy in their homes (see Figure 10).

There is some *prima facie* evidence of common features in poor relief reforms and more stringent programmes to control begging adopted by a number of European states and cities almost simultaneously.

1. *The enhanced role of the state* which led already in the sixteenth century, and also later on, to highly influential debates about the proper relationship between public and private charity. Since the late Middle Ages leading preachers and theologians demanded more positive

intervention of the civil authorities in caring for the poor. Geiler of Kaysersberg (1455–1510) advocated as early as 1498, that the municipal government and not the Church should be responsible for the poor and their relief. Especially the Nominalist school at the University of Paris at the end of the fifteenth century was already prepared to accept or even justify the extended functions of the State as compared to those of the Church. The merging of the ecclesiastical with the secular authority in the administration of poor relief can, therefore, be traced back to the eve of the Reformation. At the end of the fifteenth and the beginning of the sixteenth century many town councils were already more or less successful in attaining the right of supervision of hospitals and charitable institutions, exercising a control over their internal management and their external affairs.

2. An increasing *rationalization, bureaucratization and professionalization* of relief work. Because the number of needy became larger, reformers insisted that traditional forms of charity would never again be able to contend with the real job of poor relief. Arbitrary and unfounded alms-giving seemed to them obsolete, counterproductive and disastrous not only for the individual and his family but also for the community. More effective forms of help for the needy had to be found. Poor relief administrators began to undertake the meticulous investigation of each individual case of poverty, diligently and repeatedly. This individual and personal supervision was seen by magistracies all over Europe as solid foundation for more efficient poor relief. Professionalization and bureaucratization were the result of this new social policy. For purposes of better administration, larger towns were split up into numerous relief districts, with each district supervised by a relief officer appointed by the local government. Outdoor relief was greatly increased and also systematized. Poor relief officers and charitable institutions started to keep large registers in which they laboriously noted the name, profession, birthdate and place, occupation, illness and disability as well as the number of dependants of every pauper. Such orderly procedures signalled the emergence of a new bureaucratic spirit in poor relief. The trend towards bureaucratization and rationalization was to continue until the end of the *ancien régime*. It was particularly marked in northern and central Europe, while in Spain, France and Italy there was an embedded reluctance on the part of the state to develop highly sophisticated and centralized structures of assistance for the poor.

But even within the confines of resurgent Catholicism, the demise of traditional ties and the advent of modern social relations brought with it a new quality of charitable relations. Public institutions instead of private alms-givers dispensed aid. Hospital directors and poor relief administrators now interposed between themselves and the poor a set of clear written rules which replaced the casual procedures of the past. Some of the solutions were perceptive, especially as Catholic and Protestant reformers had argued with effect the economic advantages of such rational methods over the wastefulness of unsupervised alms-giving. Some measures (e.g. forcing the legitimate poor to wear badges) were more naively conceived and probably counter-productive. The desirability of such sweeping innovations in poor relief was, however, not accepted by everyone. Some voiced apprehension that rationalizing charity carried with it the possibility of throttling compassion as well. Another school of thought took a more pragmatic and unidealistic view of human nature and advocated coercion. The State, these thinkers claimed, should dispense aid and force all citizens to contribute. While some authors claimed that taxation was not a reasonable alternative to philanthropic works and others suggested schemes in which the offerings were not quite voluntary and yet were also clearly no tax (e.g. weekly collections from house to house), this did nothing to alter the perennial problem: since the sixteenth century all over Europe men and women, for a variety of reasons, no longer were prepared to comply with the charitable imperative.

3. The links between Catholic and Protestant attitudes towards the poor are unusually clear in the case of *education*. In the Reformation and Post-Tridentine period as well as later on within the Enlightenment reorganization of poor relief and educational reform overlapped. The education of the impoverished constituted a kind of litmus test for the ubiquity of the reorganization of poor relief in early modern Europe. The reformers saw in proper education of the lower classes a splendid tool with which to combat poverty. And even if education could not cure the present social evils right away, it nonetheless seemed to provide the best chance of reducing poverty in the next generation. No sixteenth-century author put it more plainly than an English writer who suggested that the 'poorer sorte of people, maie be sette to some good Artes, Science, Occupation, Craftes and Labours, by whiche meanes they might be able to relieve them selues of their greate nede and want'[1]. These goals easily meshed with the aims of most early modern governments. The training of pauper children in some kind of work or craft, so that they might learn habits of industry and have the ability to support themselves when they were grown up was a distinctive feature of sixteenth-century social policy. In various English towns (London, Norwich, Ipswich, York) more or less successful attempts were made to rescue destitute children

---

[1] Robert Hitchcock, *A Pollitique Platt for the Honour of the Prince...* (London, 1580), p. 20v.

from the street and to give as many poor children as possible the sort of education and technical training then thought desirable. This preoccupation with children and the need to give them a proper moral example as well as occupational training is also evident in the sixteenth-century Castilian poor laws, which forbade parents from taking a child of five years or older out begging and ordered that these children be put with master artisans to learn some sort of occupation. The drive for 're-educating the paupers themselves' (Christopher Hill) did not diminish during the early modern period and even gained momentum during the Enlightenment. In eighteenth-century Catholic Grenoble a Bureau des Écoles Charitables was established. The governors claimed that their school 'would rescue the poor from the perilous idleness where they are wont to languish with our help'.[2] In late eighteenth-century Hamburg, at that time still a predominantly Protestant city, the industry schools developed by Friedrich Eberhard von Rochow on his estate at Reckahn, by Heinrich Sextroh in Brauschweig and by the Wagemann brothers in Göttingen became the model for poor relief administrators looking for new methods of educating pauper children as useful members of society. Today historians come to a rather critical assessment of such educational reform projects. Some of them even reach the conclusion that the history of almost all poor relief reformers' endeavours in the field of education can be succinctly summarized as follows: modest beginnings, great expectations, meagre or even disappointing results.

Recent investigations of poverty and poor relief in early modern Europe have thus demolished the well-established myth about the importance of the Reformation for procuring good order and reducing physical want and suffering. Yet two major questions still remain to be answered. Even if historians have blurred the contrasts between Catholic and Protestant poor relief to the point that they are virtually invisible, were there perhaps other interesting distinctions in dealing with poverty in different countries? And if they did exist, what can be said about the effectiveness of the reformed system of poor relief in comparison to systems still much closer to medieval forms of charity? These are large questions and it is likely that they will never be fully answered by historians.

Some social historians have at least tried to offer a convincing explanation of why Catholic and Protestant communities followed almost the same principles. According to the English historian Brian Pullan the 'ubiquity of disease, crime, and crisis' caused territorial states and municipal governments to respond to an urgent social problem in similar

---

[2] Quoted in Kathryn Norberg, *Rich and Poor in Grenoble, 1600–1814* (Berkeley, Los Angeles and London, 1985), p. 160.

ways. Other historians have followed suit, pointing out several conditions which could be responsible for directing reform schemes along similar lines: first, the failure of institutions (e.g. hospitals), causing the same administrative problems; secondly an increase in the numbers of beggars on the street; thirdly, the cumulative impact of different economic crises and social problems.

Meanwhile there is no shortage of studies bearing on the social and economic background of poverty. They take us right into some of the important areas of comparative political and social development in early modern Europe. Our aim is not to trace the geographical growth of secularized or more modern systems of poor relief in Europe during the period under study, nor do we intend to treat this development in a strictly chronological order. We are likewise not interested in a quantitative measurement of poor relief agencies in either Protestant or Catholic communities. Our objective is to show how two highly competitive poor relief systems came into being and how it was possible that both civil and ecclesiastical authorities participated in the welfare reform that displaced medieval charity. In the sixteenth-century debate on the reorganization of poor relief the point of contention was not between state or church over charity, but between public or private, centralized or decentralized relief.

Centralized poor relief

A new era dawned in the social policies of many European towns in the first half of the sixteenth century. Almost everywhere magistracies had made attempts to introduce a centrally administered system of relief in their city. With the exception of some Italian, German and Spanish towns, the existing charitable funds were centralized into a 'common box' (*gemeiner Kasten, gemene beurs, aumône générale*). Today historians see little or no religious influence, either of Catholicism or Protestantism, in the development of the characteristic features of sixteenth-century poor relief organization, such as the pooling of revenues in a common fund and the centralization of relief agencies.

The first cities to centralize poor relief under the control of secular authorities were Nuremberg (1522), and one year later Strasbourg, Augsburg, and few smaller German towns. Other European cities followed later. With the exception of Ypres and Nîmes and some other cities which remained predominantly Catholic, the reorganization of poor relief in the 1520s and 1530s was the result of the town council's decision to support the Reformation. All the Protestant systems of poor relief had certain points in common: all were based upon the idea of a 'common chest', which was financed by funds that were taken from the formerly Catholic hospitals and charitable institutions, from monastic properties, from gifts and endowments, and from the current collections in the Church. But the idea of centralizing public, private and ecclesiastical charity was, as we have already seen, not restricted to Protestant cities. At Lille, for example, a *bourse commune* was established as early as 1506, placing all the revenues of the town's numerous institutions of charity under the central control of a single board of trustees, representing the citizens. And there can be no doubt that municipal poor relief reform, which ante-dated Protestantism by many years, paved the road to a centralized poor relief system, which came into being in many European towns in the course of the sixteenth century.

In *Germany* poor relief was from the later Middle Ages up to the dissolution of the Holy Roman Empire of the German Nation in 1806 a community affair. The Imperial Diet at Lindau had already declared in 1497 that each community should take measures to care for its own poor. This principle was later enacted in the Imperial Police Ordinance of 1530 and remained in force during the whole period under study. Historians suggested a twofold causality of poor relief reform in German towns. One is directly connected with the religious movement which led up to the Reformation, the other was more influenced by socio-economic and humanistic considerations.

The oldest poor relief order influenced by evangelical principles is the so-called *Beutelordnung*, passed by the town council of Wittenberg with Luther's cooperation and assistance some time in late 1520 or early 1521. This ordinance made the following provisions. A chest, locked with three separate keys, was to be placed visibly in the parish church for the deposit of money collected in regular collections. There were to be four stewards, elected from each quarter of the town. They were to be elected 'honest, prosperous, and faithful citizens ... who are well acquainted with the towns and with the poor as to their property, character, status, origin, and integrity, and who are capable of discerning those willing to work from the idle ones, judging conditions and making decisions'.[3] While Luther was in protective custody in the Wartburg Castle, his disciple Andreas Bodenstein von Karlstadt became the leader of the reform movement in Wittenberg. After intensive consultation with both theologians, the town council issued on 24 January 1522 *Ain lobliche Ordnung der Fürstlichen Stat Wittenberg*. The new Church Order did not only deal with poor relief, it also specified the form of worship the citizens were to

---

[3] English translation of the 'Ordnung des gemeinen Beutels' by Donald Durnbaugh, *Every Need Supplied: Mutual Aid and Christian Community in the Free Churches, 1525–1675* (Philadelphia, 1974), pp. 215–18.

follow, and the ecclesiastical penalties with which violators of the law were to be punished. The characteristic novelty of this ordinance was the common chest. The revenues which were to go into this chest were taken from the secularized monastic property, from the hospital foundations, from the dissolved religious guilds and from any charitable bequest or voluntary gift. The income was to be used for poor relief, but a substantial part of the money went to defray the expenses of the Lutheran pastor and his clerk, to maintain the schools and church buildings, and to provide for times of future scarcity. A closer look at the account books of the 'common chest' in Wittenberg reveals that the new institution functioned well during the first two decades. In the early years about half of its considerable income was devoted to poor relief.

In consulation with Luther the small Saxonian town of Leisnig set up in 1523 an Ordinance of a Common Chest which was more detailed, as far as provisions for the poor were concerned, than the earlier scheme at Wittenberg. It also included a new feature, the first mentioning of a poor tax in a Protestant poor relief ordinance: 'every noble, townsman, and peasant living in the parish shall, according to his ability and means, remit in taxes for himself, his wife, and his children a certain sum of money to the chest every year'.[4] The Leisnig experiment was obviously not very successful. In a letter to his friend Spalatin (1484–1545) dated 24 November 1524, Luther mentions that the poor relief reform at Leisnig did not come up to his expectation, even though, as the first of its kind, it should have served as a model. Nevertheless there can be no doubt that Luther's proposals were highly influential at that time. This is evidenced by the fact that more than twenty-five poor ordinances, containing the essentials of Luther's suggestions, and differing only to accommodate themselves to local conditions, were enacted into the local statutes of German towns between 1522 and 1530. Luther's direct influence, however, ceased to be important in the history of Protestant poor relief in Germany after 1526. At that time Bugenhagen (1485–1558) became the leading figure in this field. In 1526 he reorganized the 'common chest' in Wittenberg. Later on, other north German towns also asked for his advice and included his practical revisions in their Church Orders (Braunschweig in 1528, Hamburg in 1529 and Lübeck in 1531). Bugenhagen maintained Luther's central principle of poor relief, namely the 'common chest'. The majority of the changes he made pertained to administration and were only accidental and not substantial, with one exception: Bugenhagen thought it would be better to separate the funds

---

[4] 'Fraternal Agreement on the Common Chest … at Leisnig' (1523), in *Luther's Works*, ed. Jaroslav Pelikan and Helmut Lehmann (Philadelphia and St Louis, 1955ff.), vol. XLV, p. 192.

used for the upkeep of the church buildings and the salaries of the ministers and teachers from the relief fund devoted entirely to assist the poor. Thus the establishment of an independent *Armenkasten* (poor box), apart from the rest of the church funds, formerly merged into the 'common chest', was incorporated into these Protestant Church ordinances. After 1530, other Protestant reformers, such as Caspar Hedio at Strasbourg (1533) and Andreas Hyperius at Bremen (early 1560s), shaped the reorganization of poor relief in some German cities. Although they had Luther's model in mind, they were also strongly influenced by Ludovicus Vives. Caspar Hedio, for example, was the first German translator of Vives' influential tract *De subventione pauperum* (first Latin edition Bruges 1526). Hyperius was born and grew up in the Flemish city which Vives had in mind when he advocated a reorganization of poor relief. The significant contribution of Christian humanism which was also behind Vives' reform programme was, however, manifest in some larger German cities (Nuremberg, Augsburg) already at the beginning of the 1520s. In these economically and politically powerful communities the call for the reorganization of poor relief flowed first from the values, the view of nature, and the moral and socio-economic concern of laymen whose Christian humanistic commitment comes to light in their actions and proposals.

We have shown that the Reformation created neither the communal nor the governmental system of poor relief, since both had their counterparts in Catholic countries. But there can be no doubt that the discussion of Luther's principles of relief and their effects in the sixteenth century shaped the centralized poor relief system not only in early modern Germany but also elsewhere in Europe. The Reformation paved the way for the development of a new social policy which favoured secular systems of poor relief.

The legacy of the Reformation was still visible when German towns embarked on another major reform of poor relief at the end of the eighteenth century. A very well-researched case is the city of Hamburg. The poor relief ordinances of 1550 completed the rebuilding of outdoor relief begun in 1527–8, defining the duties of the deacons and subdeacons and delegating to them the real burden of parish relief. Assistance from the *Gotteskasten* excluded all those perceived as alien to the community, or regarded as undesirables, namely beggars, transients and pilgrims. As in other communities which had reorganized poor relief it was hoped by the governing élite that the parish would find ways to employ all the able-bodied poor, but finding work for the poor proved to be difficult, and by the end of the sixteenth century one of the cardinal features of centralized poor relief – the detailed investigation of each pauper at home in order to assess his fitness for work – was given up. All that survived of a once ambitious and comprehensive programme was 'a scattering of alms and occasional handouts of bread, clothing, and fuel' (Mary Lindemann). By the beginning of the eighteenth century, poor relief in Hamburg was hit by a crisis. Until then the patchwork of institutions inherited from the Reformation period had functioned more or less satisfactorily. The *Gotteskasten* was responsible for outdoor relief, the *Zuchthaus* provided confinement for beggars and delinquents but gradually became a refuge for the elderly and the infirm, the *Pesthof*, the old plague hospital, served as multi-purpose institution, housing in its labyrinth of buildings the invalid, the insane and the aged alike, the *Waisenhaus* offered shelter to orphans, while several dozen 'Ragged Schools' drilled discipline, religion and learning into the heads of pauper children. The plague years 1712–14 severely disrupted the old poor relief system. The economic recession, the concomitant of the plague, contributed to widespread impoverishment as well as increasing concerns about the poor. The Improved Poor Relief Ordinance of 1711, which sought to centralize funds and to ensure a more rational allotment of the money raised no longer by collections but by subscriptions, was a first attempt to disengage poor relief from parish control, to centralize funds above the level of the parish, and to establish an integrated poor relief system based on a more rigorous supervision of the registered poor and able-bodied beggars alike. Shortly after the dangers of the plague had subsided, the administration of poor relief was again decentralized, and the parishes, hospitals, and almshouses became again the most powerful agents of relief. However, when poor relief approached another major crisis in the 1770s and 1780s, the reformers took up ideas which were already guiding the reform at the beginning of the century.

The poor relief reform which was initiated by the 'Patriotic Society' followed the paradigm of centralization but preached at the same time voluntarism. The society sponsored, for example, a series of essay contests on general precepts of poor relief reform which attracted more than local interest. At the same time Hamburg's newspapers were filled with accounts of the poor relief reform in other German cities. By the mid-1780s a number of German and Austrian towns had already experimented with new (although not revolutionary) measures to cope with growing pauperism: Berlin in 1774, Lüneburg in 1776, Bremen in 1779, Augsburg in 1782/3, Lübeck and Vienna in 1784, Hanover in 1785, Mainz in 1786. The Hamburg reforms were also in close and personal contact with some eminent pioneers in eighteenth-century poor relief reform, such as August Wilhelm Alemann (died 1784) in Hanover, Johann Anton Leisewitz (1752–1806) in Braunschweig, Christian Garve

(1742–98) in Breslau, Benjamin Thompson alias Graf Rumford (1753–1814) in Munich, Friedrich Eberhard von Rochow (1734–1805) in Reckahn, Heinrich Balthasar Wagnitz (1755–1838) in Halle.

The result of this intensive debate in Hamburg was the reorganization of poor relief which centred on the three crucial spheres of reform: work, health and education. At its core was the Allgemeine Armenanstalt (General Poor Relief Agency), a semipublic institution which incorporated the principles of centralization and voluntarism. The entire city was divided into five districts, each under the direction of two citizens (*Armen-Vorsteher*). Each district was then additionally subdivided into twelve quarters, with each quarter placed under the supervision of three relief officers (*Armenpfleger*). Districts cut across old parish dividing lines. The council (*Armenkollegium*), consisting of five members of the town council, two *Oberalten*, ten directors, five parish *Gotteskasten-verwalter*, and the senior governors of the three poorhouses (orphanage, house of correction, and the *Pesthof*), was the administrative heart of this centralized and comprehensive poor relief system.

From 1491 the local government was in charge of poor relief in the *Swiss Confederation*. As in Germany each community had to make provisions for its own poor and was entitled to send foreign beggars away. In Zurich under Zwingli, poor relief had a predominantly Protestant character right from the beginning. While the Alms Statute of 1520 was still in line with the pattern of traditional structures of poor relief in Zurich, the Poor Law (*Almosenordnung*) passed by the town council on 15 January 1525 broke new ground, for it brought all forms of care for the poor under a single, local administration. Poor relief was thus to be administered by one central agency. Care of the poor was also to be local because the town council had incorporated the neighbourhoods into its structure of poor relief, appointing overseers (a layman and a priest) to each of the seven wards who were familiar with the local context. This pattern of local organization was not employed in some German cities which also had introduced a centralized poor relief system in the early 1520s. Poor relief in Zurich was therefore 'at once centralized and localized, nonpersonal and familiar' (L. P. Wandel). In other Swiss cantons (e.g. Oberwalden, Solothurn), that same localism placed within each rural or urban community the care of its own poor. In the small village of Apples (canton Vaud) a *bourse des pauvres* is first mentioned in 1638. Its assets were at that time about 266 florins. In the second half of the eighteenth century outdoor relief distributed by the *bourse* amounted to up to 11 per cent of all public expenditure in this Swiss community. In some Swiss cantons the responsibility for poor relief passed at the end of the *ancien régime* from the hands of the local government to a regional council, the so-called *Armendirektion*. This agency also made successful attempts to place private charity which still existed in Solothurn and other Swiss cantons under its supervision.

Geneva is another prominent and well-researched example of how early Protestants reformed the administration of social welfare in a Swiss city. The Geneva General Hospital (*Hôpital-Général*), a multi-purpose institution providing relief to all sorts of poor people, was a creation of the Reformation, although it was not established by Calvin who by that time had not yet arrived in Geneva. It seems much more likely that the ruling élite of Geneva, being in constant commercial contact with Lyon, was influenced by the establishment of the *Aumône-Général* in this French city in the years 1531–4. Before 1535 there were in Geneva at least eight institutions devoted primarily to coping with poverty in the city. The General Hospital replaced a number of these different and competing earlier institutions with a single, rationally organized relief agency. The direction of this central institution was entrusted entirely to laymen drawn from the urban upper class. A number of assistants and servants worked under the supervision of a full-time *hospitallier*. This officer was in turn responsible to a board of governors (*procureurs*). These men were chosen by the twenty-five members of the ruling small council. Calvin mentions the *hospitalliers* and the Hospital *procureurs* occasionally in his writings, most notably in the ecclesiastical ordinances which he drafted for the city of Geneva in 1541, shortly after his return from Strasbourg. By making the *procureurs* and *hospitalliers* into deacons he transformed them into lay ministers of the Reformed Church. After 1562 three of the four *procureurs* of the Hospital General were also elders who sat on the Church consistory. The Geneva General Hospital proved to be a remarkably durable institution. The first major reorganization took place in 1869, when it was converted into a new institution called the *Hospice-Général*, which continued to care for the local pauper population.

Calvinistic principles of poor relief only found their way into the *Netherlands* towards the end of the sixteenth century. A synod held at Wesel in 1568 changed Calvin's original specification by admitting also women of 'tried faith and probity'.[5] The General Synod of Herborn in 1586 set forth certain requirements for two independent groups of deacons and deaconesses. The one was in charge of gathering and distributing alms and relief to persons outside the charitable institutions; the other was chiefly occupied with the care of the sick, the aged and captives. But even before Calvinism made inroads upon the Low Countries, Dutch cities had secularized and centralized poor relief

---

[5] Quoted in Aemilus Ludwig Richter (ed.), *Die evangelischen Kirchenordnungen des sechzehnten Jahrhunderts* (Weimar, 1846), vol. II, p. 315 (my translation).

institutions, although rarely was the management of charity reserved to the laity to the same degree as in Geneva. The gradual 'municipalization of charity' (C. R. Steinbicker) in the Low Countries began in the early 1520s. The centralized systems of relief established at Ypres in 1525 and at Bruges in 1526 were largely the results of social, economic and political developments in those cities since the turn of the century. The Ypres plan for poor relief was published in September 1525. It began with the famous and self-assured sentence: 'It appertains no doubt to all rulers, both of the political or civil sort, to care and provide for poor folks.'[6] There were to be appointed four civil supervisors or overseers of the poor. These men should meet every week to discuss how to help the poor and supervise the relief work of groups of four or more individuals, operating in each parish. These parochial relief officers were to visit the homes of all paupers, to collect alms, and to manage the poor box, which was to be erected in every Church. The most striking feature of the new scheme is, however, the establishment of a 'common chest' (*bourse commune*), which was supposed to funnel charitable bequests and alms given by citizens in order to provide a more efficient, fairer and impartial distribution of relief. The scheme of 1525 is left general enough to go along with the existing charitable institutions. The three hospitals in Ypres, for example, continued to function after the creation of the *bourse commune* and the above-mentioned overseers of the poor cooperated smoothly with the administrators of the already established parochial poor relief organizations known since the later Middle Ages as *Hl. Geesttafels* (Tables of the Holy Ghost). Only the Mendicant Orders of the city could not come to terms with the new measures. In 1530 they formally presented a list of grievances to the city council, arguing that the prohibition of begging and forcing foreign beggars to leave the city was against the divine law and that laymen had no right to administer and distribute charitable revenues. They also maintained that they should be maintained by the Common Fund as they had been deprived of their principal source of income, viz. begging. The case was referred to the theological faculty of the Sorbonne, which decided in January 1531 that the poor relief reform in Ypres was in agreement with the Scriptures, the teaching of the Apostles, and the laws of the Church, providing that certain conditions be observed. The rich, for example, ought not to feel that their obligation of giving alms was entirely satisfied when they had contributed to the Common Fund, and if the money in the Common Fund was not sufficient to provide for the needs of all the poor, those who did not receive any assistance therefrom ought to be allowed to beg. The

[6] F. R. Salter, *Some Early Tracts on Poor Relief* (London, 1926), p. 40.

Sorbonne decision was met with mixed reactions not only in the Low Countries but also elswhere in Europe, particularly in Spain and in France. The cardinal of Lorraine and the papal legate granted indulgences to those who contributed to the Common Fund in Ypres, while a Franciscan of Bruges, Jean Royart, published a pamphlet protesting against the reform and the superior of the Franciscans in Bruges preached against the new institution. Under the threat of being charged in court, Royart publicly retracted his criticism; his confrère and superior was officially reprimanded by the Council of Flanders in 1531. And even the Emperor Charles V was most assuredly influenced by the positive Sorbonne decision when he issued at Ghent a decree which encouraged municipal welfare reforms in the Low Countries. The edict recommended among other things that all charitable revenues should be consolidated to form a Common Fund (*se fasse une bourse commune*[7]). Begging was prohibited except for mendicants, prisoners, lepers and any deserving pauper who could not be maintained by the Common Fund.

Juan Luis Vives' famous treatise *De subventione pauperum* (1526) was dedicated to the magistrates of Bruges but he cannot be credited with prompting the welfare reforms of Bruges since his tract was published only after the Flemish city had embarked on a new social policy. It is more likely that the poor relief reform undertaken by Bruges was influenced by the reforms already carried out in Mons, Ypres, Strasbourg and Nuremberg. Nevertheless his ideas achieved the dubious notoriety of being declared heretical by the Franciscan vicar of the bishop of Tournai and influenced later attempts to reorganize poor relief not only in the Low Countries but also in other European cities. Vives himself wanted his poor relief scheme to be flexible, insisting that there could be exceptions and adaptations since 'it may not be expedient at all times and in all places to do everything we have described'.[8] At the beginning of the 1560s the senate of Bruges, for example, was forced to modify its earlier reforms by taking over all the charitable institutions of the city. This radical step was defended by Gyl Wyts, pensionary of the city, in a book entitled, *De continendis et alendis domi pauperibus* (1562). Two years later a Spanish Augustinian, Lorenzo de Villavicentio, appointed to Bruges as preacher but also serving as an informer to Philip II, published his influential tract, *De oeconomia sacra circa pauperum curam* (1564), in which he criticized Wyts and Vives as well as any secular authority that attempted to take over charitable institutions or to forbid begging. He

---

[7] French text quoted is in the appendix to Carl Steinbicker, *Poor-Relief in the Sixteenth Century* (Washington, 1937), p. 246.

[8] Vives, *De subventione pauperum*, translated into English by Margaret M. Sherwood (New York, 1917), p. 34.

pleaded that the work of poor relief should again be entrusted to the Church and pointed with pride to the 'model of the modern hospital and of its nursing organisation [which] came from Spain'.[9]

Not because of Villavicentio's fervent attack but as a result of the various religious and political disturbances, Catholic poor relief reform in the Netherlands came to end in the later sixteenth century. And when finally peace was established, the reform measures of the Council of Trent became the guiding principles for the the Catholic Netherlands, while secularization of poor relief came under Calvinistic influences in the Protestant northern territories. The major reforms occurred at the end of the eighteenth century. The French poor law of 1796 reorganized public relief in the Southern Netherlands, creating in each *commune* two secular institutions under the supervision of the municipal authorities: the Commission for the Civil Hospices, entrusted with the administration of all charitable foundations and hospitals, and the Charity Bureau, controlling outdoor relief. In the Calvinistic towns outdoor relief to members of the State Church was entrusted to the deacons. It was their duty to receive all voluntary alms, ecclesiastical rents and other revenues, and to minister the poor out of these funds. The efficient functioning of this system of relief is described, for example, with much admiration by an Englishman named Bagley, who paid a visit to Leiden in 1684 and wrote afterwards a detailed 'account of the various methods by which the Hollanders raise money for the sustinance of the poore, as also how they distribute it'.[10] In eighteenth-century Amsterdam, Holland's biggest city and most important commercial centre, anyone who did not belong to a religious community or was for some reason or another not included in parochial welfare schemes could apply for assistance to one of the two *huiszittenhuizen* (municipal poor relief centres), if he had lived in the town for at least seven years and had furthermore met the required conditions. These public institutions were directly subsidized by the town, but the trustees were, except for the submitting of annual accounts, completely independent.

In contrast to the quick and almost undisputed acceptance of poor relief reform in northern and western Europe, attempts by the government to reorganize welfare encountered strong opposition in sixteenth-century *Spain*. Despite this resistance some towns at least succeeded in centralizing the local hospitals and in rationalizing outdoor relief during the sixteenth century. On 25 August 1540, the Spanish King and Emperor Charles V, who had been an advocate of reform in the Holy

---

[9] Lorenzo de Villavicentio, *De oeconomia sacra circa pauperum curam* (Antwerp, 1564), p. 168 (my translation).
[10] Unpublished manuscript, British Library, Landsdowne MS 841, fol. 27r–28v.

Roman Empire and in the Low Countries, responded to calls for a poor relief reform. He issued throughout the Spanish kingdom instructions demanding a new approach to local poor relief. He did not, however, go as far as Zamora and other Spanish towns had already done by finding alternatives to licensed begging. The only progressive element in this set of instructions is that at the same time the King urged civil and religious authorities to supply local government with information relating to the income of charitable institutions. He indicated that by applying these resources more efficiently in centralized institutions, the poor might not need to resort to begging. Although the royal decree of 1540 compelled each town to turn its attention to poor relief, only a few Castilian cities made efforts to comply with the king's order. In Zamora religious and secular leaders worked together and designed the first comprehensive poor relief scheme for a Spanish city. The Zamoran ordinances of the early 1540s closely resembled the Catholic reforms undertaken in Ypres (1525) and Bruges (1526). After their successful implementation in Zamora, the ordinances were adopted by the cities of Salamanca (1544) and Valladolid (1543). In November 1544, however, Prince Philip, regent for his father Charles V, asked two prominent Spanish theologians from Salamanca, Domingo de Soto and Juan de Medina, to present their views on the welfare reforms going on in Spanish towns. The impassioned controversy between these two men on fundamental issues raised by the new restrictions on paupers and begging was not just a battle of words, but had serious repercussions in the Catholic world. In the end the followers of de Soto, who objected on both theological and practical grounds to the new prohibitions on mendicity, kept the upper hand. According to a seventeenth-century writer, Diego de Colmenares, the arguments in Soto's book were so compelling that they put an end to any dispute over this issue.

It is therefore not surprising that the few Spanish municipalities which had followed the example of Zamora enforced the debated poor law ordinances only for a few years and then ceased. In the 1580s, however, Medina's ideas surfaced again in various attempts to centralize hospitals. In Zamora the town council finally decided after an intensive debate not to unify its hospital facilities, but in Seville, for example, 76 out of 112 small hospitals merged into two major charitable institutions (Espiritu Santo and Amor de Dios). These measures were obviously not too successful. Some years later, in 1592, the Cortes of Madrid complained that the reduction of hospitals had not been useful and representatives of the three estates petitioned that consolidated hospitals were to be returned to their previous condition. Welfare reforms were attempted again by the Spanish government in the eighteenth century but again encountered opposition. The persistence in Spain of a religiously motivated and decentralized system of social welfare until well into the nineteenth century had political as well as social and economic causes. Among the major factors were chronic fiscal difficulties of the Spanish state through the seventeenth and early eighteenth centuries which prevented the adoption of the costly system of poorhouses and municipal charity boards which existed already in some other early modern Catholic states (e.g. France, Italy).

In the *Italian* city-states, the interest of secular rulers in the supervision of confraternities and hospitals, from the late Middle Ages onwards, meant that their constitutional arrangements and even their charitable acts became more or less standardized. In Venice, for example, the brotherhoods were enlisted in a parish-based system of poor relief introduced by Senate legislation in 1529. In Rome, however, the confraternities remained on the whole independent of the parishes, for they had broader territorial limits and more powerful and influential adherents. A campaign for centralizing hospitals started in Italy well before the sixteenth century. Under the influence of the Franciscan Observants, reformers argued that, in order to improve the help administered to the poor, large centralized hospitals should be established in the city. It was also suggested that these institutions ought to absorb all or most of the existing charitable institutions in the city. In many Italian cities, however, the absorption or incorporation of small foundations remained incomplete. In Venice, for example, the reformers in the Senate talked a lot about a great hospital, as in Florence or Sienna, but they only succeeded in establishing a relatively small one in thanksgiving for the successful battles against the Turks. In early sixteenth-century Milan the ruling party was more successful. The new general hospital established by Francesco Sforza (1401–66) was designed to fit the prestige and political ambitions of its parvenu ruler. In late sixteenth-century Turin, the development of an extensive and more rationalized system of municipal poor relief seems to have been linked to power struggles between the municipal authority and the ducal government. The poor relief system which prevailed in most Italian city-states in the sixteenth and seventeenth centuries was, however, for various reasons never really fully centralized. It can be described as based on charitable institutions administered by voluntary or ecclesiastical associations under mixed or lay management, and under increasingly close governmental supervision and control, especially in times of subsistence crisis.

For political and economic reasons the towns in *France* were unable to play such an important part in the relief of the poor as the towns in

Germany, Switzerland or the Netherlands. Consequently, we find the interference of the King in the traditional system of poor relief a more important factor in France during the later fifteenth and early sixteenth century than it was elsewhere. In 1453 King Louis XI had already issued an edict which transferred the administration of all charitable institutions to appointed citizens. By the beginning of the sixteenth century, the parliament was in charge of the supervision of hospitals and institutional poor relief and often interfered in the actual management of these institutions. Francis I, who received the crown of France in 1515, gave little thought to social policy during the first twenty years of his reign. In 1536, however, he issued a decree on the reform of French poor relief. Whether he had been moved to this by the schemes introduced in various French towns in the early 1530s, or by the welfare reform activities of the Emperor Charles V in the Netherlands, cannot be said with any degree of certainty. This ordinance contained a general prohibition of begging and the strict command that all the able-bodied poor should be put to some form of work. Those unable to work were to be assisted by the parish; indigent persons without abode were to be taken temporarily into the hospitals. Appointed citizens were to collect alms at stated times and places, and should people not have an open hand, there was to be a house-to-house solicitation. In 1547 the king introduced further regulations into this scheme: the homeless poor were to become special objects of municipal charity, while poor persons with homes in the locality were to be cared for by parochial poor relief. In 1561 and 1566 further orders came from his successors, Francis II and Charles XI, which ruled that the community was to assume charge only of those who had their home or their birthplace there; the other poor persons were to be sent to their former place of residence. And in order to provide sufficient money for relief of the local poor, every citizen should contribute to the financing according to his financial means.

Prior to this royal initiative, Paris, Lyon and other French cities had been active on behalf of the poor. In Lyon, welfare reform was launched in 1531 by a coalition of notables and lawyers, among the Catholic and Protestant sympathizers. In this year the Lyonnais preacher and humanist Jean de Vauzelles published his tract *Police subsidaire à celle quasi infinie multitude des povres* in which he advocated among other things the centralization and rationalization of poor relief. In 1532 the local dominican prior Nicolas Morin attacked these reform plans in his *Tractatus Catholice*, but he obviously could not prevent the group of reformers in the town council from carrying the day. In 1534 the *Aumône-générale* was finally established (see Plate 4). This event marked the culmination of an almost century-long shift in the control of welfare

Plate 4 Anonymous, *Distribution of alms out of the common chest in Lyon*. Frontispiece, *La police de l'aumône générale*, Lyon, 1539.

from ecclesiastical to secular hands. As in other European cities, two essential principles became manifest in this reform: centralization and rationalization. According to Nathalie Zemon Davis the *Aumône* assisted in money and in kind about 3,000 people every week in the first thirty years of its existence, which means that about 5 to 7 per cent of the population were on the dole. In the same year (1534), the city of Rouen enacted a poor relief ordinance which surpassed all that had gone before it. The magistrate sought to purge the traditional ecclesiastical system of relief from abuses without, however, wresting this work from the hands of the local clergy. The municipality of Paris received through Letters Patent from the French King in 1544 the authority 'to supervise and conduct all things required for the treatment and relief of the poor'.[11] Paris was also the first city which introduced a poor tax in 1551. Thus England's famous poor rate of 1572 had its equivalents in the municipalities of Catholic France. There were, however, striking differences. In France compulsory taxes for the poor were raised on occasion as a reaction to crisis circumstances and never became a permanent feature of French social policy. For reasons which have not yet been sufficiently studied, the poor rate system of French cities fell into abeyance in the seventeenth century, and the municipalities returned towards a more voluntaristic method. The economic and demographic consequences of the French civil wars and religious struggles in the sixteenth and early seventeenth centuries may well have contributed to this.

Another distinctive feature can be noticed as well. Although many villages and towns had a *bureau de charité*, a central pool of alms which provided outdoor relief, the keystone of social policy towards the poor down to the end of the *ancien régime* was the *hôpital général*, an institution for the punishment of sturdy beggars, relief of the sick and orphans and employment of the idle, which spread through France during the seventeenth century. In contrast to many other European countries, in France, at least in theory, the centralization of political authority allowed poor relief schemes to be implemented on a far larger scale than anywhere else in Europe. Acting particularly through the office of the Grand Aumônier du Roi, the King's personal chaplain, the French government intervened in the management of institutional relief and encouraged the municipalization of poor relief in the sixteenth and early seventeenth centuries. Later on the French crown tended to support the existence of a mixed system of public and private charitable institutions rather than to push as far down the road of centralized poor relief as once had seemed likely in the reign of Francis I. The post-Tridentine religious revival in

---

[11] Quoted in Steinbicker, *Poor-Relief*, p. 8.

France gave a boost to private charity. The French state therefore never achieved the kind of uniformity and community obligation in the relief of poverty that England accomplished through the generalization of the parish-based poor rate from the late sixteenth century onwards. The 'charitable imperative' (Colin Jones) in France had the effect of reducing municipal involvement in outdoor relief and hospital management which was increasingly in the hands of confraternities. From the seventeenth century onwards the French absolutist government, balancing its own centralizing drive with considerateness for local, ecclesiastical and corporative liberties, slowly returned to a decentralized system of poor relief, which will be described in more detail in the next paragraph.

From the early sixteenth century onwards *England* saw slow but steady progress towards statutory poor relief. The consequences of the political and religious changes of the 1530s upon local poor relief were disastrous. It is at this point that the central government had to intervene. The Act of 1531, however, was also a direct result of the economic depression of the late 1520s. It was the first attempt by the English crown to distinguish between the impotent and the able-bodied poor. The former were allowed to beg, albeit only within their own community. The government soon realized the deficiencies of this Act, particularly the fact that no real provision was made for the 'deserving' poor. A further statute was drawn up in 1535. It was most probably prepared by William Marshall, the English translator of the famous poor law ordinances of Ypres which were presented in the same year to the English public as model for what must urgently be done in the realm. The Act finally passed in 1536 followed in many aspects the lines of Marshall's scheme and introduced three elements into English poor relief which were of major importance for its later development. First, it stressed the need for public employment alongside the usual repressive measures against idle vagabonds. Secondly, it expanded slightly the provisions for impotent poor, creating a parish-based relief system financed by alms which were not to be given to individuals but to common boxes in each parish. Specially appointed officers were to be responsible for any money collected. Thirdly, it discouraged casual doles and indiscriminate alms-giving. The Act of 1536 was thus in line with the principles which characterized the innovative poor relief legislation in many parts of the continent in the first half of the sixteenth century: centralization, rationalization and professionalization.

The following decades saw the crucial shift from voluntary to compulsory support of the poor. By the middle of the the sixteenth century the Church's assistance had practically vanished. Lay collectors had become the key figures within a parish-based relief system. The infamous Act of 1547 with its draconian measures against vagabonds took things a stage further, although it proved to be impractical and was repealed in 1550. Like the Statute of 1536, it proscribed weekly collections for the impotent poor and prohibited all begging without exception, but it also ordered local officials to provide housing for all 'idle, impotent, maimed and aged persons' who were not vagabonds. Another Edwardian statute of 1552 stipulated that anyone who refused to contribute to the weekly collections was to be 'exhorted' by the parson, thus paving the road to a national poor rate. The principle of compulsory giving became the main feature of Elizabethan poor-law legislation. The 'Act for the Relief of the Poor' of 1563 continued the statutes of 1531 and 1549, but also contained the stipulation that anyone refusing to contribute to collections was to appear before justices with threat of possible imprisonment. The Acts of 1572 and 1576 were mostly concerned with the repression of vagrancy and added little regarding the relief of the impotent poor. With respect to the 'deserving' poor, the Act of 1572 authorized the Justices of the Peace to supervise parish and town relief. The Act of 1576 mentions for the first time those 'poor and needy persons willing to work' who could not find employment. All corporate towns were therefore ordered to raise stocks of wool and other materials, and to establish 'houses of correction' with the typical mixed function of punishment and support which characterizes so many innovations in social welfare in the early modern period.

The later Acts of 1598 and 1601, one for the relief of the poor, the other for the punishment of rogues, vagabonds and sturdy beggars, completed the Elizabethan poor relief legislation. It was the completion of more than a century of experiment, ranging from the brutally repressive to the preventive and ameliorative. The legislation of 1598 and 1601 contained only a few new features as far as the relief of the 'deserving' poor is concerned: overseers of the poor were to replace the collectors in the parishes; outdoor relief financed by poor rates became commonplace; county treasurers were to be appointed to administer the funds for the relief of prisoners, soldiers and mariners passing through the county. What distinguishes these laws from similar legislation in parts of the continent is not the novelty of their approach but rather that they were implemented nationwide and that they remained in effect until 1834, though modified by the Settlement Act of 1662 and the 'Speenhamland system' in the later eighteenth century. Before turning to the later development of the Old Poor Law, let us consider shortly some of the more important local responses to poverty in Tudor England.

The central government's major concern was domestic security, hence it focused its legislation on vagabondage and then on poor relief. The municipalities favoured different strategies, concentrating their efforts on centralized institutions rather than parish collections. In the 1520s several English towns for the first time provided stocks of corn for their poor. Between 1531 and 1547 licences, badges or other means or regulating begging were introduced in Southampton, Cambridge, Chester, York and other English cities. In London five hospitals were either founded or remodelled between 1544 and 1557. This attempt to reorganize poor relief not through regular parish collections and more efficient distribution but through the confinement of different categories of pauper in centrally managed civic institutions funded by private philanthropy has been called 'the greatest experiment in social welfare in Tudor England' (Paul Slack). These hospitals, which resembled in form and function some continental schemes, attracted nearly half of the charitable bequests of London testators in the 1550s. Other English towns followed. The aldermen of London soon found out that institutional relief could not solve the problem of casual labourers and 'decayed householders', and regular provisions for outdoor relief on the parish level therefore had to be made. By the 1560s the London parishes were retaining in their own hands the alms for outdoor relief which ought to have been paid into Christ's Hospital for central distribution, thus undermining the intended centralizing functions of the large hospitals. The towns pioneered a number of other novel poor relief measures. There were censuses and surveys of the poor in Chester in 1539, Coventry in 1547 and Ipswich in 1551. Schemes for setting the poor to work were introduced in Oxford and Kings Lynn between 1546 and 1548. Parish collections were replaced by compulsory levies for the poor in Norwich in 1549 and York in 1550, some years before parliament began to move in the same direction. Local initiatives therefore helped to shape national legislation. The Acts of 1531 and 1536, for example, had been anticipated in London, while the later legislation was often based on local experience in other English towns (e.g. Norwich). The central government could only set the guidelines, although it was influential in the localities as well, either through direct pressure from the country or through the activities of individual councillors in towns as well as in the provinces. The Act of 1598, for example, stated that mayors and aldermen should enforce it in corporate towns. And we can see a little bit later that several municipalities (e.g. Norwich) responded willingly by centralizing poor relief and transferring funds from one parish to another.

Seventeenth-century practice revealed some deficiencies in the national legislation of 1598–1601. The period of implementation reached its peak during the 1630s, when Charles I made poor relief one of the objectives of his personal rule. After the Civil War the central government withdrew slowly from its role of enforcement, but was still active in legislation. The most important problem which arose from the Act of 1598 was how to save the parishes from the liability for the relief of every casual visitor or passenger. The Act for Settlement of 1662 was a direct result of the pressure from parishes needing stronger powers to rid themselves of unwanted and potentially indigent immigrants. This Act statutorily reaffirmed the traditional assumptions of the individual parish's exclusive responsibility for its own poor and granted the overseers the legal right 'to remove and convey to such parish where they were lastly settled either as native Household Sojourner or Apprentice or Servant for the space of forty days at the least' any new immigrant whom they suspected as likely to become a charge on the local rate 'unlesse he or she give sufficient security for the discharge of the said Parish'.

Settlement was not the only problem which gained the attention of the English legislators after 1601. In the sixteenth and early seventeenth centuries the central goverment had been busy in stimulating and guiding local actions for the relief of the poor, first through legislation and later through administrative enforcement. Now the roles had changed. Local government was going ahead, finding it necessary to ask the central authorities for the legal authority to organize relief as efficiently as they wished. The solution to these problems was the local Act of Parliament. A convenient, although not complete list of those Acts passed before the end of the eighteenth century can be found in F. M. Eden's famous book *The State of the Poor* (1797). Among the local acts one is worth mentioning. In 1782 the so-called Gilbert's Act was passed in an attempt to spread to rural areas the advantages enjoyed by local act districts. One of the most significant results of the eighteenth-century debate over poor relief was the Roundsman system which was later combined with the Speenhamland system that started informally in Berkshire in 1785. The first was, in fact, a system of billeting the unemployed pauper upon the parishioners in rotation, each in turn having to provide maintenance and being free to exact service. The latter system stipulated for the first time allowances in aid of wages. The Speenhamland system spread to other parts of the country after 1795 and became most prevalent in the southern agricultural counties. From then on poor law authorities were required to subsidize the wages of every labourer below a certain level according to a scale tied to the price of bread and the size of his family. The year 1795 was, for various reasons, called the 'turning point in the history of the old poor law' (G. W. Oxley). This becomes clear, looking at the overseers' accounts from the rural parishes in the areas which had introduced this system. Down to 1795 the pension list was rather brief, mentioning mostly females, children and widows. Then the list becomes much longer and the majority of the new names are male. The Speenhamland system brought about a permanent change in the pattern of English poor relief.

Scotland and England created their post-reformation poor laws within a few year of each other. The Scottish Act of 1574–9 is a close copy of most of the provisions of the Elizabethan Act of 1572. In Scotland, however, the development was different. The Act of 1574–9 was not put into practice, although poor relief on a parochial basis did exist in late sixteenth-century Scotland. As there was already a church organization which was active in poor relief, it does not come as a surprise that parliament, in issuing a new Act for the poor in 1592, should accept the lowest court of the new church structure, the kirk session, as the agent of relief. The lack of an effective lay system of relief was therefore one of the most significant differences between England and Scotland in the sixteenth and seventeenth centuries. Although the Union with England in 1707 led to the progressive assimilation of Scottish institutions to those of England, the poor relief system remained almost unaltered. In 1781 a Scottish writer described the main features of the Scottish poor law, making the differences quite obvious for those familiar with the English system: no relief except to those permanently disabled and recognition that the main source of poor relief was voluntary contribution.

As for the *Scandinavian Countries*, Lutheran poor relief ideas were adopted along with the Reformation. In Denmark, for example, the law which established the duty of each community to support its own poor was passed in 1558. The parishes were obliged to put up a common box (*fattigblok*) for the donations and were supposed to erect a poorhouse for the local paupers. Some of the parish registers and account books of the 'alms chests' (*fattigkasser*) kept by local pastors from the pre-1700 period have survived. Another important step forward in Danish poor law legislation is the paragraph on 'Hospitals and the Poor' (*om Hospitaler og Fattige*) in the Danish Law Code of 1683. The aged, sick and infirm should be the first to be admitted to hospitals. The resident poor (*husarme*) were to be given aid by local welfare officers (*fattigforstandere*). The money should come from voluntary collections and donations. The Danish kings were obviously more interested in erecting hospitals than in outdoor relief. In one district alone (Fionie) about forty-eight hospitals were founded in the various parishes up to 1850. In Norway the Church Ordinance of 1539 stated that a Common Fund (*menige Kiste for de Fattige*) should be set up in each parish. Three year before, a royal decree had made stipulation for a reform of the hospitals. The Norwegian Law Code of 1687 also contains some paragraphs on poor relief. Poor relief should be in the hands of the Protestant Church. In the towns certain officers (*forstandere*), supervised by the local pastors and the council, were in charge of outdoor relief, while in the countryside this was the responsibility of the churchwardens who were also to be controlled by the parish priest.

Decentralized relief

With the Counter-Reformation, the traditional system of charity recovered, but only partially. For many European states, especially for those which had convinced Catholic rulers, the decentralized system of poor relief still seemed to be a competitive model. And at the end of the eighteenth century an English traveller to southern Europe, Joseph Townsend, could be amazed at the extent of charitable services provided in some of the poorer regions of Spain, as Luther was at the beginning of the sixteenth century when he visited Rome in 1511 and saw the many hospitals and foundling asylums. By about 1700, the decentralized system of relief was composed of four distinctive layers. They can be identified as those of the confraternities, of the hospitals, of the parish, and of the Monti di Pietà. These different elements originated in the Middle Ages, but were still developing and adapting in the sixteenth and seventeenth centuries (see Plate 5).

By far the most important organization for dispensing outdoor relief was the confraternity. In religious terms, confraternities were associations which prepared their members for death and pursued the hope of salvation by amassing a common store of merit through the performance of good works. In pursuing acts of mercy, confraternities sometimes cooperated with private individuals, priests, friars and nuns, creating a comprehensive welfare programme for the poor. The timing of charitable activities reflects the awareness of the sacred nature of charity. Alms distributions coincided with births, marriages, funerals and saints days. The most basic form of aid to the poor was the visitation of sick brothers and sisters; the most elaborate form of mutual help was the administration of hospitals for the poor and the development of sophisticated insurance programmes for their members. The confraternities of the Middle Ages were less specialized than those founded in the sixteenth and seventeenth centuries. Some of the larger and richer brotherhoods not only visited the sick, but also cared for women in childbed, established hospitals for the aged and sick, managed hospices for pilgrims and travellers, provided spiritual and material comforts for prisoners, buried not only their members but also the poor who could not afford a decent Christian burial, and last but not least distributed alms to all those

Plate 5 Pieter Bruegel the Elder, *Caritas* [*Charity*]. Drawing, 1559.

who were in need. The post-Tridentine Church attempted to draw the
confraternities closer to official notions of orthodoxy but did not succeed
in eradicating the local religious cult connected with this form of
charitable and penitential devotion. In some Catholic states (e.g. Venice),
however, the interest of the secular rulers in the supervision of
confraternities, from the fourteenth and fifteenth centuries onwards, led
to a standardization of constitutional forms and devotional formulas.
Confraternities lost none of their popularity during the early modern
period. In some Catholic countries they became the central pillars of the
welfare system. In those towns where exact statistics are available for
comparing listings of confraternities before and after the Counter-
Reformation, it is evident that their number varied little between the two
periods. In the Spanish town of Zamora, for example, the ratio dropped
slightly from one confraternity for every fourteen households in the
sixteenth century to one for every seventeen households two centuries
later. Although we lack similar data for early modern France, we have
evidence which indicates that the reforms initiated by the Council of
Trent significantly altered the corporate structure of French society. One
of the most practical aspects of this traditional welfare system was that
without the help of a large bureaucratic apparatus the Catholic Church
had a blueprint by which communities across Europe could develop
similar expressions of welfare assistance. The ubiquitous arch-confra-
ternities of the *Misericordia*, for example, buried paupers in various parts
of Europe with identical techniques and similar religious aspirations.

Since hospitals were often managed by confraternities (e.g. those
named after the Holy Spirit), it may seem artificial to distinguish between
two distinctive layers or elements of the traditional welfare system. In
principle the hospital, the major function of which was to shelter all kinds
of people, differed from the confraternity, whose major concern was
some form of outdoor relief. More than 10,000 hospitals are known to
have existed in Europe at the end of the later Middle Ages, the majority
of them in urban communities or in the neighbourhood of towns. Larger
cities had six or more hospitals, some of them specializing already in the
care of the sick and poor (e.g. leper houses, hospitals for syphilitics).
They varied as institutions from more or less well-endowed groups of
priest and brethren living under the rule of an ecclesiastical order (e.g.
that of the Augustinians), with charity as one of their major concerns, to
those establishments which offered some kind of medical care or provided
shelter and spiritual services to aged and sick persons under the
supervision of a warden or a prior. Hospitals were supervised by a variety
of external authorities, such as bishops, monasteries, kings, territorial
rulers and last but not least town governments. From the late fifteenth

and early sixteenth centuries secular authorities controlled to a varying degree hospitals and similar charitable institutions almost everywhere in Europe. Most hospitals gave some kind of temporary relief to the poor, the old and the sick. Some issued doles to the poor living outside the hospital walls. By the beginning of the early modern period, the great majority already provided long-term residential places for people selected on the grounds of their poverty. Since the middle of the sixteenth century and even before, more and more hospitals accepted lodgers, who gave a substantial endowment of land or cash in exchange for their keep for the rest of their lives. In general the medieval and early modern hospital had three functions: to offer hospitality to pilgrims and travellers, to care for the sick, and to look after other persons imprecisely described in the sources as *pauperes*.

The late fifteenth and early sixteenth centuries saw the rise of the so-called 'great hospitals'. The uncontrolled building and bad administration of a large number of small hospitals had disquieted many European governments even well before the Reformation. Since the merging of small hospitals was considered as an infringement of private and ecclesiastical rights, approval by the Church and intervention by secular rulers were often necessary. The administrative board of the new general hospitals included, at least in the beginning of this shift of power and control, both clerics and representatives of the state or city council. Throughout the early modern period the general hospitals continued to expand and to act both as institutions for the care of the sick and as relief agencies for the poor in and outside the hospital. The inmates in some hospitals often numbered several hundred, greatly increasing during epidemics or periods of dearth. In early seventeenth-century Venice, for example, about 16 per cent of the population were 'hospital poor' according to the census of 1642. In cities with a centralized poor relief system, this figure was, for obvious reasons, much smaller. In the north German town of Braunschweig, for example, only 3.1 per cent of the population were inmates of the various municipal hospitals in 1671. Recent research on indoor relief suggests, however, that the total number of persons either in hospital or dependent on hospitals was in fact far greater than the official censuses indicated. After a decline in the sixteenth century, hospitals and almshouses grew in numbers in many Catholic territories and communities.

The character of the post-Tridentine hospital foundation reflected new attitudes towards the poor. The 'new philanthropy' (Brian Pullan), which had asserted itself already in the sixteenth century, put more emphasis on the selection of the genuinely indigent. The catch-phrase was 'redemptive charity'. Outdoor relief was important, but generally there was more resort to closed, quasi-monastic institutions or hospitals whose purpose was both to help the poor and to inculcate social discipline through regular work and religious devotion. Although hospitals drew an increasing amount of support and publicity in the sixteenth and seventeenth centuries, this trend is not always corroborated by some recent studies of charitable testaments. In early modern Sienna, for example, the change in post-Tridentine patterns of charity was to return to medieval practices. During the seventeenth and eighteenth centuries the hospitals, formerly so central to the religious and social fabric of the medieval and Renaissance city, fell on hard times, relative to total charitable bequests. Hospitals had earlier attracted as much as 17 per cent of all pious gifts; with the Counter-Reformation they would never receive more than 3 per cent. The decline in importance is less evident in the case of another Catholic city. In early modern Münster, for example, the Catholic renewal did not bring about such a major fall in charitable bequests to hospitals and almshouses. Between 1530 and 1618 the hospitals (twenty altogether) hovered on average at about 34 per cent of all gifts. While there was a slight drop in the later sixteenth century, the hospitals in this north German city recovered somewhat their pull on the pious at the beginning of the seventeenth century.

The Counter-Reformation made significant inroads into strategies of philanthropy. In Sienna, Münster, Cologne and other European cities another traditional agency of charity profited from the shift in pious donations after the early sixteenth century: the parochial relief organizations known since the later Middle Ages as 'poor tables' (*Armenbretter, Hl. Geesttafels, plats dels pobres, maison de l'aumône*). In terms of the scale of relief provided for the poor, these institutions undoubtedly gained in importance in the early modern period, but one should not forget that even in the post-Reformation period outdoor relief was still complementary and not in opposition to institutionalized charity. The 'poor tables' were pools of voluntary alms, parish collections and small legacies by parishioners, which were to be administered to the deserving poor of the parish by confraternities, churchwardens, or some other individual or group capable of judging the needs of the recipient and the validity of his claims. The outdoor relief agencies on the parish level were so to speak the Catholic equivalent of Luther's 'common chest'. While there is a high degree of uniformity in regard to the nature of the provisions for the poor (distribution of bread, cloth, footwear, meat, money, herring, peas, lard, wine and beer), the quantity of the items which were regularly and occasionally dispensed as well as the number of poor supported varies from one 'poor table' to another (cf. Table 10). In fact, what little evidence we have on Spain, France, Germany and the Low Countries,

Table 10. *Amount of aid and number of persons receiving poor relief in each Toledo and Cologne parish in the sixteenth century*

Toledo

Parish	Inhabitants (1561)	Recipients (1558)	% of poor	Weekly amount (per person)
S. Andrés	2,250	398	17.68	3.5 lb bread
S. Antolin	535	85	15.75	ditto
S. Bartolomé	1,605	492	30.65	ditto
S. Cipriano	2,600	573	22.03	ditto
S. Cristóbal	1,190	370	31.09	ditto
S. Ginés	495	38	7.67	ditto
S. Isidoro	3,320	154	4.63	ditto
S. Juan Baptista	580	64	11.03	ditto
S. Justo	2,950	555	18.81	ditto
Sta Leocadia	2,720	508	18.67	ditto
S. Lorenzo	3,945	998	25.29	ditto
Sta Maria Magd.	3,205	723	22.55	ditto
S. Martin	1,740	232	13.33	ditto
S. Miguel	3,855	1,283	33.28	ditto
S. Nicolás	3,060	663	21.66	ditto
S. Pedro	1,890	251	13.28	ditto
S. Román	2,185	575	26.31	ditto
S. Salvador	645	76	11.78	ditto
Santiago	7,475	1,110	14.84	ditto
Sto Tomé	8,635	1,719	19.90	ditto
S. Vicente	1,390	238	17.12	ditto

Cologne

Parish	Inhabitants (1568/74)	Recipients (16th c.)	% of poor	Weekly amount (per person)
Kl. St Martin	2,695	35	1.29	?
St Brigiden	1,985	20	1.02	$\frac{1}{12}$ fl.
St Alban	805	53	6.58	$\frac{1}{16}$ fl.
St Laurenz	1,145	33	2.88	$\frac{1}{12}$ fl.
St Peter	3,345	36	1.07	in kind
St Kolumba	3,995	25	0.62	$\frac{1}{12}$ fl.
St Aposteln	2,890	75	2.59	$\frac{1}{12}$ fl.
St Lupus	1,050	12(?)	1.14	in kind
St Paul	1,255	?	?	?
St Maria Ablass	1,475	?	?	?
St Kunibert	1,210	12(?)	0.99	?
St Maria Lysk.	575	8	1.39	1 lb meat
St Jakob	1,135	24	2.11	$\frac{1}{24}$ fl.
St Johann Bapt.	2,760	50	1.81	$\frac{1}{12}$ fl.
St Christoph	1,300	?	?	?
St Mauritius	1,380	?	?	?
St Severin	1,615	10(?)	0.61	?
St Johann Ev.	365	10	2.73	$\frac{1}{24}$ fl.
St Maria i.P.	?	?	?	?

Source: Martz, *Spain*, pp. 114, 134; R. Jütte, 'Parochialverbände als Träger städtischer Armenfürsorge', *Geschichte in Köln* 12 (1982), 27–50, Table 2.

from the mid-sixteenth to the mid-eighteenth century, leaves no doubt that the commodities and money distributed by these parochial relief agencies never represented more than a proportion of institutionalized alms-giving and that the monetary value of this type of relief never reached more than a third of the contemporaneous earnings of an employed male labourer.

Many of these parochial relief organizations survived until the end of the *ancien régime*. In France the reforming zeal concept of the late seventeenth century created a new form of outdoor relief which was partly modelled on the late medieval 'poor tables'. The *bureaux de charité* were charitable institutions which also functioned at parish level. They distributed bread and cloth to the needy of the parish every Sunday in much the same way as did 'poor tables' in other European countries. Recipients were chosen according to a strict residence qualification and often on an attestation by the parish priest on good conduct. Apart from the residence qualification, physical disability and widowhood were other important criteria which determined the types of parishioners to whom assistance might be accorded. These new parochial charity organizations were founded all over France from the late seventeenth century under the influence of the Jesuits. Because records of the *bureaux de charité* seldom survived, there is almost no information on how many people benefited from their aid. In a provincial French town (Mende), for example, one hundred poor received one meal twice per week while there were at least 1,000 destitutes living in this town. The early hope of the Catholic reformers that a *bureau de charité* would be set up in each parish met with scant response. The dioceses of Clermont and Limoges, for example, never knew such an outdoor relief agency outside the diocesan centre. The financial difficulties of the parochial poor relief funds, not only in France but also in other countries in which the 'poor table' remained in existence for the whole period under study, help to explain the limited success of these charitable institutions. Deficits equalling or exceeding the annual revenues were quite common – a situation which could not be completely reversed until the end of the eighteenth century when these institutions fell into oblivion. Two conclusions can be drawn from this: first, that many 'poor tables' failed utterly during periods of greatest need (subsistence crisis) since they were then forced to curtail their assistance severely at times of rising numbers of indigents; second, that the many and prolonged economic recessions of the seventeenth and eighteenth centuries had a long-lasting effect on the budgets of these institutions despite the fact that the attractiveness of parochial outdoor relief shows no loss of charitable enthusiasm in the post-Tridentine period.

With respect to the communal pawnshops (*montes pietatis*), the fourth feature of traditional charity was a Christian reaction against Jewish money-lending. It first developed in central and northern Italy in the fourteenth and fifteenth centuries. There special charitable institutions had been set up in an attempt to free the less affluent sectors of society from both Christian and Jewish money-lenders who took advantage of the temporary financial problems of the working poor and small artisans alike. These pawnshops were established in the late medieval period under the influence of the Franciscans. Shortly after their beginning in 1463 at Orvieto, under the auspices of Pope Pius II, similar institutions sprang up in Assisi, Mantua, Pavia, Ravenna, Verona, Lucca and other Italian cities. Bologna had one in 1506. The Roman Monte di Pietà was established as late as 1539. Only in Venice had the Council of the Ten vetoed this charitable institution in the 1520s because of the complexities of the government's relationship with the Jews. By the end of the eighteenth century, these communal pawnshops were relatively numerous in Italy. There were at least eleven in the department of the Arno, some even in small communities like Laterina and Modigliana. Outside Italy, communal pawnshops had been set up for the most part in the sixteenth century. And even some Protestant municipalities such as Frankfurt am Main made special provisions for low-interest loans from the 'common chest' which referred explicitly to the successful Italian model of *montes pietatis*. In France, the bishop of Grenoble, in conjunction with a number of pious laymen, established a charitable pawnshop, the *prêt charitable*, which made interest-free loans to the poor, as late as 1699. The extraordinarily rapid diffusion of these charitable institutions is the best proof that they responded to a real want. The charitable pawnshops were officially approved by the Church in 1515. There were, however, some contemporaries whose attitudes towards the *monti di pietà* remained ambivalent through fear lest they encouraged improvidence among the poor. In late eighteenth-century Florence, for example, the local authorities fought a losing battle against poor people who pawned or sold the bed or bed-clothing they had successfully requested from a municipal charitable institution. Most of these pawnshops advanced small sums of money against household objects, however petty, at low rates of interest (4 to 6 per cent) or even free of interest. The *monti di pietà*, with or without subordinate branches, were administered (as were the new great hospitals) by a board or a large body of governors. Its members were either elected by the town council or were magistrates with ex officio seats. Although their prime function was to lend money to the indigent, these communal pawnshops were regarded as an integral part of the decentralized system of poor relief and were sometimes required to finance other charitable institutions. There can be no doubt that the *monti di pietà* were an important safeguard against impoverishment for the small peasant in the months just before the new crop, and for the craftsman and petty trader during a slack period.

Previous government intervention in the field of poor relief in the late fifteenth and early sixteenth centuries in a punitive and regulative direction and the increased criticism of religious charity for its indiscriminating character by humanists and segments of the Catholic Church in the 1520s and 1530s indicated a shift in attitude on social welfare, although such views did not seriously affect the structure of traditional charitable activities. The sixteenth-century Church movement to reform charitable institutions without giving up the framework of a decentralized system of relief began with individual Catholics (amongst them bishops and priests as well as laymen). Church leaders were aware of these attempts and responded to a call for reform in various provincial councils during the sixteenth century. Under the impact of the inroads which the Reformation had made upon German towns and territories, and considering its concomitants in the welfare system, the Provincial Council of Cologne (1536) devoted seven decrees directly to the reorganization of charity. The assembled bishops declared, for example, that it was both their right and duty to erect new and to supervise existing institutions of charity in the Cologne Province and that their authority in the field of poor relief extended also over the finances of such institutions. One of the great obstacles to effective correction of the abuses in some of the hospitals and charitable institutions, namely exemption from episcopal jurisdiction, was removed by the Council of Cologne. Another abuse, indiscriminate alms-giving to beggars, was also condemned by this Provincial Council. All succeeding Councils in Germany, prior to 1563 when the decrees of the General Council of Trent were published, repeated the reforms suggested by the Cologne bishops in 1536.

The decrees pertaining to charity issued by the Council of Trent are, on the one hand, a re-statement of legislation which had been enacted previously and, on the other hand, an attempt to adjust principles of universal Christian charity to local circumstances. While officially recognizing a place for the State in the work of charity, the Fathers at Trent nevertheless indicated a line of strict demarcation between the two powers. While allowing the legitimately established right of patronage to civil rulers over Church property within their own domains, the Council denied, for example, the right of secular rulers to supervise or to inspect the accounts of hospitals. According to the decrees the administration of such charitable institutions belonged to the bishops and not to laymen. It also fell to the bishops to determine, for instance, how much of the diocesan revenue should be devoted to the care of the poor and to what other pious use the funds of defunct charitable institutions should be turned. As far as the institutional relief is concerned the Tridentine charity legislation was almost comprehensive. Less attention was paid to outdoor relief. The bishops and cardinals assembled in Trent made no direct regulations for it.

The charity legislation of the Council of Trent was first put into practice in northern *Italy*. In 1565 Cardinal Borromeo (1538–84) and his suffragans saw to it that the Tridentine poor relief reforms were enforced in the Archdiocese of Milan. In spite of these practical reforms of poor relief at Milan, the great plague which struck the city in 1576 proved that there were still some deficiencies within the decentralized system. The three important charitable institutions which grew out of the plague of 1576/7 were the College of St Sophia, a refuge for orphaned girls, the large beggar hospitals in the old Benedictine monastery, and the order of the Oblates of St Ambrose, which later took the name of St Charles Borromeo. This institution was known for its cooperation with the city's rulers, and rose to prominence in charitable work at the the close of the sixteenth century.

In the year that Charles Borromeo died (1584), one of the most important Catholic organizations in the history of institutional relief began at Rome under the guidance of St Camillus de Lellis. The religious society which he founded, the Ministers of the Sick, was dedicated to the care of the sick and the poor in hospitals and private homes. It was recognized as a religious order by Pope Gregory XIV in 1591. When St Camillus died in 1614, there were more than three hundred members of his Order involved in poor relief in sixteen different Italian cities. Fifty years later, the Order had spread already to Spain, Portugal, France and the Catholic Low Countries. While in some Italian cities (e.g. Venice), the confraternities were tied to the parish after the Council of Trent, the confraternities in Rome survived as a network of associations which rivalled the parishes, as far as poor relief was concerned. And by the end of the sixteenth century Rome could boast of a series of new charitable organizations which comprised religious houses for penitents, refuges for married women quarrelling with their husbands or accused of loose behaviour, and conservatories for poor and morally endangered children.

In Turin traditional charity displays a quite specific trend. In this Italian city private charity remained a marginal phenomenon for a rather long period, during which the funding of the decentralized poor relief system derived essentially from the municipal budget as well as from the revenues of the local hospitals. Only in the eighteenth century can we observe a rise in private charitable initiatives, resulting in growth of the number of bequests and donations. An exception is the Ospedale Maggiore di S. Giovanni Battista. It attracted pious gifts from the middle of the sixteenth century onwards, and managed thus to establish itself as a major centre of poor relief in this north Italian city. The great charitable impulse behind its development took place, however, only from the last decades of the seventeenth century.

In Venice the new principles of Catholic philanthropy were applied from the 1540s onwards. During this period, the most important charitable initiatives, which restructured the decentralized poor relief system in this city, came not from bodies that can be easily identified with either Church or State, but rather stemmed from mixed groups of clerks and laymen, who shared common values. The charitable acts of these 'societies' were influenced by spiritual and moral aims and were governed by discrimination on economic and moral grounds. Their advantage was the high value which they placed on personal contact with the poor. Many of these societies therefore gained support both from ecclesiastical authorities and from the Venetian government. This applies, for example, to the Compagnie del Divino Amore, the Compagnie della Carità, and the various fraternities for the care of the shame-faced poor. The essential coincidence of aims between the city-state and these societies also prevented a storm of protest, when the Venetian poor laws enacted in the first half of the sixteenth century were endorsed and employed in the post-Tridentine era.

It does not come as a surprise that in *Spain* the crown was willing to cooperate to the utmost with the Tridentine reforms. Philip II considered himself the protector of the Catholic Church. Although he renewed the old poor law which was based on the teaching of Domingo de Soto, poor relief remained basically in ecclesiastical hands. In 1565–6 Philip sent a crown delegate to all the provincial synods which had been convened in order to to put the Tridentine legislation into practice. In the second half of the sixteenth century, the hospitals of Castile were subjected to reforms fostered by the hospital decrees of the Council of Trent which demanded episcopal supervision of the services, expenditures and administrators of such charitable institutions. Only the Royal Hospitals were exempt from episcopal visitation. But also the Crown did attempt to locate, supervise and improve those hospitals which belonged to the so-called 'royal patrimony'. Hospitals were but one institution that the Tridentine legislation urged should be put under episcopal control. Also included were the confraternities which provided some sort of charitable assistance. Of the 143 confraternities which existed in late sixteenth-century Toledo, there were some twenty that were engaged in public charity, as opposed to charity acts for members only. Of the twenty, four offered charity on a large scale, either by operating a hospital or by offering home relief in all the city parishes. Because of the rivalry which occurred between the confraternities, resulting in negative effects on the distribution of relief, the diocesan council tried either to reach an agreement between the large confraternities or to see to it that appointed visitors kept close watch over the execution of pious bequests. Judging by the continual reiteration of these recommendations and proscriptions, the Church had little success in eliminating the rivalry of the brotherhoods. In the two centuries following Trent, the Spanish populace continued to hold confraternities in high esteem. In Madrid, for example, the brotherhood of San Fernando picked up beggars in the street and furnished them with food and lodgings; the brotherhood of the *Refugio* carried out a relief programme which assisted an average of 5,000 persons a year during the eighteenth century. The charity activities of the numerous voluntary associations (*hermandades, cofradias, congregaciones*) were supplemented by the Church, through bishops, cathedral chapters, monasteries, convents and religious associations which dispensed alms, food and clothing to the indigent. There can be no doubt that Spain lagged far behind the initiatives taken elsewhere in Catholic Europe, to place decentralized poor relief on a better organized and indirectly secular basis. In eighteenth-century Spain, charity was still haphazardly and undependably distributed by a plethora of charitable institutions, most of them working under ecclesiastical supervision.

In *France*, too, the bishops strove to put the principles of the Tridentine poor relief reform into practice. They insisted upon receiving annual reports from charitable institutions. However, their jurisdiction was consequently denied by the Crown. By the time of Louis XIV (1656) all ecclesiastical authority over hospitals had passed to the secular powers. Hospitals remained the keystone of poor relief in France down to the nineteenth century. An inquiry in 1791 undertaken by the Public Assistance Committee of the Legislative Assembly suggests that at the end of the *ancien régime* there were more than 2,000 hospitals in the whole of France which lodged at least 120,000 individuals, compared to England which could muster only 3,000 hospital inmates in 1800. As important as the extensive reorganization of hospitals in the seventeenth and eighteenth centuries was the remarkable input of energy into the administration and support of charitable institutions by France's social and ecclesiastical élites in the post-Tridentine era. Not only bishops but also the parish clergy showed a new spirit of confidence in the charitable sphere. The Council of Narbonne (1609) and that of Bordeaux (1624) paved the way for a strong and more effective system of parochial relief. The Counter-Reformation in France also brought about a greater involvement in church affairs by the laity, but the charities of St Vincent de Paul (1581–1660), which began with the opening of the first mission in Paris in 1625, operated through confraternities of men and women under strict ecclesiastical supervision. Some of the confraternities which sprang up in seventeenth-century France were attached as tertiaries to the houses of established religious orders; others were operating at parish level within the current conciliar legislation. The most important agencies in the domain of non-governmental poor relief in early modern France were the Company of the Holy Sacrament (Compagnie du Saint-Sacrement) and the community of women which came to be known as the Daughters of Charity (Filles de la Charité). The first one was an organization of religious activists including high-ranking clerics as well as laymen from the French upper class. The company was founded in the 1620s and became very active in the reform of poor relief (including hospital care, home and outdoor relief, prison visits) all over France. The other charitable offshoot of the post-Tridentine religious revival in France was a mixture of a confraternity and a regular order. The Daughters of Charity were founded by Vincent de Paul and Louise de Marillac (1591–1660) as an ancillary organization to support and implement the charitable activities of the numerous confraternities which had sprung up in Paris and in other parts of France in the 1620s. Its members were drawn from the less affluent social groups. This community of religious females was soon operating on a nationwide scale, gaining approval and support by clergy and laity alike. They were active in education, home relief, nursing, institutional care, in short, they showed every imaginable form of charitable commitment. The philanthropic zeal of the Daughters of Charity did not, however, with some important exceptions, outlast the immense charitable impulse of the seventeenth century. But here and there new institutions were created on the lines envisaged by St Vincent de Paul and his supporters. In the eighteenth century not only the recipients of poor relief changed but also those men and women who ministered to them. In seventeenth-century Grenoble, for example, charitable institutions were founded, funded and administered by judges from the sovereign courts and nobles from the highest rank of the army and the Church. In the eighteenth century, the social élite had already pulled out, and another group took charge of poor relief: the bourgeoisie, comprising lawyers, businessmen, bankers, doctors and local officials.

It was primarily in those *German* territories and cities governed by ecclesiastical rulers (e.g. Salem, Fulda) or by Catholic magistracies (e.g. Münster, Cologne) that acts of mercy retained their traditional functions as channels of grace. The traditional evaluation of the poor and feeble as representatives of Christ persisted longer in these societies. Catholic welfare was on the whole decentralized and embraced a variety of needs, showing a relatively high level of social tolerance. Its major aim was to give a helping hand to various groups of the population in general and to reform the moral habits of the population through compassion, alms-giving and religious instruction. In Germany as elsewhere in early modern Europe the Counter-Reformation was a campaign for the conquest of the soul. The beggar dying in the street was a lost soul because he died without the benefit of the sacraments and the idle vagrant lived in permanent danger of hell. Poor relief in the eyes of Catholic reformers was therefore more than just 'corporal' relief, it involved in fact a total moral transformation of the receiver. Prince-bishop Julius Echter of Mespelbrunn (1547–1617), for example, proclaimed an ordinance for the city of Würzburg, in which the receivers of poor relief were subjected to a stricter church discipline and moral control than they had experienced in the past. Before they were given alms the recipient had to prove that he attended mass regularly and that he lived decently and according to Christian values. Thus the poor became not only objects but also instruments of large-scale ecclesiastical and moral reform. Catholic rulers were aware of the fact that centralized poor relief gave both religious and civil authorities greater control over the private lives of their subjects. The movement to centralize hospitals and outdoor poor relief institutions was in Catholic territories very strong although the battle between the adherents of public and private relief was not always an easy one. In the city of Würzburg, for example, Bishop Julius Echter's plan to centralize hospitals and charitable foundations en-countered serious obstacles when brought to the attention of the Magistrate. At the outset the city council was prepared to block the reform. The magistrates were, however, by no means opposed to centralization. The important question for them was who would be in charge of the centralized poor relief: the bishop himself or the city council?

Such sixteenth-century developments as the collection of alms by civil officers, a stricter regulation of begging, and the re-allocation and centralization of funds were in no way opposed to the aims of the church hierarchy and Catholic rulers. On the contrary, these measures were in line with Tridentine charity legislation and attempts by the Catholic Church to get rid of the inadequacies of unregulated charitable activities but, at the same time, to save as much of the spirit of traditional Christian charity as possible. The Council of Trent provided an ideological means by which Catholic communities across Europe developed similar expressions of welfare assistance. And even where Catholic rulers or magistrates stopped short of establishing a central agency of poor relief, similar to the Lutheran 'common chest', the government exercised tight administrative and financial supervision over the dispensation of alms to the poor. Thus two systems of public relief developed. Parallel to the partly centralized or centrally supervised system of welfare was the often more important sector of private charity. Giving alms directly to the poor or to charitable organizations not under government control (fraternities, hospitals, etc.) continued to be an important way to earn salvation in post-Tridentine Catholic Europe.

Formal versus informal relief

Much more spontaneous, however, and much less discriminatory, even in Protestant communities, were straightforward gifts to beggars – in the street, outside church, in the yards of inns. There can be no doubt that throughout our period this uncontrolled form of alms-giving was far from being eradicated but still proliferating despite all attempts to outlaw begging from the sixteenth century onwards. And it is only a myth that in Protestant communities the massive condemnation of mendicancy and the availability of alternative forms of poor relief had some effect on individual alms-giving in the long run. An outstanding example of the continuity of private and individual charity is provided by the Protestant clergyman Ralph Josselin (1617–83), who sometimes fasted and the saving of one or two meals a week he gave to the needy. And it is estimated that throughout his life he had spent something like £200 on 'charitables uses', of which £160 went towards helping the poor. In Catholic cities, however, there was – according to some well-known travellers' reports of the eighteenth century – a vast number of beggars in the street, and they would not have been there if there had been no response from passers-by. In eighteenth-century Paris, for example, the vast majority of the beggars caught by the police had on average 47 sous in their pockets, presumably the money which was given to them by passers-by as alms. This was more than double the daily income of a day-labourer in the building industry. And those who did not have money with them when arrested for begging had on average four morsels of bread, which they had recently collected. Nevertheless, we should not generalize these findings or take this evidence at face value. There are also sources which indicate that even in Catholic towns citizens gradually became fed up with distributing alms to beggars who went from door to door, although they were aware of the fact that mendicancy filled some gaps in welfare-provision.

In rural areas things were a little bit different. Recent studies argue that personal alms-giving persisted longer in the countryside because of its traditional piety and more personalized social ties. How this system worked in the diocese of Tours in 1774 is described by a French village priest. Each morning the women and children who went to church and were known to be poor received after attending Mass a slice of bread. Later in the morning, by arrangement with the parish priest, the children were divided up and were given a bowl of milk by specific richer households. After midday the mothers of the children called at the same houses, and received a crust dipped in stew or gravy, or the scrapings of the main meal of the day. The aged poor were similarly divided up among the more comfortable households. And in 1601 the overseers of Holkham in Norfolk reported: 'There be dyverse pore allsoe within the said parishe wch have noe Contribucon of money: by reason they have by order dayly relieffe at the houses of the inhabitantes.'[12] This informal relief applied, however, only to the local poor. But even the wandering beggar might expect some help in kind and – most important – an overnight shelter in a barn. But such alms – either in kind or money – were both small and erratic, and could do little to alleviate the chronic poverty of the countryside.

For obvious reasons it is almost impossible to measure the growth of formal relief since the emergence of a social policy in the sixteenth century, both in centralized and decentralized systems of public welfare. The most useful quantitative indicator is perhaps the total payments on public poor relief in selected European towns, measured in relation to population size. Figure 11 shows estimated expenditure per thousand people at various dates in some English and German towns. Although limited by deficiencies in the records, and in some cases based on population estimates, the figure gives a suggestive picture of the importance of formal poor relief in early modern European towns. Public expenditure on the poor increased, with an initial leap at the end of the sixteenth century, and then more gradually over the following centuries. The figure also shows that even in those German towns which had been rather reticent in introducing schemes for public welfare before the late eighteenth century – unlike the English towns which were very much encouraged by legislative initiatives by the central government – the financial outlay doubled between the beginning and the end of our period. From this necessarily tentative statistical picture emerges the fact that social welfare gradually became a rather important feature in the

[12] Quoted in Tim Wales, 'Poverty, poor relief and the life-cycle: some evidence from seventeenth-century Norfolk', *Land, Kinship and Life-Cycle*, ed. Richard M. Smith (Cambridge, 1984), pp. 359ff.

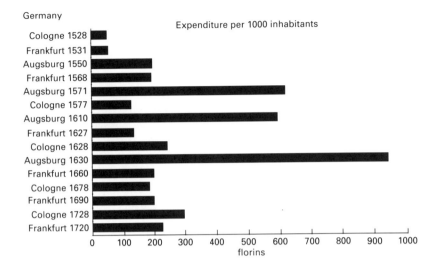

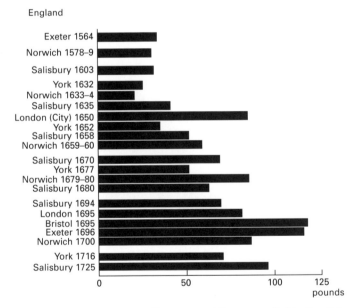

Figure 11 Expenditure on public poor relief in English and German towns in the early modern period

Source: R. Jütte, 'Poverty and poor relief', Germany: A Social and Economic History, vol. II, ed. Robert Scribner and Sheila Ogilvie (in press), Figure 4; Paul Slack, Poverty and Policy in Tudor and Stuart England (London and New York, 1988), p. 181, Figure 4.

provision for the poor in most of the European urban centres during the early modern period.

It is difficult to ascertain if the centralized relief programmes of Protestant communities, designed to allocate resources efficiently, provided for the poor better than the basically decentralized system of Catholic towns. In any case, neither system was intended to do more than alleviate the worst ills of poverty. While historians have been aware of the shift in policy in the sixteenth century, they have not – except in some case-studies – systematically studied long-term developments. There can be little doubt that expenditure on formal poor relief grew slowly but steadily in many European countries during the seventeenth and eighteenth centuries, outstripping price inflation and population growth.

At least in the urban centres of early modern Europe public poor relief became a powerful element in controlling disorder among the needy and enforcing social discipline. Town council records show that local government could often cope successfully with short crises such as harvest failures, trade slumps and epidemics. In addition to poor relief, other forms of government action discouraged begging and vagrancy. In the countryside, however, the situation was quite different. The traditional forms of poor relief in rural settlements were overcharged and could not remove the need to wander. In order to cope with the situation the local authorities saw no other solution than to remove the transient pauper to his or her place of origin where – at least in theory rather than in reality – he or she should receive statutory relief. This system of

passing on paupers (often combined with additional punishment) was an expensive and time-consuming business. But only by the end of the eighteenth century did many European governments lose interest in it.

8   Forms of deviance

Crime and poverty

For the Church as well as for the State, crime and sin always accompanied poverty. Contemporaries therefore saw in the poor not only Christ but sometimes the Devil himself. An English author who had some influence in early Tudor government circles wrote in 1532/3 that poverty is 'the mother of enuy and malyce, dyssensyon and debate, and many other myschefys ensuying the same'.[1] And there seems to be no difference in opinion on this matter between Catholic and Protestant authors. A pamphlet published by the Company of the Holy Sacrament in Toulouse in the early seventeenth century gives a detailed description of the material and spiritual dangers that ensued from poverty:

> They [the poor] live outside the Church in blasphemy and against God ... They never hear the holy mass and never pray to God ... The beggars who live there in the city, and some for more than ten years, despoil their host and make them weak by their vice and libertinage ... in giving alms one does more harm than good, because it seems ... that one thereby maintains a network of weaklings, tavern haunters, fornicators, villains, robbers, and thieves, in short, a network of vice.[2]

Everywhere in early modern Europe the poor in general and the able-bodied beggar in particular were increasingly looked upon as the source of social discontent as well as moral and civil disorder. William Perkins (1558–1602), the first English Calvinist theologian, wrote that the life of rogues, beggars and vagabonds resembled the life of a beast. A similar attitude can be found in contemporary literature written by non-theologians. Poverty and its concomitants, sin, crime and vagrancy, were problems not only for the secular authorities, but also for the Church. The mobile beggar, living in misery and in immediate danger of harming

---

[1] Thomas Starkey, *A Dialogue between Cardinal Pole and Thomas Lupset*, ed. J. M. Cowper (London, 1878), p. 50.
[2] Quoted in Kathryn Norberg, *Rich and Poor in Grenoble, 1600–1814* (Berkeley, 1985), p. 34.

Plate 6 Giuseppe Maria Mitelli, *This is the numerous company of the ruined into which one can be admitted without references or recommendations* (detail). Etching, 1687.

his body and soul, could not easily be integrated into the parish community and was therefore lacking special supervision and instruction in Christian virtues. In the eyes of both Catholic and Protestant theologians, those who, in the words of John Dod and Robert Cleaver, 'live without calling, without magistracie, without ministry, without God in the World, that neither glorify GOD, nor serve the Prince, nor profit the common-weale'[3] had to become a target of ecclesiastical as well as social discipline.

With the increase in the ranks of paupers in the late fifteenth and early sixteenth centuries, contemporary legislation began to discriminate between the deserving and the undeserving poor. The definition of the 'true' poor (e.g. children, the aged, the sick and the infirm) reflected the new policy of early modern governments all over Europe of refusing to recognize unemployment *per se* as an excuse for beggary. The magistrates held that, apart from those who were rendered incapable of earning a living by age or physical condition, all who begged should be considered wilful idlers and treated severely. It was therefore declared that the beggary of the able-bodied poor was criminal. The intention was, as we have seen, to help those unable to take care of themselves, whereas able-bodied persons unwilling to work were not entitled to poor relief, but, on the contrary, were subject to a variety of disciplinary measures. The dangerous poor were, according to a stereotype which developed in the sixteenth and seventeenth centuries, typically rootless, masterless and homeless (see Plate 6). The beggar who took to a life of crime, and abused the conventions of a Christian society of 'orders' and 'callings', became suddenly a vagabond, a member of a deviant subculture, who had to be punished. The type of punishment varied, however, according to the various degrees of deviance, as can be seen in Table 11 which shows the various punishments of various types of 'licentious poor' in early sixteenth-century Bordeaux (1542). In its justification of these punishments, which became even more severe during the seventeenth and eighteenth centuries, the government stressed the connection between beggary and criminality. According to a declaration by the French Crown of 12 October 1686, the sturdy poor, instead of working, 'give themselves up to beggary, and in becoming addicted to idleness, commit robberies and fall unfortunately into many other crimes'.[4] The equation between begging and crime became a commonplace in poor law legislation from the sixteenth century onwards. It was used to justify

---

[3] John Dod and Robert Cleaver, *A plaine and familiar Exposition of the Ten Commaundements* (London, 1603), p. 238.
[4] Quoted in Robert M. Schwartz, *Policing the Poor in Eighteenth-Century France* (Chapel Hill, 1988), p. 19.

Table 11. *Punishment of various types of 'licentious poor' in early sixteenth-century Bordeaux (1542)*

Person concerned	Deviance	First punishment	Second punishment
1 foreign poor	not working	whipping	discretionary
2 idlers	begging	compulsory work	whipping
3 fraudulent beggars	disturbance	whipping	–
4 poor in general	begging	hospital	discretionary
5 poor criminals	crime	arbitrary	–
6 loafers	gaming	compulsory work	–
7 concubines	concubinage	whipping	–
8 pimps and bawds	prostitution	putting under water	discretionary
9 vagabonds	idleness	whipping and deportation	

Source: Martin Dinges, *Stadarmut in Bordeaux, 1525–1675* (Bonn, 1988), p. 267, Table 59.

harsh but futile measures against those who supposedly showed an ingrained laziness and a stubborn preference for living from charity, and, inevitably, went astray, becoming used in the end to a disorderly and criminal style of life (vagrancy, theft, smuggling and prostitution).

Vagrancy

Vagrancy was a socially defined offence which reflects the dual problem of geographical and social mobility in early modern Europe. Offenders were arrested and punished not because of their actions, but because of their marginal position in society. The implication was that vagrants were no ordinary criminals; they were regarded as a major threat to society, and therefore pursued by all authorities and stigmatized as deviants. The offence of which they were accused posed a serious challenge to the moral and physical well-being of the Christian commonwealth. Vagrants should not be confused with the outsiders known in medieval Germany as *fahrende Leute*. The latter included a variety of people, from wandering scholars to minstrels and knife-grinders. Many of them were engaged in ill-famed itinerant trades or professions whose form of work involved wandering (entertainers, transient healers, hawkers, tinkers). They were also despised, ridiculed, stigmatized and marginalized, but not prosecuted for their deviant way of life. However, during the course of the fifteenth century a new social phenomenon grew up alongside these traditional 'vagrants': the fraudulent beggar and the idle, sturdy vagabond. Their appearance caused governments to react accordingly. In early modern Württemberg, for example, all officials were put on alert for idle vagrants from 1495, and by 1508 those arrested were increasingly charged with 'suspicious wandering'. The legal concept of vagabondage is based on the distinction between able-bodied and 'impotent' poor, which had been propagated by the critiques of the traditional view of poverty since the later Middle Ages, but was only fully accepted by governments of all persuasions from the sixteenth century onwards. The ideological underpinning was provided by the rhetorical flourishes of humanists and preachers and the attacks upon vagrants in popular literature. A marginal comment on Acts 17:1–6 in the Geneva edition of the Bible describes the 'lewd fellows of the baser sort', who appear in the text as 'vagabonds ... which do nothing but walk the streets, wicked men, to be hired for every man's money to do any mischief, such as we commonly call the rascals and very sink and dunghill knaves of all towns and cities'.[5] The menace of vagrancy is no less ubiquitous in poor law legislation, but is, of course, more precisely defined, usually referring to some of the five main characteristics of a vagrant pointed out by A. L. Beier: being poor, unemployed, capable of earning a living, rootless and suspicious. The English vagrancy Act of 1531, for instance, defined the vagabond as 'any man or woman being whole and mighty in body and able to labour, having no land, master, nor using any lawful merchandise, craft or mystery whereby he might get his living'. A much more impressionistic prescription can be found in contemporary popular literature, as, for example, in Thomas Dekker's *Bell-Man of London* (1608), where the vagrant is painted in broad strokes:

A rogue is known to all men by his name, but not to all men by his conditions: no puritan can dissemble more than he, for he will speak in a lamentable tune and crawl along the streets (supporting his body by staff) as if there were not life enough in him to put strength into his legs: his head shall be bound about with linen, loathsome to behold; and as filthy in colour as the complexion of his face; his apparel is all tattered, his bosom naked, and most commonly no shirt on ... only to move people to compassion, and to be relieved with money, which being gotten, at night is spent as merrily and as lewdly as in the day it was won by counterfeit villainy.[6]

Related to the image of the vagabond and idle beggar was the view that vagrants were poor not so much by circumstances beyond their control as through their own fault. In 1524 the Nuremberg artist, Barthel Behaim,

---

[5] Quoted in Christopher Hill, *The World Turned Upside Down* (Harmondsworth, 1975), p. 39.
[6] Quoted in John Pound, *Poverty and Vagrancy in Tudor England* (London, 1971), p. 98.

depicted twelve different kinds of vagrants, presenting also the reasons for their descent into the ranks of beggars. Only one was poor by birth, the others were described as deviants unable to live up to contemporary social standards. Five were beggars because of moral failure: the rake, the gambler, the wastrel, the glutton and the brawler. Three became poor as a result of their foolish actions: the alchemist, the old student, and the man who lost his inheritance. The last three cases (all of them women) have been brought to poverty by their moral failures: the lazy maid, the servant girl who allowed herself to be seduced, and the woman who took too little care of her female honour.

The omnibus statutory definitions of vagrancy and even those to be found in the learned or popular tradition remained not purely theoretical. Not every offender, of course, showed all the characteristics of the stereotype, nor were these traits absolutely necessary for prosecutions or arrests to take place. According to contemporary sources the number of vagrants had been increasing over the sixteenth century, but it is difficult to substantiate these estimates statistically. The clearest evidence of a real growth in vagrancy during the early modern period lies in the figures which refer only to people who were arrested, convicted or punished for vagrancy alone, and not for any other crime. In late sixteenth-century England only hundreds of vagrants were to be found in the special searches in the aftermath of the Rising in the North (1571/2), while sixty years later reports to the Privy Council recorded the local arrest and punishment of many thousands of wandering rogues and sturdy beggars (nearly 25,000 in thirty-two English counties between 1631 and 1639). It is likely that the number of people who could be labelled as vagrants continued to increase well into the seventeenth century, not only in England but also in other European countries. But there was worse to come. In the eighteenth century vagrancy was exacerbated not only by deteriorating demographic and economic conditions but also by growing government efforts to eradicate the problem. Comparative statistics for the total number of vagabonds in various European countries are complicated by the variety of ways in which vagrants could be punished. Despite numerous uncertainties, it is possible, for example, to compare the number of people detained as vagrants (broadly defined) and interned in 'houses of correction' or *dépôts de mendicité* in England and France in the later eighteenth century. While in England 3,000–4,000 vagrants and idlers were interned annually, the French police arrested in the same period (1770s and 1780s) between 10,000 and 13,000 vagrants each year. Comparing the rates of internment for every 100,000 inhabitants in the two countries shows that, as far as the repression of vagrancy was concerned, the French government was obviously more successful and its police more efficient in enforcing the vagrancy laws which had been in force in both countries since the sixteenth century. These numerical results are thus quite significant in terms of the capabilities of the two most powerful eighteenth-century European states and their respective policing organizations, but there can be no doubt that other countries made similar efforts to suppress vagrancy. In 1780 the Bavarian security police arrested over 1,000 people during a roundup of all vagabonds and knavish elements. Between 1786 and 1788 the same police force reported arrests of 5,843 beggars and vagrants.

Yet it would be misleading to take the above mentioned figures as indicating the real extent of the problem. We cannot ignore the fact that many records are incomplete and that therefore we underestimate their true numbers. On the other hand, one has to take into account the rather 'high visibility' (A. L. Beier) of this group, which made them in the eyes of contemporaries who provided estimates more numerous than they were. And finally one should not forget that even numbers of arrests are misleading, because they may only reflect 'tidal waves', as the ranks of beggars and roaming people swell enormously during the summer (particularly in the countryside), after military campaigns (because of the masses of demobilized soldiers and uprooted victims of the war), and during slumps or subsistence crises.

The sources tell us also something about the structure of vagrancy. Vagrants, for example, were more mobile and travelled longer distances than other migrants. According to an English study the large majority of apprentices and journeymen moved less than 40 miles, while among the vagrants whose place of origin can be determined, more than 70 per cent had gone farther, and a substantial number of them (22 per cent) had even covered a distance of more than 100 miles. It is often impossible to state the average age of those arrested as vagrants because of the patchiness of the data. The few statistics which we have for the sixteenth to eighteenth centuries, however, leave no doubt that vagrancy was mainly a young person's crime. In Tudor and Stuart England the proportion below age 21 declined from 67 to 47 per cent in the years 1623–39 as compared to 1570–1622, but was still rather high. In late eighteenth-century Germany the comparable figures were a little bit lower, but in Holstein, for example, where officials noted children consistently, the very young ones among the vagrants formed at least 28 per cent of the total. Most vagabonds were single and male (cf. Table 12). That is precisely the group which is under-represented in listings of the resident respectable poor. The vagrants were, as we have already seen, distinguished from the latter also in being predominantly young.

Almost unanimously, contemporary observers and legislators assumed

Table 12. *Sex distribution among vagrants and wandering beggars*

Place	Year	Male abs.	%	Female abs.	%	Category
Cologne	1568–1612	74	93	5	7	arrested beggars
Toledo	1597	136	82	33	19	expelled beggars
Cheshire	1570–1600	129	51	48	19	vagrants (singles)
Essex	1597–1620	69	67	18	17	vagrants (singles)
Norwich	1597–1609	186	50	106	28	vagrants (singles)
London	1624–5	453	56	320	39	vagrants (singles)
Chelmsford	1620–80	143	72	56	28	arrested beggars
Salzburg	1675–90	–	70	–	30	arrested beggars
Aix-en-Provence	1724	834	70	360	30	interned beggars
Bavaria/ Franconia/ Suebia	1750–90	4,739	65	2,518	35	expelled vagrants
Meaux/ Melun	1768–90	–	83	–	17	interned vagrants
Rennes	1777	135	66	68	34	interned vagrants
Grenoble	1772–90	–	63	–	37	interned vagrants
Madrid	1786	374	82	84	18	arrested vagabonds
Holstein	1794–1809	–	53	–	28	arrested vagrants

that vagabonds chose to be unemployed. The evidence of vagabonds' previous and present occupations suggests that unemployment was a growing problem and that opportunities were contracting, and that, as a result, the poor were taking up less secure positions such as casual labour, soldiery and entertainment, which had at that time close links with vagabondage. According to a study on the profile of vagrancy in England in the sixteenth and seventeenth centuries roughly a third of all vagabonds who could report work-histories were engaged in the production of food, leather goods, cloth and metal wares, and in mining or building; at least a quarter were servants, apprentices, journeymen, labourers and harvest workers; almost a fifth were petty tradesmen and tinkers; and a tenth soldiers and mariners. This profile of occupations is strikingly similar to that established for vagrants arrested in eighteenth-century Bavaria. The other major group which figures prominently in the German reports of arrest was a medley of tramping artisans and members of 'dangerous trades', consisting largely of flayers and knackers' men and their families.

All these features and social traits provided ample grounds for abhorrence of the idle rogue and sturdy beggar and for his accidental confusion with the simple migrant or pauper.

Theft

In 1789 a French clergyman reiterated what other writers had expressed in a similar way in the three centuries before the French Revolution, namely that 'beggars do not have much religion and less honesty' and that therefore 'they do not long resist the temptation to steal'.[7] The contemporaries may have been terrified of vagabonds and the many crimes which they allegedly committed, but citizens of early modern towns actually had more to fear from their next-door neighbours whether they were poor or not. For the needy, one other alternative to poor relief and begging always existed. This was, of course, petty crime, especially theft. Theft of course was not the monopoly of the poor, but the crimes of the poor in general were those most likely to come before the courts, especially when they were committed by strangers and not by the local poor.

There is contradictory evidence that the incidence of theft rose markedly in years of dearth. In late sixteenth-century England, for example, the number of indictments for theft rose in the counties around London immediately after bad harvests. Other studies show that this correlation between theft and grain price becomes for various reasons less obvious. In seventeenth-century Bordeaux, for instance, there are only two years for which a positive relationship between economic distress and crime can be established, and these two incidences (1614 and 1630) are certainly not typical because there were other years in which the grain price rose even higher and the delinquency rate as far as property crimes are concerned shows a distinct downward move.

Unfortunately court records only seldom offer detailed information about the economic circumstances of the offender, for these courts were not very much interested in extenuating circumstances until the eighteenth century, when criminals blamed their destitution much more frequently than did their predecessors in the previous centuries. According to a study on crime and poverty in early modern Grenoble, during the Enlightenment the judges were more willing to take into account mitigating circumstances, and the thieves were, of course, all too happy to provide them. One of them was Marie Mansion, a destitute, sixty-year-old secondhand dealer, who told the court that 'misery' caused her to filch some bread, while another, much younger thief, an eighteen-year-old, unemployed apprentice mason, explained that 'hunger' had forced him to steal some iron from a blacksmith. Such claims and pleadings, however, are rare, even in the eighteenth century,

---

[7] Quoted in Norberg, *Grenoble*, p. 258.

and any information on the correlation between crime and poverty can only be based on rather shaky parameters such as profession, place of origin, and the nature of the crime. Information on the types and social background of people arrested for theft in eighteenth-century Aix-en-Provence indicates that those who turned to theft came from the neediest sector of the population. The bulk of the offenders were poor labourers and textile workers, the same sort of people who also filled up the ranks of the city's beggars and charity recipients.

This does not mean, of course, that there was no professional crime in an early modern city. On the contrary, the increase in organized crime was alarming in the eyes of contemporary writers and magistrates alike. The greater availability and accessibility of money and valuables, the size, density and transient character of the population in urban centres, and the trend towards popular consumerism offered ideal prospects for earning a dishonest living. And it is therefore no surprise that from the sixteenth century onwards men suddenly became aware of the existence of a 'criminal underworld' (Christopher Hill). Despite the efforts of such professional thieves, the crime rate in early modern Europe was still rather low in comparison to modern post-industrial societies.

Allied with the correlation between poverty and crime is the pattern of goods stolen by petty thieves. In some urban modern French towns over half of all thefts were thefts of clothing or materials and a certain amount of ancillary metalwares (shoebuckles, buttons, brooches, etc.). And we have also studies on the ubiquitous theft and resale of stolen clothing among the poorer classes in early modern England. In seventeenth-century Essex, for example, clothing and household items constituted 14 per cent of all thefts, while in eighteenth-century Surrey clothing was the most commonly stolen item in reported larcenies. According to a recent study on Paris there was even a tremendous increase (from 24 to 37 per cent of all criminal cases tried before the judges of the Châtelet) in this type of delinquency during the eighteenth century, suggesting that the trend towards popular consumerism which centred first on appropiate apparel must have had a decisive impact on the criminal targeting of certain goods. A sociological analysis of those tried for the theft of clothes in eighteenth-century Paris reveals that the poor often stole from the poor, although the two commonest victims were the keepers of boarding-houses and their lodgers and the employers of any casual labour or domestic servants. Two-thirds of the offenders belonged to the bottom of the workforce, working in lowly positions as apprentices, labourers and journeymen. Eleven per cent were domestic servants, while military persons constituted only 3.5 per cent of all the thieves tried for stealing clothes. Although historians have characterized much of the theft of clothing in early modern Europe as being opportunistic in nature, there can be no doubt that there were also professional thieves at work. Organized gangs who specialized in stealing clothes were known in sixteenth-century English cant as 'anglers' or 'hookers'.

In the countryside the pattern of stolen goods remained similar, the theft of clothing being the second most common type of theft. The commonest things to steal in the rural areas were foodstuffs designed for immediate personal use: food, corn, honeycomb, cheeses, fruit, eggs, meat, sausages and flitches of bacon (from more affluent farms). The limited scope of stolen goods reflects the interplay between economy and criminal opportunity and bears witness also to the fact that those from whom the goods were stolen were not people of considerable means. The occasional thieves who constituted the bulk of the cases which appear in Quarter Sessions records in England and in the legal procedures started by the *Prévôtés* in France were normally not those who filled the countryside with fear. Peasants and farmers were more afraid of banditry, especially in the eighteenth century. They shared with the local authorities the general feeling that pilfering beggars and occasional stealers of food and wood among the local poor were something one knew how to deal with. Robber bands, however, as well as vagabonds and gypsies travelling in groups of varying sizes were both more incalculable and more dangerous.

Smuggling

Another crime often associated with poverty was smuggling. In many early modern countries the villagers and citizens of the boundary areas found in smuggling an important subsidy to a precarious livelihood. Jacques Necker (1732–1804), the Swiss-born French progressive minister of finance under Louis XVI, estimated that 2,300 men, 1,800 women and some 6,600 children annually came before French courts for smuggling. In reality the figures were certainly higher than in Necker's dubious statistics. In the court of Laval which dealt only with salt smugglers caught in the area over 12,000 children on both sides of the French frontier were arrested for defying the law against smuggling. Smuggling was in France under the *ancien régime* a national industry, which employed not hundreds but thousands of men, women, children, civilians, soldiers and bribed government officials. In other countries smuggling was comparatively underdeveloped, with the exception of England, where smuggling became almost a national sport in the eighteenth century with popular sympathies on the side of the smugglers against customs officers. In 1773 illicit trade with France and Holland was estimated at one-third of the legitimate trade England had with these two countries. At the end of our period scarcely one third of the tea consumed in the British Isles seems to have been imported legally. And even a man like Adam Smith sympathized with the smuggler who in his opinion 'would have been, in every respect, an excellent citizen had not the laws of his country made that a crime which nature never meant to be so'.[8]

The penalties imposed were steep but ineffective, since they could only be applied if the smugglers, who were always familiar with the area in which they operated, were caught. The police force was small and had to rely on a few informants willing to give away names. The smugglers' knowledge of the territory in connection with an almost general complicity and support by the local population rendered capture unlikely. Those who were caught were often children and pregnant women who got away with either no punishment or much reduced penalities. In late eighteenth-century France smuggling salt and tobacco without arms, the goods carried upon one's person, was to be punished in the first instance by a fine of 200 livres, the second by a fine and six years in the galley. Women and girls caught smuggling goods on their persons were to be punished in the first instance by a fine of 100 livres, the second by one of 300 livres and a public whipping, the third by banishment from the province. For Cologne in the time when it was ruled by the French (1794–1814) we have detailed statistics on the number of people punished for smuggling. More than 13 per cent of the accused were acquitted, about 10 per cent got a prison term over six months, a third of the offenders were imprisoned for less than six months, but the vast majority of the smugglers got away with a fine.

Smuggling was undoubtedly a lucrative business not only for the big entrepreneurs who provided the capital but also for the many petty smugglers. For eighteenth-century France we have evidence that every child could smuggle easily a couple of pounds of salt and gain thereby a profit of fourteen *sols* (equal to the daily wage of an agricultural labourer). An adult could multiply these profits which, in some cases at least, must have constituted a substantial and attractive additional income for the labouring poor. Evidence of small-scale smugglers is abundant. Sometimes customs officers and the small police force made their swoop and brought the small offenders to justice. The largest single occupational group tried before the courts in Cologne for smuggling were day-labourers. In the second rank we find all kinds of people who specialized in the transport of goods and merchandise. According to English and

---

[8] Quoted in Christopher Hill, *Reformation to Industrial Revolution* (Pelican Economic History of Britain, vol. II; Harmondsworth, 1969), p. 238.

French evidence, even the local clergy were engaged in the smuggling business. A parish priest from the Lorraine area who was also a deputy to the Estates General in 1789 justified in his memoirs his activities as a tobacco and salt smuggler, pointing out that he needed the money for his poor parishioners. And the British founder of Methodism, John Wesley (1703–91), had the greatest difficulties in persuading his fellow-priests in Cornwall, Sussex, Cumberland and Dover to give up smuggling for moral reasons.

The typical smuggler was not the romantic figure which we find in contemporary literature: the smuggler, docking his vessel in some picturesque cove or loading his pack-horse in the morning mist and proceeding over the hills with his contraband (brandy, tobacco, textiles), while a conniving populace offered him shelter and support. The commonest smugglers were, as we have seen, children, at least in eighteenth-century France where salt smuggling enabled poorer families to make their children self-supporting at an early age. When caught these children often told heart-rending stories which were not merely fiction but reflected the grim reality of family economy in the poorer sectors of the French rural population. An eight-year-old boy, for example, told the judges that his father, stricken with fever and unable to earn his bread, lay helpless in bed while his mother had problems in breast-feeding her baby daughter. Other children pleaded in court that their parents had left them to fend for themselves and that they had no other alternative for making a living than to smuggle salt in small quantities.

More lucrative was, of course, large-scale smuggling, and the entre-preneurs were often respectable merchants. But these businessmen did not take any risks. They left the actual smuggling to professional bands of smugglers. These bands consisted of full-time accomplices recruited among deserters, ex-servicemen, demobilized soldiers and vagabonds, and *porteurs* or *journaliers* who were usually engaged for a particular job and who were young and adventurous enough to carry packs on their backs. There were two types of large-scale operators in the smuggling business: on the one hand, the long-distance smugglers operating with a large armed band (often up to a hundred people and more). On the other hand, there were the small family-based bands which relied on the usual camouflaging of goods hidden on the person. Both types recruited manpower from the urban and rural poor who did not have a sufficient and regular source of income and who therefore were willing to take upon themselves such a risky job. While small-scale dealing with contraband goods was not a male monopoly, smuggling bands certainly were predominantly male. According to the study by Olwen Hufton on eighteenth-century France the smuggling of certain goods (in this case tobacco) ceased to be a popular sport and fell more decisively into the hands of those who were vagabonds or brigands, and who committed also other serious crimes than just smuggling contraband. The smuggler who once had been a popular figure had turned into a bandit.

Prostitution

For many prostitutes practising their illicit profession in early modern towns it can be stated with certainty that poverty was the result as well as the cause of their taking to prostitution, and it was also the condition in which most of them lived while engaged in their immoral activity. Some historians seem to be suprised that there were only few prostitutes under the recorded poor in pre-industrial towns, but after all, prostitution was often a temporary alternative to poverty and it is was not an occupation that one was willing to declare.

It is clear that poverty itself was not necessarily sufficient to drive a woman onto the streets or into insalubrious bawdy houses, for had this been the case then far more women would have been whores in an early modern town in which, as demonstrated in Chapter 3, between 20 and 30 per cent of the population, most of them women, were living below the poverty line. Although prostitution might flourish among the poor in the bigger cities, in particular in the European metropolitan centres (e.g. London, Paris, Venice, Nuremberg, to name only those famous for the number of whores in their streets), it was relatively rare in provincial cities. In Aix-en-Provence, for example, only four cases of prostitution were recorded in the years 1773 to 1790. A special hospice (*l'hôpital de la Refuge*), in which prostitutes from all over Provence were interned for correction, had therefore a surprisingly low number of female inmates (between sixty-five and seventy) during the eighteenth century. Things were somewhat different in Montpellier, a city which was to gain a reputation in the eighteenth century as a mecca for all the prostitutes of southern France. Between 1700 and 1709 the *bureau de police* sentenced seventy-two prostitutes. In the period between 1780 and 1790 ninety-three women received various punishments for being prostitutes in this French town alone. In Venice, for comparison, the institution which tried to rehabilitate prostitutes (Santa Maria Maddalena delle Convertite) housed between 200 and 300 women in the sixteenth century; not all of them were, of course, strictly speaking, reformed prostitutes, some were poor women who could not afford the dowry required by more respectable convents.

As the demand for prostitutes in urban centres of early modern Europe was always comparatively high, it is obvious that the prostitutes themselves were never in scarce supply. The main cause for this was the great extent of poverty in both towns and villages. There is limited evidence regarding the initial cause of individual women resorting to prostitution. For some French cities it has been shown that the prostitutes often stemmed from a poor family and that prostitution tallies with the geographical pattern of urban recruitment. The prostitutes in Paris were Alsatians and Lorrainers, the streetwalkers of Lyon came from Bresse, Bugey and Forez. In Strasbourg, Dijon, Lille and Troyes, however, the prostitutes were usually locally recruited. The girl most likely to end up on the streets of the big cities was not the seduced and naive country girl, but the servant girl between jobs or unable to find an employer. Ideal candidates for the vice trade were also female workers in the textile industry confronted with a slump. A girl might start out on her dubious career also because of an unwanted pregnancy. Once pregnant, dismissed by the employer, abandoned by the man who seduced her, and with no family to which she could return, the unmarried mother faced a bleak future. The odds would seem heavily weighted on her becoming first a part-time prostitute, realizing only when it was already too late that prostitution in the economy of the poor was a 'one-way ticket' (O. Hufton).

Poverty almost certainly awaited those prostitutes whose beauty had departed or who became infested with veneral diseases. The inevitable downfall of the temporarily successful harlot provided ample material for moralistic popular literature in the early modern period. Poems, sermons and broadsheets traced the descent of the prostitute ruined by disease, aged, to begging on the bridges or brought to a hospital for syphilitics, which according to popular opinion was the symbol for the punishment awaiting all those who had ruined themselves by their debauched and scandalous way of life. In 1692 the Italian artist Giuseppe Maria Mitelli published a broadsheet entitled *The Unhappy Life of the Prostitute divided according to Twelve Months of the Year*[9] in which he depicted the misery awaiting an offensive prostitute who (in month of July) still 'offered on the altar of the common pleasure' and becomes only four months later according to this 'infallible calendar' an impoverished woman, 'afflicted, oppressed with disease, a beggar upon the public streets', before she finally dies in utmost misery. Such grim stories were meant to reinforce the close link between poverty, vice and prostitution, and draw public support for many attempts of a spiritual conquest of prostitution in Counter-Reformation Europe.

[9] A translated version and a reprint of the original broadsheet can be found in David Kunzle, *The Early Comic Strip* (Berkeley, CA, 1973), Figure 9–26, p. 292.

9 Strategies of marginalization

Stigmatization

Since the 1960s is has been fashionable to speak of a 'stigma of poverty' in the social sciences. The term 'stigma', not coined by but popularized by the American sociologist Erving Goffman (*Stigma. Notes on the Management of Spoiled Identity*, Englewood Cliffs, NJ, 1963), draws from one of the two major sociological conceptualizations and explanations of the relationship between values and social structure. It refers to people becoming different, or deviant, with respect to a whole set of patterns of behaviour. This is shown to be the case with the marginal groups and minority subcultures which existed not only in twentieth-century post-industrial society but also in medieval and early modern Europe. That behaviour which does not accord with certain conventions will be subject of collective negative regard.

Since our analysis focuses upon the stigma of poverty, we mainly deal with a labelling process which is based on moral judgments concerning beggars. The belief that the undeserving poor have no morality (i.e. steal, cheat, are loose sexually), are lazy, work-shy and do not want to be educated and improve themselves, emerged in the late Middle Ages and persists in one form or another to this very day. Social activity of deviant nature, as it pertains to the patterns of behaviour and values of the poor, entails a variety of legal and collective sanctions including marginalization and contempt. Where contempt is institutionalized in such a manner, stigma (and its consequent contribution to social and personal identities) is said to result in reactions of stigmatized persons. Goffman suggests various strategies which stigmatized persons might adopt in order to cope with the situations and degrees of stigma. The question is, however, whether this was a realistic option for the heterogeneous deviant poor in early modern Europe.

Stigma, then, can be seen as deriving not so much from the occupation of institutional or social roles as from the way in which such roles are expressed through an individual's performances and from the manner in which he develops his moral career. 'Moral career' is again a term borrowed from Goffman, which implies a more dynamic perspective which 'takes cognizance of the norms, values, and aspirations of the poor, and relates them to the interaction of the poor with the non-poor' (Chaim Isaac Waxman). To demonstrate and examine the stigma of poverty, three modes of stigmatization have been selected: signs, gestures or language, and rituals.

At the end of the fifteenth and the beginning of the sixteenth century the moral categories of deserving and undeserving poor were long established. In the twelfth century already, the body of papal laws and decrees known as 'Decretals' prohibited alms to be given to 'followers of infamous professions'.[1] What is new in the poor relief legislation of the early modern period is the detail of description of those whose livelihoods were immoral and the efforts by local government to catalogue the variety of patterns of behaviour excluding them from communal aid. Such criteria were included in most of the poor laws formulated and passed by European municipalities and territorial rulers in the sixteenth and seventeenth centuries. Moral judgments were used, for example, to discriminate among the poor in Zurich even before the Reformation. Drawing on the city fathers' experience with the problems of unworthy and deserving poor, begging and itinerant poor, the Alms Statute of 1520 mentions two kinds of poor. The first are the 'pious, honourable, home poor ... who have also worked, plied a trade and nourished themselves willingly'.[2] The second category of poor were those whose deviant nature was expressed both in appeareance (ruinous and presumptuous clothing) and behaviour (gambling, squandering, fornication). With the Poor Law of 1525 the Zurich town council moved beyond the Alms Statute of 1520. The deserving poor were, for the first time, to be publicly distinguished within the community:

And in order that the home poor folk may be recognized, they shall have and wear publicly a stamped or cast metal sign, and if anyone becomes healthy or comes into possession of goods such that he no longer needs the alms and no longer wants to receive them, he should return the same sign to the guardians again. But if any of them were formerly persons of substance, or males who want to work for the people but who still need alms, then one may permit them not to wear the sign.[3]

These badges served not only to distinguish the worthy poor from the undeserving beggars but were also meant to make visible to people who

---

[1] Quoted in Brian Tierney, 'The decretist and the deserving poor', *Comparative Studies in Society and History* 1 (1958/9), pp. 363–4.

[2] Quoted in Lee Palmer Wandel, *Always Among Us: Images of the Poor in Zwingli's Zurich* (Cambridge, 1990), p. 151.

[3] Quoted in Wandel, *Images*, p. 153, German text *ibid.*, Appendix B, pp. 191ff.

did not know the local poor other than those living in their neighbourhood the recipients of municipal poor relief. In the eyes of a
Protestant or Catholic government the poor were to be recognizable, not
only as worthy recipients of public relief, but also as objects of Christian
brotherly love.

The decree that recipients of public relief had to wear a sign was
nothing unusual in the sixteenth century. The demand that certain
beggars wear a sign can be found as early as the late thirteenth century in
France. In the Holy Roman Empire Nuremberg was the first Imperial
city to introduce such a sign for beggars in 1370. Other German cities
followed in the course of the fifteenth century (Frankfurt am Main in
1488, Augsburg in 1491). In the late Middle Ages, however, municipal
authorities issued badges or tokens to show that the beggars wearing
them were begging with the approval of the authorities, as was still the
case in seventeenth-century Scotland, where the Kirk made such signs or
begging licences compulsory. Later on, when begging had become
prohibited, the same sign served as a distinctive mark for those who were
on the dole. The form and colour of these badges as well as the material
of which they were made varied from place to place. In some towns they
were made of metal (often shaped as the local seal) and had to be fixed to
the clothing. More often they were made of cloth, varying in shape (T, A
or other letters, fleurs-de-lis, etc.) and colour (most often yellow, red or
blue).

While the form of the semiotic code might change, the readability and
meaning of the sign acting as a distinctive feature of social identity was in
this case almost universal. And there was nothing wrong in using such
signs as social markers in the Middle Ages. The famous Dominican
preacher San Bernardino made it in 1427 quite clear to his native
Siennese audience, why sartorial signs both describe and develop the
social identity of its wearer:

How do you know where to borrow money? By the sign on the awning. How do
you know where wine is sold? By the sign. How do we find an inn? By its sign
... But tell me what sort of person would approach a woman who puts on clothes
or decorates her head with vanities that are the sign of a whore.[4]

By the late Middle Ages signs and badges had already become a
legitimate means of (mostly negative) social distinction and they were
also extended to include all marginal groups of the Christian commonwealth such as public prostitutes, heretics, hangmen, the Jews and
even lepers. Jewish women were marked with yellow veils or circles on

---

[4] Quoted in Diane Owen Hughes, 'Distinguishing signs: ear-rings, Jews and Franciscan
rhetoric in the Italian Renaissance', *Past and Present* 112 (1986), 53ff.

their costumes. Some cities identified the hangman by either special, flamboyant clothes or a sign depicting a gallow. Heretics were marked with a yellow cross. The bell was a common sign of a leper, but on a prostitute the same sign can be associated with those daughters of Zion whom Isaiah would smite because they walked 'with stretched forth necks and wanton eyes, walking and mincing as they go, and making a tinkling sound with their feet' (Isaiah 3:16–17). In some Italian cities prostitutes were assigned a yellow stripe on the shoulder, reminiscent of the yellow circle that Jews had to attach to the clothing of their chest.

By assigning humiliating marks to deviant individuals and groups the medieval and early modern legislators pushed them into a separate social category. Other people the clothing regulations sought not to separate but to incorporate. This was the case of the deserving poor who in Zurich and elsewhere in Europe were obliged to wear a special badge identifying them as recipients of municipal poor relief. In theory at least part of the law's purpose was more positive than contemporary reactions might seem to suggest. By denying the unworthy poor badges as an emblem of respectability and honour, magistrates hoped to solve the proper application of charity. Yet these signs marked in a more indelible way than town councils may have been willing to allow. We certainly cannot ignore the transvaluation of the signs for the deserving poor in the course of the sixteenth century. The Spanish physician Cristóbal Pérez de Herrera, for example, thought it necessary to refute the arguments of his contemporaries who considered such badges as degrading and 'infamous'. A Strasbourg poor relief official, Alexander Berner, who went on a fact-finding trip to south Germany and Switzerland in the 1530s, discovered that the badges met with strong opposition from those who were obliged to wear them:

It is a sign which is supposed to be a sign of love (so that it is visible that we do not neglect our brethren and that those who want to give alms to them may see that they were considered worthy to receive alms by the relief officers), and which now has become a mark of infamy [*Schandzeichen*] so that people trust them less and do not want to give them work.[5]

With such a contrast in the air, is it any wonder that the deserving poor wanted to cast off those badges that had become signs not only of dependency on charity or public relief but also of a man's loss of honour? If the 'honorable' poor were to be marked like deviants and marginal groups with a sign that served not only to distinguish, but also

---

[5] Quoted in Otto Winckelmann, *Das Fürsorgewesen der Stadt Strassburg vor und nach der Reformation bis zum Ausgang des sechzehnten Jahrhunderts* (Leipzig, 1992), pt II, p. 271. My translation.

(unintentionally) to suggest infamy and dishonour, could respectable citizens who had fallen into poverty be compelled to wear those signs? The answer by many recipients of public relief was 'no' and they therefore asked the town council to exempt them and their families from the infamous signs. In some cases the request were granted, but often the magistrates turned it down and insisted that the petitioner display the badge. According to the report by the above-mentioned traveller, Alexander Berner, only the south German city of Memmingen seems to have followed a more liberal policy in this delicate matter. This Imperial City left it finally to the poor to decide whether they wanted to wear such a sign or not. Other cities were at least willing to make a distinction between the 'shame-faced' poor, persons of status within the community who were so ill or oppressed that they were no longer able to support themselves, and the majority of poor people, who would be publicly designated as worthy recipients of charity or civic relief.

The transition of badges for poor relief recipients from a sign of distinction and mark of official recognition to a sign of dishonour and a mark of the marginalized brings to an end the long struggle between ideals of poverty and the necessity of coping with a growing and disturbing social problem by more rigorous measures, including marginalization.

Although the poor in general were characterized by a lack of economic means to sustain themselves, they still had at least one important asset to defend: their individual and collective honour. Two English sixteenth-century theologians, John Dod and Robert Cleaver, stated that 'every man is bound to have a charitable opinion and good conceit of his neighbour with a desire for his good name'.[6] The deviant poor, however, were deprived of this privilege. Those people described and attacked by contemporary writers as 'idle counterfeits' and 'lazy' had obviously lost or forfeited honour, a good name and credit. Defamation was therefore another strategy in the marginalization process. Different stereotypes pertaining to behaviour, habits and actions designated some poor not only as unworthy of charity but also as despicable. These stereotypes ranged from an abominable way of life, physical and moral corruption, criminal conduct to libertinism. Using terms like beggar or rogue must have had for many contemporaries the same notions and implications which we encounter in most western societies in some of today's equivalents (e.g. anarchist, terrorist). In the early modern period allegations were frequently brought by a respectable person against another for uttering such slanderous statements. One of the many ways

---

[6] Quoted in John Addy, *Sin and Society in the Seventeenth Century* (London and New York, 1989), p. 114.

of insulting someone was to refer to various kinds of dishonesty, infamy
and deviant behaviour. In seventeenth-century England, for example,
somebody was brought before a church court because he had called a
fellow-citizen 'a burn cast rogue, drunken bad fellow, rascall, rogue'[7]
publicly in the street. In eighteenth-century Paris the obsessive fear and
widespread contempt of social outcasts created insults such as night
prowler (*rôdeur de nuit*), rascal (*bougre*), beggar (*gueux*), knave (*coquin*),
rogue (*fripon*), spendthrift (*mangeur de biens*) and rabble (*canaille*). Some
of these slanderous terms had equivalents for females. Yet one must keep
in mind that the literal meaning of such insults is only significant up to a
point, for many of them, like beggar and rogue, being so frequently used,
retained in everyday life little of their original meaning. In the social
context in which they were produced, they gradually had acquired a more
general and symbolic semantic quality.

Another favourite linguistic technique used to stigmatize persons was
the use of derogative nicknames. In sixteenth-century Cologne, for
instance, persons punished for vagrancy and petty crimes were often
referred to not by their real names but by their various nicknames. One
was known as *placknaeß* (because of his broken nose), another was called
paßbortutt (i.e. master key). In Nuremberg, a city for which we have a
long list of nicknames derived from sixteenth-century records, social
outcasts were labelled with reference to names and places of their past
(e.g. *Wolf aus der Findel*, obviously a man brought up in an orphanage),
to their begging practices (*Groschenpumpel*, penny-borrower), or occasionally to their physical appearance (*Lumpenbub*, rag-a-muffin man).

Closely related to these insults and marginalization techniques were
accusations of criminal convictions, which of course lent themselves to
combination with an attack on a person's life. Claiming that somebody
had been publicly shamed, whipped or branded (a favourite punishment
for sturdy beggars and vagabonds in the *ancien régime*) was a strong case
for libel action because it implied that the incriminated person had
suffered degrading punishment and had therefore become infamous. In
seventeenth-century England, for example, a man was brought to court
because he had stated that a widow by the name of Alice Parre deserved
'a whip and cart for an old bawd',[8] implying that this woman should be
punished as the Tudor and Stuart legislation for vagrants prescribed.
Such accusations against men were more frequent, according to evidence
from eighteenth-century Paris police records. Cases involving impu-
tation of degrading punishments against men were more frequent than
those against women. This reflects possibly the real distribution of this

---

[7] Quoted in Addy, *Sin*, p. 115.   [8] Quoted in Addy, *Sin*, p. 115.

mark of infamy among the sexes. The late eighteenth century manifests a loss of confidence in the morality and efficacy of such ritual punishments. It became common to argue that public scourgings and brandings 'served no better purpose than to mark with indelible infamy those who suffer it and to give offence to every decent inhabitant'.[9] Vagrants, beggars and other petty offenders bearing the stigmata of punishment would be shunned by employers, and hence driven back onto criminal paths.

In early modern legislation the sturdy beggar was characterized as the incarnation of idleness. Flogging, branding, hard labour in the galleys, and all other penalties introduced against begging and vagrancy which involved public disgrace, were justified because they were meant to constrain the poor from following their unlawful and un-Christian inclinations and impel them towards their moral and social duty, i.e. to work. Branding and ear-boring were ritual punishments which left ever-lasting marks of infamy on the body of the offender. According to the Edwardian statute of 1547 vagrants were to branded with a 'V' on their breasts. Ear-boring is first mentioned in a statute passed in 1572, requiring all apprehended vagabonds to be 'grievously whipped and burned through the gristle of the right ear with a hot iron' an inch in diameter. We have evidence that this degrading punishment was in fact executed on several vagrants caught in late sixteenth-century England. At the beginning of the seventeenth century branding became common practice, not only in England under James I. The English Act of 1604, for example, stated that recidivous rogues were to be 'branded in the left shoulder with a hot burning iron of the breadth of an English shilling, with a great Roman "R" upon the iron'. That the branding was to be done so thoroughly 'that the letter "R" be seen and remain for a perpetual mark upon such rogue during his or her life'. Female vagabonds, however, were usually let off with a whipping, although we have a few cases where a woman was branded for vagrancy. In France beggars and vagrants brought to court were subjected to the ritual of corporal punishment including branding (M for *mendiant*, V for *vagabond*) and public flogging. Both police and judges examined suspects' bodies for the marks of branding and whipping when they took their disposition. Sometimes the most obscure mark (e.g. the fact that a patch of skin on the shoulder was lighter and of different texture from the rest) was used as proof of criminal record.

Further forms of corporal punishment for deviant paupers included hair-polling, the pillory, and ear-cropping. Each of these rituals implied

---

[9] G. O. Paul, Address to the Justices of Gloucester (1789), quoted in Michael Ignatieff, *A Just Measure of Pain* (Harmondsworth, 1989), p. 90.

various degrees of public disgrace. The pillory for example, had been employed against fraudulent beggars since the late Middle Ages. Other forms of degrading punishments for vagrants were of local origin, as for example the 'cucking-stool' which was in use in some early modern English towns. This is an special instrument of punishment for prostitutes or dishonest tradesmen but also for other offenders, consisting of a chair in which an offender was tied and exposed to public derision or ducked in water.

Whipping, branding and ear-boring was for a long time and until the eighteenth century the easiest way of dealing with sturdy beggars and vagabonds. Whether these corporal punishments alleviated the problem of poverty and its concomitant, vagrancy, is doubtful. But it had at least one great advantage: it gave the local governments the feeling that they were at least doing something against the rising number of 'masterless men' on the road.

Segregration and expulsion

The official construction of deviance was shaped by the government's assumptions about its own statecraft as well as its perception of the governed. In the course of the early modern period writers, officials and legislators not only expressed these assumptions with unusual freedom, but also developed them to their logical extreme and further were able to manifest them in practice. The sturdy beggar and vagabond, it would appear, became the focus of the most terrible anxieties which the poor evoked in the imagination of the authorities. Town and countryside appeared to be a territory of potential, sometimes hidden, dangers, political and corporeal, moral and cultural. Among the most awesome and compelling dangers represented by the deviant poor was the threat of crime, moral corruption, sedition and disease. If, in the eyes of contemporaries, the masses of masterless men on the road were a repository of all kinds of dangers, there were two possible prophylactic measures. Since most problems caused by wandering beggars were supposedly caused by idleness, one obvious solution lay in a massive programme of educative and disciplinary measures undertaken by the state. Alternatively, a minimalist answer might be found in segregation and the rigorous maintenance of a substantial distance from the marginal groups.

In the larger urban settlements of early modern Europe segregation was fervently imagined but in most cases only ineffectually maintained. And with the exception of the late medieval Jewish ghetto there was never an urban section serving as a compulsory quarter for the deviant poor. However, some cities used a certain parish or quarter as a convenient dumping ground for all the morally or physically suspect persons not welcomed in the inner city. In sixteenth-century Toledo, for instance, prostitutes, persons with contagious diseases and beggars were all housed in the parish of San Isidoro. In Medina del Campo and Segovia beggars were concentrated in peripheral areas as in Toledo, while in some other Spanish towns the pattern was distinct. When at the end of the fifteenth century more and more beggars settled in the town centre the Frankfurt magistrates decreed that the beggars should no longer be permitted to dwell in the area called Liebfrauenberg but should be moved to the Gilergasse (beggars' lane). At about the same time the Nuremberg town council ordered the prostitutes to settle in an area known as Judenpühel (Jews' hill) where the detritus of early modern urban society was at home.

Whether the beggars and other marginal groups were relegated to peripheral quarters or preferred to live in certain districts which provided not only cheap accommodation but also refuge and protection, these districts never had the character of a coercive ghetto. Embankments, cemeteries, harbours, the areas next to the city walls as well as suburban parishes were early modern slums populated by new immigrants, debtors, prostitutes, criminals and beggars. One of the most famous recognized criminal 'sanctuaries' of this period was the Kohlenberg district in Basel. This area had the status of a liberty until the beginning of the sixteenth century although it was never a private enclave outside city authority. Despite its floating population it was a relatively stable district. It was endowed with certain jurisdictional privileges and established styles and institutions of collective life. In other cities there were no such self-enclosed areas with special jurisdiction and own codes of exclusivity. Although they were denied the status of liberties, these quarters or parishes were functionally and historically akin to those ill-reputed areas which law enforcement agencies found it difficult to penetrate. Street names such as Bedelerstraße (beggars' street) in Hildesheim and rue de la Truanderie (roguery street) in Paris suggest that these areas were dwelling-places not only of notorious beggars but also of adulterers, thieves, murderers and other criminals. Despite such topographical concentrations of marginal groups in certain areas, early modern European society was too complex and too turbulent to be segregated along social lines. The spatial separation of outsiders remained more a conceptual than a physical reality during the *ancien régime*.

Local authorities seldom used their legislative powers either to lock up the wandering or deviant poor (confinement) or to restrict their freedom to move within the municipal area (segregation). More often than not magistrates turned to the ancient remedy of expulsion. There was almost no town in early modern Europe which at one time or another did not prohibit begging and ordered the removal of all sturdy beggars and vagabonds. Gatekeepers and constables were admonished to redouble their efforts in order to keep the unwelcome poor outside the city. Some municipalities (e.g. Cologne and Bordeaux) were less successful in barring foreign beggars from entering the city once again because of the lack of a police force and loopholes in their fortification system. Other European cities managed better in keeping an eye on the floating populations. In early eighteenth-century London, for example, gate-keepers and constables could boast about such a good catch quota that the town council was able to reduce the award from a shilling to six pence.

Although expulsion proved in general only temporarily successful, the same remedy was used at different times in the same city. It seems that only a few beggars obeyed out of fear of being whipped or imprisoned, the rest came back and ran the risk of being driven out again by bailiffs, constables and tip-staffs, the so-called *chasse-gueux* or its popular equivalent in the various European languages. Driving the non-resident and undesirable poor out of cities shifted the burden onto the countryside or other urban communities. Expulsion, then, was neither an effective deterrent to beggary nor a means for an overall settlement of the problem of poverty.

In view of the various weaknesses connected with the expulsion or mass banishments of beggars, national governments tried out more effective forms of removal for outcast rogues and sturdy beggars. In England the transportation of vagabonds to the colonies dates back to Elizabeth I's reign. The Vagrancy Act of 1597 stipulated that dangerous rogues should be banished overseas. A Privy Council order of 1603 mentioned various destinations: Newfoundland, the East and West Indies, France, Germany, Spain and the Low Countries. Most of those exiled for vagrancy and other crimes were, however, sent to the American colonies. The exact figures are not known as it is difficult to distinguish vagrants who were misdemeanants from convicted felons or children who were sent away. France, another colonial power, adopted the same harsh policy about one hundred years later. In 1718, 1719 and 1720 the Regency government ordered the transportation of sturdy beggars, vagabonds and *gens sans aveu* (masterless men) to Louisiana and other French colonies in the New World. Although this measure had been suggested many times before during the seventeenth century, it had never before received royal approval. In the beginning support came from merchant companies and investors. In a proposal sent to the French

Ministry of the Marine in May 1718, merchants of the city of La Rochelle argued that vagabonds and idlers should be recruited for the colonies because 'it would be good for the Kingdom to be discharged of this vermin'.[10] Support came also from the directors of the General Hospital in Paris who drafted lists of proposed deportees who were imprisoned for a variety of charges that ranged from begging and vagrancy to theft and murder. Therefore it does not come as a surprise that the royal government urged judges to impose the penalty of transportation on men and women convicted of begging and vagrancy. In 1719 about six to seven hundred captives were shipped to Louisiana, most of them convicted smugglers, petty criminals, vagrants and beggars.

The deportees often included a large proportion of younger men and women. The circumstances under which these young captives bound for exile were awaiting departure for the colonies were regarded with mixed feelings by contemporaries. The description in some eye-witness reports suggests that deportation was often seen as a person's ultimate degradation. The deplorable conditions of those waiting for embarkation and the uncertain fate awaiting the deportees as well as the abusive arrests of people who did not fall under the law incensed public opinion not only in England but also in France. The Duke de Saint-Simon, for example, approved in general of the plan to remove the masterless and dangerous from France, but he was critical of the indiscriminate arrests and the indifference and brutality involved in bringing the deportees to their place of embarkation. In some cases the guardsmen were attacked and captives were set free by an angry crowd. Transportation provoked not only opposition and resistance but also fears among the lower classes. Farmers in the Paris area, for example, could not find day-labourers, as migrant workers from the provinces had returned home or did not come because they were frightened by the threat of being rounded up and transported to the colonies. According to an English source, in 1618 some forty 'poor maidens' had fled one Somerset village alone because they were afraid of being sent to the colonies. Some years later a revolt broke out among the children locked up in the Bridewell, the famous house of correction in London, expressing thus their 'unwillingness to go to Virginia'.[11] Their protest was, however, to no avail. While England continued to send convicts to the American colonies and later to Australia, in France the penalty of transportation was officially revoked

[10] Quoted in Robert Schwartz, *Policing the Poor in Eighteenth-Century France* (Chapel Hill, 1988), p. 29.
[11] Quoted in R. C. Johnson, 'The transportation of vagrant children from London to Virginia, 1618–1622', in H. S. Reinmuth (ed.), *Early Stuart Studies* (Minneapolis, 1970), pp. 143–4.

in 1722 as a consequence of violent resistance and widespread criticism of this ill-administered social policy.

'The Great Confinement'

Compared to stigmatizing corporal punishment and other traditional measures of social control such as expulsion and transportation, a new reformative policy of punishment in the form of so-called 'proto-penal institutions' offered the authorities a kind of control over the offender without abusing his body. One should not forget, however, that despite this humanitarian impetus, in most bridewells and houses of corrections or similar institutions which were founded in many European countries during the late sixteenth and early seventeenth centuries, chaining and beating of the inmates were common practice until the end of the *ancien régime*.

The most distinctive product of early modern thinking on social welfare was the creation of a new kind of hospital. The practice of confining beggars in gaol-like institutions certainly gained favour in the eighteenth century, but as a means of providing work for the needy and punishing the disreputable and deviant, it had a long history, dating back to the second half of the sixteenth century.

In 1553 Edward VI, influenced by Bishop Nicolas Ridley, conveyed an old, decayed palace, the Bridewell, to the city of London, for the safekeeping, punishing and setting to work of idle poor and vagabonds. Other English towns (e.g. Norwich, Ipswich) followed in the 1560s. The poor relief Act of 1576 ordered the establishment of so-called 'houses of correction' in all counties and corporate towns of the realm. In this prototype of an institution which was later to become known as the 'workhouse' punishment by imprisonment was given a new importance and labour was, for the first time, introduced as corrective discipline. The English statutes of 1576, 1597 and 1610 all listed punishment, work and discipline as intentions for the establishment of such houses. While some contemporaries regarded bridewells as a definite improvement on gaols, others were more sceptical about the result of their reformative programme, as for example a Middlesex justice by the name of Jacob Stoit, who drafted a petition in 1605, arguing:

that it [bridewell] is a charge every parish in the countie knoweth in particular, and that it beares noe fruit, but is rather a stepp and an inevitable degree unto the gallowes as most men doe observe. And for this reasons, because when any vagrant is committed he is there kept to hard worke and labor, and beats himself both out of Metall and out of clothes, and [there]for departs worse for service then when he did come in, being also disabled for entertainment, yf it be knowen he hath been there.[12]

There can be no doubt that a stay in a house of correction stigmatized a person and that it was therefore very difficult for an inmate of such an institution to find work outside these 'proto-penal' institutions. We have also evidence that the discipline in these institutions terrified some vagrants who begged instead to go to gaol. And indeed, most English houses of correction maintained a strict discipline. Admission was accompanied by a whipping, followed by incarceration and hard labour. The day was regimented. The inmates of the Norwich house of correction, for example, were supposed to work form 5 a.m. to 8 p.m. in summer, with half an hour to eat and fifteen minutes to pray. If the prisoners refused to work they were 'ponnissed by the whipp at the discrecion of the wardens'[13] or their food allowance was cut.

By the beginning of the seventeenth century the high expectations for the houses of corrections were largely dashed, mainly because of abuses and disorders due to bad management and insufficient budgets. And we also find an attitude of resignation in view of the scale of the problem, or as one contemporary author put it: 'the number of such vagrant poor within every shire, if they be all taken up, will be over large for one common receipt, or house of correction'.[14] The houses of correction also failed to employ significant numbers of vagabonds, because they were in most cases released soon after punishment. To incarcerate and to employ them for a longer period and thus subject them to reformation through work was expensive. Because of such financial and administrative problems, most English houses of correction lost their original purpose of combining social discipline with economic gains. The idea, however, retained some currency until a new poor law was passed in England in 1834. The modern workhouse movement started in 1696 when Bristol obtained a local act to govern poor law administration in the town. In 1722 workhouses were given a formal and permanent place in the old poor law. The new institutions proliferating in the early eighteenth century differed little from the former bridewells and houses of correction, but shared many of their administrative and financial problems.

At about the same time when Bridewell became the English model for a new type of institution to combat vagabondage, the Dutch humanist

---

[12] British Library, Add. MSS 12496, fol. 258r.
[13] 'Orders for the poor' (1571), reprinted in R. H. Tawney and E. E. Power (eds.), *Tudor Economic Documents* (London, 1924), vol. II, p. 320.
[14] Quoted in A. L. Beier, *Masterless Men: The Vagrancy Problem in England 1560–1640* (London and New York, 1985), p. 166.

Dirck Volckertsz Coornhert launched the idea that the idle poor be disciplined by hard work and that in every town a gaol-like institution should be erected for the punishment of sturdy beggars, rogues and deviants. In his *Boeventucht* (Discipline of Knaves), written in 1567 but first published in 1587, Coornhert argued that corporal punishment had failed and that loss of freedom and forced labour were the proper solution to a growing social problem. His ideas were taken up by two prominent Dutchmen, Jan Laurensz Spiegel and Sebastiaan Egberts, who held various offices in the Amsterdam magistracy at the end of the sixteenth century. In 1589 the magistrates of this Dutch city decided to establish a *tuchthuis* for men, to be followed by a similar institution for women known as *spinhuis* in 1596 (see Plate 7). The name of the institution derived from the type of labour the inmates were compelled to do. The men were forced to chop and rasp Brazilian dyewood, while the women and young children were required to spin, knit or sew. The purpose of these two new institutions was, according to a report by one of its founding fathers, Jan Laurensz Spiegel, the disciplining of the inmates. The reformative programme attached great importance to personal hygiene, industriousness and piety. Another aim was to avoid the stay in such an institution bringing shame or dishonour on the former inmates. Spiegel suggested that for this reason the confinement to the *tuchthuis* should be kept secret. One way of achieving this aim was that the entire staff of the institution should swear an oath to remain silent on the identity of the persons under their custody. It is interesting to note that on this issue there was obviously no consent between the magistrates who set up the Amsterdam *tuchthuis*. Sebastiaan Egberts, for example, argued that those who feared becoming tainted with infamy should try to wipe it out by working hard and living an honest life. He was, of course, not so naïve as to believe that everybody thought that way. He therefore suggested that released prisoners should move to another town and thus remain anonymous about their past. The book by Coornhert and the reports by Spiegel and Egberts reflect the intellectual and political discussion which preceded and accompanied the initiative for a new, clearly penal institution with reformative character. The foundation of the Amsterdam *tuchthuis* was a landmark in the history of a vast programme of social engineering, known since Michel Foucault's work in this field as 'the Great Confinement'. In the Netherlands, confinement of beggars and criminals became a regular practice during the seventeenth century. About twenty-six Dutch towns imitated the example of Amsterdam, by establishing similar institutions for the employment of the idle poor and the correction of offenders.

The various beggars' hospitals which were founded in late sixteenth-

Het Tucht huys

Plate 7 Anonymous, *The inner courtyard of the house of correction in Amsterdam (Rasphuis).*
Broadsheet entitled 'Miracula San. Raspini', (1612).

century Italy were also new institutions rather than adaptations of existing ones. They also sought to discipline and to punish beggars who otherwise would have been expelled or sent to the galleys. Pope Sixtus V established the famous beggar's hospital of Ponte Sisto in Rome in 1587. Similar hospitals were founded in Turin (1583) and Modena (1592). In Venice the Senate converted a decayed leper colony into the Hospital of the Mendicanti in the years after 1594. In Florence the Conservatory of San Salvatore began with the same reformative régime in 1621. In Genoa the local beggars' hospital developed out of the public pesthouse in the mid-seventeenth century. The new Albergo dei Poveri there was an Italian equivalent to the General Hospital of Paris, established in 1656. The institutions in Italy were neither initiated nor run by the State or by the Church alone. Finance and management were private as well as public matters. Pope Sixtus V, for example, entrusted the administration of Ponte Sisto both to officers chosen by the Roman Senate and those of a very experienced confraternity, the Trinità, which had cared successfully for pilgrims and for convalescents. In the seventeenth century also some Italian reformers and philanthropists dreamt of total enclosure of all kinds of poor people. However, most of these ambitious programmes of admitting every beggar failed because of insufficient financial resources. The example of the beggars' hospital in Florence shows that is was possible to run an institution comprising 200–300 inmates but not more. It was not able to cope with the influx of beggars from the countryside during an economic crisis in the shape of famine and prolonged stoppages of work. Sharing thus the fate of many institutions with similar purposes in early modern Europe, the Italian beggars' hospital differed at least in one important aspect from its European counterparts. In post-Tridentine Italy the enclosure of the poor was seen primarily not as an act of discipline, but as one of humanity and Christian charity.

In Spain the city of Toledo was among the first to proclaim the foundation of a beggars' hospital in 1581. Two years before, Miguel de Giginta, a canon of the cathedral of Elna, had published his *Tratado de remedio de los pobres* (1579), in which among other things he made hardly constructive suggestions about how to discipline sturdy beggars by confining the poor. It was not so much Giginta's rather vague reformative programme but Toledo's pragmatic move which inspired other Spanish cities. In July 1581 the *procuradores* (councillors) of the Cortes voted on a petition to the king, asking that 'the universal confinement of the poor be effected throughout the kingdom'.[15] The president of the Royal

---

[15] Quoted in Linda Martz, *Poverty and Welfare in Habsburg Spain: The Example of Toledo* (Cambridge, 1983), p. 72.

Council, however, discouraged this petition on grounds that it was a 'novelty' and that the King was already flooded with proposals. Despite this unfavourable answer from the court, a few more beggars' hospitals were founded in the years after 1581. The most important one was opened in Madrid in January 1582. In Barcelona Giginta himself was behind the establishment of the Hospital de la Misericordia in 1583. All these hospitals were financed by a variety of complicated money-raising schemes, all indirect or voluntary. Most of them were therefore short of funds and could not fulfil the functions their founders and benefactors had originally in mind. Despite the fact that in some cases the idle poor, especially the younger ones among them, were incarcerated and subjected to work discipline in those hospitals, they never became proto-penal institutions as was the case with the English bridewell and the Dutch *tuchthuis*. The voluntary and idealistic aspects of Gigintas's reform plan remained prevalent in the Spanish experience with the 'Great Confinement'.

The Amsterdam *tuchthuis* became the most influential single model for similar reformative institutions in the southern Netherlands too. In 1613 the pesthouse at Antwerp was turned into a house of correction, where beggars and vagabonds were incarcerated and set to work. Some years later, similar houses were erected in Bruges, Ghent, Ypres, and Malines, but they were bound to fail after a short while because it proved to be impossible to make those institutions self-financing owing to the fact that most Flemish towns were confronted with the decline of their traditional wool industry in the late sixteenth and early seventeenth centuries.

In Germany the first *Zuchthäuser* were founded in the early seventeenth century, for example in Bremen (1609–13), Lübeck (1613), Hamburg (1614–22) and Danzig (1629). After the Thirty Years' War more German towns followed their example (e.g. Vienna 1670, Frankfurt am Main 1679 and Königsberg 1691). Most German *Zuchthäuser*, however, were founded in the eighteenth century, when these institutions proliferated not only in Germany but also in Austria. When the Holy Roman Empire of the German Nation came to its end in the year 1806 there were at least a hundred smaller or larger institutions of this kind in the various German states alone. For Austria sixteen *Zucht- und Arbeitshäuser* were counted, while Prussia could boast the largest number of such houses of any German territorial state, namely twenty-two. Like its European counterparts the German *Zuchthaus* was founded with the illusory expectation of the possibility of self-balancing budgets through the inmates' labour. The economic returns of workhouse production were rather disappointing for the government, uneasy about the permanent quest for subsidies, as well as for the private entrepreneurs who in the beginning saw in workhouse production a means of avoiding corporative restrictions (*Zunftzwang*) but sooner or later realized that without the continuous financial aid of the State they had to declare themselves bankrupt. Because of such economic problems, the German *Zucht- und Arbeitshäuser* lost their original purposes of employing and correcting the unwilling and idle poor. By the end of the eighteenth century they dealt overwhelmingly with criminal offenders: of all the persons sent to the *Zuchthaus* in Pforzheim in the second half of the eighteenth century, only 20 to 30 per cent were described as vagrants, the rest were runaways, thieves, burglars and quite a number of immorality cases (prostitutes, mothers of bastards, bigamists, fornicators, etc.). The pattern was similar in other German *Zuchthäuser*, judging by the evidence from Prussia, Austria and some German city-states (e.g. Cologne and Frankfurt am Main).

The development in Scandinavia was very similar to the German one. Only a few houses of correction were founded before the eighteenth century. In Denmark, for example, the first *tugthuse* outside Copenhagen was erected in Stege (Isle of Mön) in 1739. In late seventeenth-century Finland female beggars risked – at least in theory – being sent to the local *spinnhus*. In Norway a *tukthus* was established, for example, in the city of Trondheim in the 1630s. A statute of 1683 prescribed the erection of workhouses (*arbejdshuse*) in all Norwegian towns. Recent research, however, makes it quite clear either that such instructions were not carried out everywhere or, if such institutions were established, that they did not house many beggars.

The example of France is particularly interesting, because it shows that political as well as ecclesiastical aims could bring about the movement to incarcerate the poor. The prototypical institution was the General Hospital known as Notre Dame de la Charité, used from its opening in 1622 to set to work the poor and to discipline them. By that time, some French reformers had already supplied the ideological foundations for such a reformative programme. At the end of the sixteenth century Barthélmy de Laffemas, for example, published two booklets in which he advocated that idle beggars were to be coerced by confinement in a public institution and that workhouses should be established in the principal towns of the kingdom. His ideas were revived and elaborated in the early seventeenth century by numerous French writers. They believed that confinement helped in the suppression of begging and the treatment of moral corruption among the poor by imposing on the inmates of such institutions a disciplinary régime consisting of religious instruction and regular work. Soon after Louis XIV had come to the throne, the royal government was convinced that enclosing the poor in general hospitals was the perfect solution for the problem of mendicity.

In 1656 the General Hospital was founded in Paris and came under the management of the Order of the Holy Sacrament. Only six years later, a royal decree stipulated the founding of similar hospitals in every French city or town where none existed. This edict of 1662 remained in force until 1724, when another legislative attempt was made to put beggars to work. But the new system lasted only for nine years. A further impulse to legislate drew support from the Physiocratic movement within French government circles. 'The Declaration of the King concerning vagabonds and shiftless persons' of 2 August 1764, was only the first of a series of new measures regulating charity, assistance and mendicity, but it contained already the important instructions which led to the establishment of so-called *dépôts de mendicité*. By law, after arrest and conviction, beggars had to be transferred to the *dépôt* nearest to their parish of origin.

A few years later most French *généralités* had three or four such penal institutions holding between 100 and 200 offenders. The task of providing work for the inmates was in most places put into the hands of a single company. While the public had a rather favourable opinion of the new institution, even if it soon turned out that the *dépôts* were little if any deterrent, the local government was, of course, aware of the many administrative and economic problems of confining beggars and all sorts of deviant persons in workhouses. Recent studies make it quite clear that in most cases never more than half and usually less than a third of the inmates of these institutions were the sorts of vagrants feared so much by contemporaries. For this reason the *dépots* have been regarded for a long time as an institutional failure. Only recently have these institutions been judged more favourably by historians. One of their many positive features is, for example, what one American historian has called the 'elaboration of a clinical-therapeutical model for the rehabilitation of delinquents' (Thomas MacStay-Adams) which influenced nineteenth-century prison reform in France.

The policy of the 'Great Confinement' has attracted considerable interest among historians and social scientists alike because of its multiple implications, practical and theoretical. Whether or not one agrees with Foucault's theory of continuity of the carceral system and the common disciplinary features of workhouses, asylums, prisons and factories, there can be little doubt about the 'symbolic significance' (Stuart Woolf) of such attempts to repress vagrancy and mendicity by segregating and putting to work those caught begging without permission. In the sixteenth century, labour still had strong religious-moral connotations as a remedy against sinful idleness. By the seventeenth century, when the workhouse movement had gained momentum all over Europe, the earlier quality of labour as the means to fight the supposedly main cause of poverty, viz. idleness, had been overlaid by a more pragmatic concept in which confinement and compulsory labour were seen as the appropriate instruments of penal correction of beggars and other deviants. Thus, the paternal State of the late *ancien régime* attempted to combine social discipline with economic gains. Consequently, the workhouse became the distinctive feature of poor relief right to the nineteenth century, even if this English institution and its European adaptations and mutations failed to meet the high expectations of contemporaries.

10   Reactions to marginalization

A subculture of poverty?

The problem of the reality of the subculture of poverty is a much debated issue in the social history of sixteenth- and seventeenth-century Europe. It is also one of the most uncertain. One school of thought views beggars and vagabonds as a professional group, fraternally organized and cohesively structured. Another suggests that the extent of organized, professional crime among vagrants and beggars has often been exaggerated and that the anti-heroes of the so-called 'literature of roguery' (F. W. Chandler) bear no more relation to the underworld of early modern London or Paris than the protagonists of eighteenth- and nineteenth-century operas to real gypsies. It is not for a literary historian to pass judgment in this dispute, much as he may suspect that the root of the problem is that many historians looked in the literature of roguery for fictional details in their historical reconstruction of the criminal underworld, not taking into account the aims of each author and overlooking the function of particular narratives in the wider context of the story.

Not the least value of historical anthropology is, according to Peter Burke, to help us discriminate fact from phantasy in literary sources like these. Were there really 'orders' of beggars and vagabonds in early modern Europe, and how much reliance can be placed on essentially literary sources in the absence of independent evidence of their accuracy as accounts of social reality? To answer these questions one has to look at judicial records, which yield a wealth of information on organization and cohesion among beggars and vagrants as well.

Very few records tell us, however, how members of the marginalized groups themselves may have viewed their social world. The formal, often literary descriptions of the 'fraternity' (John Awdeley, 1561) or 'brotherhood' of vagabonds (Thomas Harman, 1566) suggest a contemporary social terminology which may well be misleading. These sources provide what are essentially views from above, even if some pamphlets which deal with the sixteenth-century underworld may be regarded as 'proto-

Plate 8 Anonymous, *Liber vagatorum*. Frontispiece (1510).

ethnographical', in the sense that their authors, Thomas Harman, for example, or Mathias Hütlin, the putative author of the *Liber vagatorum* (1509/10) (see Plate 8), were interested in describing beggars and vagabonds in their own categories, moved by a curiosity not unlike that of modern anthropologists. While these basically literary sources provide a rather static, conventionalized picture of the social organization of marginal groups in the early modern period, the informal language of social classification which can be gleaned from such sources as glossaries of *Rotwelsch* or cant terminology reveals a world of social meanings untapped by most of the fictional or literary descriptions of the 'dangerous classes' of the period under study here. A survey of the contemporary social terminology quoted in a recent study of sixteenth-century canting vocabulary (*Rotwelsch*), not only reveals in exemplary fashion that division and specialization of labour and petty crime identified by Olwen Hufton and other historians as the essence of the 'economy of makeshifts', but also suggests the existence of simpler, cruder perceptions of society among socially marginal groups of people in late medieval and early modern Europe. Cant words for masters and servants, for the authorities and the anonymous mass of credulous victims of various counterfeiting practices, were often of a more practical significance in the daily life of beggars and vagabonds than the graduated hierarchy of the subculture of poverty described by learned contemporaries in works intended for publication or circulation. In everyday discourse a much simpler and more informal terminology could be adopted by the people who only had one thing in mind: how to survive in a still pre-industrialized world without sufficient means and without the opportunity or ability to work.

The evidence adduced to show that vagabonds and beggars formed distinctive and cohesive social groups is considered by some English and French historians as not convincing. Although the legendary *monarchie d'argot*, the kingdom of socially marginal people in sixteenth-century France, certainly did not exist, there can, however, be no doubt that outlaws and outcasts had some kind of informal organization in order to survive in a hostile world. We know, for example, that some fraudulent beggars (cony-catchers, counterfeiters *et al.*) 'worked' together in 'companies' or professional gangs. Gangs of five members or more were, however, quite exceptional among beggars in contrast to the rather large groups of vagrant youths and gangs of burglars and highwaymen which frequented and endangered the roads of early modern Europe. Only the Irish tinkers and gypsies travelled in extended families. According to evidence from early modern England and Germany, most vagabonds travelled in rather small groups or even by themselves in order not to raise suspicion. They formed what has been termed 'quasi-groups' by sociologists. This form of social organization lies half-way between the entirely temporary 'action set' and the permanent 'group'. A clear indicator of cohesion among wandering beggars and marginal groups is, for example, the frequently mentioned fact that they often referred to one another as 'brethren' and 'walk-fellows' and that they showed signs of solidarity if one of them was arrested or in trouble. Two young beggars, for example, who were apprehended and questioned by the police in Salzburg in the early seventeenth century, admitted that they had solemnly sworn ('by their soul') not to betray each other.

With the exception of the literature of roguery we have little additional evidence of hierarchies among beggars and vagrants. The descriptions in pamphlets and popular broadsheets vary in their purposes and in the degree of detail which they provide. Each has its own idiosyncracies. They are nevertheless a reliable indicator for the prevailing patterns of social relations, the fundamental alignments and dynamics of the traditional system of stratification from which also socially marginal groups of people such as beggars and vagabonds could not free themselves. It would therefore seem to be a mistake to regard these outsiders as having distinct social attitudes which might justify the terms 'subculture', 'contra-culture' or 'crypto-culture' used by some historians with respect to certain traits which are crucial to the analysis of the stigma of poverty. If there were distinctive behaviour patterns of the poor (e.g. the use of canting vocabulary), they must be seen not as products of a unique value system but as normal results of situations where the dominant social structure is unfavourable to those who are at a disadvantage and who are marginalized for some reason or another. The contemporary conceptions of social order among early modern outsiders may be helpful abstractions, but cannot be used without historical evaluation. They will, however, help us order our thinking about the complexities of social reality at the margins of a 'world we have lost', although these classifications may encourage us to assume falsely that highly mobile and complex societies can be neatly divided with each group tagged and placed in its niche.

In most cases, contemporaries described socially marginal groups either in terms of the functional 'orders' or 'estates' of medieval social theory or as a single hierarchy of 'occupational' (guilds, companies) or semi-religious groups (brotherhoods, fraternities). When social order was presented as the conventional social hierarchy, those who sought to describe it were forced to define varying degrees based upon qualities which involved either legal status or way of life. The Italian Teseo Pini, for example, listed in his *Speculum cerretanorum* (1484/6) about forty different 'occupational' groups among beggars. The German *Liber vagatorum* differentiates twenty-three 'occupations' (the cant word is *narungen*). The English author John Awdeley refers to a 'fraternity of vagabonds' consisting of nineteen different groups with their 'proper names and qualities', while Thomas Harman, writing a few years later, presents us with a collection of stories based upon hearsay or personal experience and clustered about a list of twenty-three 'odious' orders. A much more hierarchical view of these marginal groups can be found in the famous French chapbook *Le Jargon ou langage de l'argot réformé* (1629) written by Ollivier Chereau. The conception of a kingdom of beggars organized in sixteen 'degrees' which even have their Estates General, i.e. their regular meetings, was certainly influenced by contemporary political thought and social reality.

To socially marginal people living in a society preoccupied with hierarchy, it was natural to develop concepts of hierarchical arrangements similiar to existing ranks and degrees. Therefore, it is not surprising that an English vagabond told Kent officials in 1597 that he was the 'Lord of the Rogues'. In France the leader of a gang arrested by the police was known as the king (*roy de la Coquille*). Such perceptions of social order by members of marginal groups must not however, be taken at face value. They involved, like other popular beliefs of the period, both 'a mental accommodation to the socio-economic realities of the day' (Keith Wrightson) and a tribute to various systems of thought. Thus the social hierarchy referred to as the 'kingdom of argot-speakers' was less a reality than a by-product of a social institution enforced upon marginal groups by the authorities. The beadles and constables in charge of chasing and disciplining beggars and vagabonds were officially known, for instance, as *roi des ribauds* (France) or *Bubenkönig* (Germany).

No single characteristic of the life of wandering beggars was so unique as the binding force of their language known as *Rotwelsch*, Pedlars' French, *Gergo* or argot. This canting jargon belongs by definition to a socially marginal group of people. Its main function is to conceal meaning from outsiders. While the etymology of the German name for cant (*Rotwelsch*) is quite clear, there is some disagreement between philologists about the linguistic origin of the term 'cant'. Some scholars think it was taken from Latin or French words for chanting used for soliciting alms, others believe that the word has an Irish or Gaelic origin.

The structure of such 'secret' languages is such that an eavesdropper does not necessarily become suspicious, because when a conversation in cant is overheard it gives the impression of ordinary English or German etc. with a few garbled words. While canting vocabulary was undoubtedly useful in counterfeiting practices for which beggars and vagabonds were often blamed by contemporary authors (including Luther who wrote a preface to a later edition of the famous *Liber vagatorum*), it was far more important as a kind of watchword which signalled that somebody was part of a vagrant community with its own codes of honour and its various, often illegal, strategies of survival.

Cant was thus a kind of protective mental buffer between the beggars on the road and the outside world.

Rotwelsch or rogues' cant was partly derived from the Latin jargon used by mendicant monks and wandering students. Hebrew and Yiddish terms and some elements of Romany (the Indic language spoken by the gypsies) contributed to the 'secret' character of most European canting vocabularies. Research by some specialists on European argots demonstrated, however, that the majority of canting words were formed out of the vernacular by applying various linguistic devices: either change of meaning (e.g metaphor) or formal techniques such as substitution, affixing or reversal of consonants, vowels and syllables. In addition each cant has a certain residue of words which were by that time already obsolete in the vernacular. As early as the middle of the sixteenth century the Englishman Gilbert Walker published a popular book on tricks used in diceplay in which he claimed that cheaters used cant 'to the intent that ever in all companies they may talk familiarly in all appearances, and yet so covertly indeed that their purpose may not be espied'.[1] It should be pointed out that the many linguistic devices could be combined in various ways and that no simple linguistic rule can be established for the making of a canting vocabulary.

The origins of cant are obscure but the English author Thomas Harman is certainly wrong when he stated in his well-known *Caveat for Common Cursitors* (1566) that it first developed in the 1530s. The German *Rotwelsch*, for example, dates back to the thirteenth century. Italian and French canting words can be found in texts written in the fourteenth and fifteenth centuries. The earliest English references to canting expressions do, however, appear about the middle of the sixteenth century. The first Englishman who had a real and almost ethnographic interest in the strange language used by beggars and vagabonds was the above mentioned Thomas Harman who wrote in 1566: 'as far as I can learn or understand by the examination of a number of them, their language, which they term peddler's French or canting, began but within these thirty years, little above; and that the first inventor thereof was hanged'.[2] Harman, for example, recorded almost a hundred phrases and words, while later authors noted several hundred canting expressions. Evidence which comes not from literary sources but from judicial records of Elizabethan and Stuart England is scarce. There were, however, a few beggars or vagrants who confessed to being familiar with cant. Mary Roberts, a vagrant questioned by Dorset justices in 1613, admitted that she knew cant expressions like 'glimmer maunderer' (a counterfeit beggar who claimed that his house or belongings had been burnt by fire) and 'fakers' (makers of false passports). German court records reveal the great variety of expressions for rogues who used tricks when begging. There were *stabülers* (professional beggars with many children), *klenckner* (almsmen who sat in churchyards and market-places with broken limbs and legs, sometimes self-inflicted or merely feigned)

---

[1] Gilbert Walker, *A Manifest Detection of the Most Vile and Detestable Use of Diceplay*, reprinted in A. F. Kinney (ed.), *Rogues, Vagabonds, and Sturdy Beggars* (Amherst, 1990), p. 72.

[2] Thomas Harman, *Caveat for Common Cursitors*, reprinted in Kinney, *Rogues*, p. 111.

and *grantner* (beggars claiming to be affected by falling sickness, using soap to froth at the mouth).

To what extent vagrants and other marginal groups employed their argot is difficult to establish. The authors of the literature of roguery implied that it was in general usage among various socially marginal groups of people (vagrants, beggars, highwaymen, prostitutes, mercenaries, etc.). Its knowledge must have been really rather widespread according to the additional evidence which we have from judicial records and the findings of comparative research undertaken by linguists. Some cant words were used later on in colloquial speech, others formed a residue in local dialects until the twentieth century. This linguistical process indicates that the argot slowly disseminated from the fringe to the core and permeated a larger population which was in direct or indirect contact with the socially marginal groups of people. The cant vocabulary of beggars and vagabonds gradually lost its orginal function at the time when poverty changed its multi-faceted character and became mass pauperism with the beginning of the industrial revolution. It was succeeded by the various types of pedlars' French or travellers' cant of the early nineteenth century and the prisoners' terminology of the twentieth century, which according to many linguists and historical anthropologists suggest that these groups formed a kind of 'subculture'. When the cant spoken in the sixteenth and seventeenth centuries is compared to the slang spoken by contemporary marginal groups (tramps, tinkers, prostitutes), one immediately sees a close similarity between them despite the semantic and lexicological changes which have taken place. The *Rotwelsch* expression for 'bread' (*lehm*), for example, which derives from Hebrew *lechem* [lexem] is still used with the same meaning in modern German argots. Others have slightly changed their form and meaning, e.g. *Rotwelsch* 'fleb' (playing-card) which became in contemporary German jargon 'fleppe' (papers, documents).

On the whole it remains doubtful whether cant or argot spoken by beggars and vagabonds can be interpreted as an 'alternative ideology' (A. L. Beier) or as an indicator for the existence of a fully fledged subculture among marginal groups. Their 'secret' language certainly provided an important means of communication characterized by the need to keep something important from the knowledge of others. Its most important function was, however, to give its speakers the feeling of belonging to a rather dispersed in-group, scattered all over the place. The socially marginal groups of people were united not so much by common beliefs and attitudes but by their highly mobile life-style and their mutual interest in surviving in a mostly hostile world. Cant was thus more than just a special vocabulary typical of certain highly specialized professions.

It not only has terms for the various ways in which beggars and vagabonds made a living in early modern Europe, it also contains many expressions which tell us much about the *images mentales* or the mental world of its speakers. A closer look, for example, at cant expressions for basic clothes worn by people who spent most of their life on the road reveals a similar semantic pattern, if one compares the images or associations which governed the creation of 'exclusive' canting terms in various Europeans argots. The etymology of the various expressions for shoes (*dritling* in German *Rotwelsch*, 'stampers' in English cant and *passant* in French *argot*) points to the weariness of mind and body caused by long-distance walking often even without suitable or high-quality footwear.

Socially marginal groups of the early modern period were often true itinerants. Most of them lived by a variety of occupations. Some of them were tinkers, repairing and manufacturing tinware. Others were pedlars trading with all kinds of goods. But as occasion demanded and opportunity permitted they accepted also other menial and temporary jobs. When this 'economy of makeshifts' (O. Hufton) failed, they had, as we have already seen in Chapter 8, also an accomplished hand at begging, small-time swindling and petty theft. Canting was therefore not a standardized language used by those who were forced by some reason or another to be on the road. There was, however, something like a basic vocabulary which reflects the primary motive of all these groups, which is to escape starvation by all and if necessary illegal means.

Rebellion and resistance

In order to simplify the discussion of the possible violent reactions towards marginalization and criminalization of a growing sector of early modern society, we assume that opportunities of resistance fell into three principal groups – rebellions, food riots and social banditry. In addition we assume that it is possible to discuss all these forms of violent resistance together, even though the circumstances and conditions which triggered such social disturbances and disorders might differ with time and place.

Only in recent years has it been made plain that begging, vagrancy and popular revolts were often closely connected, but that rogues and sturdy beggars took only a remarkably small part in peasant risings and town revolts. This does not mean, of course, that the poorer or lower classes were absent or played only a rather inactive role in the popular rebellions which frightened early modern European governments. Contemporary writers as well as the governing élite expressed their fears that harvest failures could threaten the fabric of the social order and cause turmoil in towns as well as in the countryside. 'Nothing will sooner lead men to sedition than dearth of victuals',[3] noted a prominent Elizabethan statesman. Other contemporary authors, in England as well as on the Continent, wrote in the same vein. Local governments also expressed a growing concern about the problems associated with the spread of urban and rural poverty. And there is some evidence that the poor were a real and potent force for discontent both in towns and in the countryside. In 1528, the peasants near Aquila in the Abruzzi mountains, in fear of dying of starvation, started an uprising to the cry *Viva la povertà*. Thomas Walker, the mayor-elect of an English provincial town, reported on the chaos which reigned in the city of Exeter in 1625:

There hath happened many dangerous tumults in so much that the poorer sort assembling in bodies of 2 or 300 have resisted the officers and threatened by violence to relieve themselves; and the number of poor being 4000 or thereabouts and many of them infinite needy.[4]

Similar events took place in other towns in England and on the Continent, where the poorer classes rioted in the streets, resisting attempts to control their activities and demanding relief.

Not only the poor in general but the vagrant population in particular were thought to spread sedition and rebellion. Francis Bacon, for example, was of the opinion, which he shared with many others, that rogues were 'a seed of peril and tumult in a state'.[5] The Englishman Richard Morison published in 1536 a pamphlet which suggested 'A Remedy for Sedition'. He too differentiated between the poor and sturdy beggars as far as they might constitute a possible threat to the political order:

Some say povertie is the cause, that men come to be theuves, murderers, rebelles: But I thynke, nothynge so. For I knowe dyvers realmes, where povertie reyngeth moche more than in England, yet rebels there be none ... the lacke of honest craftes, and the habundauncie of ydlenes, all be it they be not the hole cause of sedicyon, yet as they breede theves, murderers, and beggers, so not a lytel they provoke men, or thynges like men, to rebellion.[6]

Of the actual involvment of beggars and rogues in uprisings there is, however, limited evidence. After the *Bundschuh* revolt which struck southwest Germany in 1513, the authorities issued a warrant for several

---

[3] William Cecil, quoted in John Walter 'The social economy of dearth in early modern England', in John Walter and Roger Schofield (eds.), *Famine, Disease and the Social Order in Early Modern Society* (Cambridge, 1989), p. 76.

[4] Quoted in Paul Slack, *The Impact of Plague in Tudor and Stuart England* (Oxford 1990), p. 258.

[5] *Letters and the Life of Francis Bacon*, ed. J. Spedding (London, 1861–74), vol. IV, p. 252.

[6] Richard Morison, *A Remedy for Sedition* (London, 1536), sig. Dii r/v.

persons who were described as *Hauptmann Bettler* (commanders or ring-leaders of the beggars). One of them was called Lorentzen von Pfortzen. The circular mentions the following distinguishing marks: 'a young, stout person who wears no jacket and who cries in the street, asking for alms in the name of St Cyriac, and has an open wound near his right ellbow which he does not let heal up'.[7] During the urban uprising in Lyon in 1529 known as *La Grande Rebeine* posters or bills appeared on the walls of the city signed by an anonymous writer with *Le Povre* (the poor). 'Captain Poverty' and 'Lord Poverty' were similar pseudonyms used by the ring-leaders of the Pilgrimage of Grace (1536/7) in the Lake Counties. This does not mean, of course, that the rebels were led or instigated by beggars or vagrants. These popular names simply reflect social motives of the insurgents as well as prejudices and fears of the governing élite, but they do not touch the visible reality of most urban and rural uprisings of the early modern period.

The frequent popular rebellions scared princes, landlords and magistrates all over Europe, forcing them into action. Local authorities struggled to master the instability and the social dislocations created by poverty, adopting a double-track strategy: the reform of poor relief on the one hand and the repression of mendicity and vagrancy on the other. Especially vagrant beggars were regarded as trouble-makers, spreading not only diseases but also dangerous rumours which could instigate an uprising. Edward Hext, the Somerset JP, wrote in 1596 to Lord Burghley, giving an impression of general disorder caused by wandering soliders and other rogues in this shire. He refers particularly to a certain sturdy beggar who had frightened the judges by swearing 'a great othe that yf he weare whipped yt should be the dearest whippping to some that ever was'.[8] In Stuart England a man from Chesterfield who was labelled a vagrant by the authorities came under arrest because he had shouted 'Arm, arm together, a mutiny and tumult' on the eve of the English Civil War. The only English rebellions, however, in which vagabonds took a remarkably active and leading part were the disturbances caused by demobilized soldiers in Westminster after the abortive Portugal expedition in the summer of 1589. Some of them formed a band of about five hundred people and threatened to loot Bartholomew Fair. It took 2,000 municipal militia men to deal with this danger. In addition to these military measures a proclamation was set up threatening all ex-servicemen and masterless men with death, unless they obtained

---

[7] Quoted in Friedrich Kluge, *Rotwelsch. Quellen und Wortschatz der Gaunersprache und der verwandten Geheimsprachen* (Strasbourg, 1901), vol. I, p. 81 (my translation).
[8] R. H. Tawney and Eileen Power (eds.), *Tudor Economic Documents* (London, 1924), vol. II, p. 346.

passports to return home within two days. Even then, it took some months before the panic caused by this rather large band of demobilized soldiers ceased. In Germany also and in other European countries wandering and begging soldiers (*Gartknechte*) were held to be one of the greatest threats to law and order, even where they travelled not in gangs but singly, usually with their concubine.

Like other more respectable persons, vagrants and beggars, especially when they were discontented about the cool reaction when asking for alms and charity, uttered not only curses but sometimes also seditious threats. The authorities did not make light of such thoughtless remarks and immediately arrested persons wandering about and spreading opinions which were in their eyes evil and dangerous. A vagrant arrested in Hertfordshire in 1602 had threatened that 'if he were a soldier again as he had been, he would rather fight against his country than for it'.[9] Judging by judicial records, vagrants did not, however, figure very prominently in what can be called the criminality of seditious words. According to a case-study on early modern Cologne, only 12 per cent of those arrested for verbal attacks on the political system and the social *status quo* were members of marginal groups (compared to 20 per cent in the total sample). These findings are corroborated by recent research in other European countries, showing that this particular infraction of the law was a misdemeanour or in some cases even felony committed predominantly by the urban middle class and not by the underdogs of a pre-industrial society.

What distinguished the popular rebellions in early modern Europe from the food riots was the clear causal relationship in the latter between dearth, high prices of food and the incidence of revolt. They were also more frequent and showed a greater social coherence. Contemporaries were aware of the close connections between famine and riots. According to Francis Bacon the rebellions of the belly were the worst. When the whole of Europe was hit by bad harvests resulting in a severe subsistence crisis in 1595–7 an English miller told the authorities that he had 'heard divers people say that there must be a rising soon, because of the high price of corn'.[10] Again, the leaders of such actions were not sturdy beggars, vagrants or criminals. The instigators as well as the crowd acted from a real fear of famine and destitution, although vagrants sometimes were suspected of spreading information on projected corn riots. However, most of these food riots were local affairs, and not the evil work of outsiders. In a small English town a violent attack on the local grain

[9] Quoted in Beier, *Masterless Men*, p. 95.
[10] Quoted in Henry Kamen, *The Iron Century: Social Change in Europe 1550–1660* (London, 1976), p. 370.

dealer was planned by a widow who claimed that she was unable to obtain wheat from overseers of the poor. Women especially took a leading part in these disturbances. In seventeenth-century Newbury as well as in eighteenth-century Paris poor women were responsible for stopping carts containing grain. Food riots in other European countries had similar features and sometimes identical social groups of participants.

Discontent of the underprivileged, impoverished and sometimes marginalized sectors of the population might erupt into popular or mostly local food riots; but it also expressed itself on a smaller scale in a phenomen which has been referred to by Eric Hobsbawm and others as 'social banditry'. It was a form of crime that rose out of political and social crisis, especially in areas over which the government could exercise only very little control, above all mountainous regions and often in frontier zones. The major haunts of bandits in the early modern period were the Dalmatian highlands between Venice and Turkey, the vast frontier region of Hungary, Catalonia, the Pyrenees near the French border, and some of the low mountain regions in the Holy Roman Empire (e.g. Westerwald, Hunsrück).

Many contemporaries stressed and often exaggerated, as we have already seen, the dangers presented by armed vagabonds organized in gangs. Here we shall only deal with a special sort of itinerants travelling in gangs and using force during burglaries, and highway robberies or when they were refused alms, namely those who were not regarded as simple criminals by contemporary public opinion and whose reputation among the poor made them suitable candidates for idealization and later on for romanticizing. According to an English social historian the characteristic feature of social bandits is that 'they are peasant outlaws whom the lord and state regard as criminals, but who remain within peasant society, and are considered by the people as heroes, as champions, avengers, fighters for justice, perhaps even leaders of liberation, and in any case as men to be admired, helped and supported'.[11] The legend of Robin Hood who robbed the rich, switched clothes with beggars and helped the poor has been popular not only in England but also in the rest of Europe for many hundreds of years. All other bandit-heroes are much more recent, many of them living in the period under discussion. There is, for example, Stenka Razin, the insurgent leader of the Russian poor in the seventeenth century. In Italy the bandits also came from an agrarian background. Marco Sciarra, the famous Neapolitan brigand chief of the 1590s, declared himself a 'scourge of God and envoy of God against usurers and the possessors of unproductive wealth'.[12] There is evidence

[11] Eric J. Hobsbawm, *Bandits* (Harmondsworth, 1972), p. 17.
[12] Quoted in Hobsbawm, *Bandits*, p. 98.

that he really practised redistribution of wealth and that he was therefore highly esteemed by the poor of Naples. Robert Mandrin (1724–55), a famous French bandit-hero, who was engaged on a campaign of vengeance, was also rather familiar with the 'economy of makeshifts', starting his criminal career as a professional smuggler in the Franco-Swiss border region.

Indeed, the records sometimes confirm the image, insofar as it represents reality and not wishful thinking on the one side and social prejudices on the other. There is ample proof, though hardly needed, that vagrants and social bandits were brothers in hardship and frequently mixed with each other. Impoverished day-labourers and domestic servants often joined a gang where young beggars rubbed shoulders with old soldiers, deserters, murderers, ex-priests and prostitutes. Social bandits did, in some cases, begin their career with some petty crime or offence which sooner or later brought them into contact with the itinerant underworld. In early modern England many 'masterless men' were, according to the study of A. L. Beier, arrested on suspicion of theft (45 per cent) and vagrancy (16 per cent). For the second largest group, numbering 23 per cent, the reasons for their apprehension are not known for sure, while a third, counterfeiters of passports and licences to beg, accounted for 5 per cent of cases.

(E)migration

Between 1660 and 1700 alone at least 100,000 persons emigrated from England to America. The majority were young able-bodied males who had formed the mass of vagrants in the early seventeenth century. In the Spanish port of Seville gathered a large crowd of emigrants to America, among them impoverished nobles, soldiers and mercenaries looking for adventure or employment, young men without any means hoping to make a fortune abroad, and along with them what Fernand Braudel described as 'the dregs of Spanish society', namely branded thieves, beggars, bandits, tramps and others, all hoping to improve their lot overseas. To all of them, the Spanish colonies represented the promised land, as we can learn from the beginning of perhaps the most delightful story in the 'Exemplary Tales' (*El celoso extremeño*) written by the world-famous Spanish author Miguel Cervantes. It is the story of one emigrant who returns from the Indies, now rich, invests his money, buys a house, settles down to a respectable living, but than makes a big mistake by marrying.

Besides transatlantic migration, poverty and the repression of mendicity prompted long-distance migration within Europe. According to some modern definitions of migration, vagabonds were not migrants at all, since they lived in a state of almost continuous motion with almost no chance of finding or founding a settled home elsewhere. As far as the so-called 'subsistence migration' (Peter Clark) is concerned, the decision to leave home, even for a short period of time, was forced upon the migrant by the impossibility of making a living in his native town or village. For the socially marginal groups of people, however, things were different. They could not cling to well-trodden paths, which usually makes it easy to distinguish quite clear patterns of migration and hence to generalize about the mobility of the poor in the early modern period. They had to react to the attempts at repression which characterized the attitude of most European governments towards the wandering beggars since the late fifteenth and early sixteenth centuries.

The beggar on the road is a figure as old as the phenomenon of poverty itself. What is new to the sixteenth century and the following centuries is the fact that the problem of vagrancy had progressed beyond the narrow confines of towns which were hostile towards idlers and itinerant poor, reaching nation-wide and European dimensions. This game of beadles and the undeserving poor, of magistrates versus vagrants, had no beginning and no end, but was a continuous spectacle which in a way ridiculed the repressive measures taken against vagabonds by local and national governments all over Europe. The problem was that expelled beggars did not simply move to other places; many times they preferred to return to their former temporary abode – much to the displeasure of the statutory authorities which nevertheless continued to believe in the efficacy of their measures. There is also some evidence that to expel the idle poor from one place merely meant to drive them to another – unless one followed the example of some European countries (France, England and Spain), rounding up vagabonds and transporting them to the colonies with the intention that on arrival they should start a new life, gaining their livelihood as farm workers and craftsmen. That beggars expelled from one city or region showed a flexible response to attempts to repress mendicity in the old-fashioned way, can be seen in the case of Spain. In 1586 the viceroy had taken firm action against idlers and vagabonds. The expulsion order applied to all towns and villages in the kingdom of Valencia and referred to beggars and foreigners, and all people who were unwilling to work for their living. Those affected by these measures reacted swiftly, as we can see from a Venetian letter of 24 July 1586, reporting the situation on the roads to Saragossa:

One has to travel in blazing heat and in great peril from cut-throats who are in the countryside in great numbers, all because at Valencia they have issued an order compelling from the kingdom all vagrants after a certain time limit, with the threat of greater penalities; some have gone to Aragon and some to Catalonia. Another reason for travelling by day and with a strong body-guard.[13]

Wandering beggars used all the means at their disposal, legal or otherwise, to move if necessary and not only when they were forced to do so. Thus it could happen that a beggar relieved as 'poor traveller' in one place might be arrested in the next if he acted suspiciously or was considered troublesome. Where he went, for how long, and who accompanied him were parameters determined by a number of factors. Something depended upon geography, something upon one's age or sex; a great deal depended upon what certain towns and regions offered to the imaginations and the experiences of the wandering poor. Those vagrants who moved from villages or provincial towns to the large urban centres of early modern Europe (London, Paris, Rome, Madrid) often never left again because they died soon after their arrival, not knowing or ignoring the fact that these conglomerates of people posed a high risk to somebody with poor health. Others who perhaps dreamt of a new beginning and emigrated to the Americas soon found that living conditions there were no Garden of Eden either.

[13] Quoted in Fernand Braudel, *The Mediterranean and the Mediterranean World in the Age of Philip II*, translated by S. Reynolds (London, 1973), p. 741.

11 Conclusion

Since the 1960s, the discussion of the 'new poverty' in industrial societies has once more drawn attention to the making of the welfare state and the problem of poverty in the past. Social scientists were often inclined to do historical research of more use to social workers and government officials than, say, to social historians. They welcomed assistance from professional historians who wrote case-studies of poverty and poor relief, often paying less attention to power relationships, family cycles, demographic changes and economic structures than to institutional and administrative problems of social policy in the past. The significance of history to an understanding of the acute problem of poverty in industrialized nations as well as in developing countries can be further demonstrated by the discussion about the concept of poverty in the social sciences since the sixties.

As in the late nineteenth and early twentieth centuries when social reformers like Sidney and Beatrice Webb studied the development of the Old English Poor Law, a comparative historical perspective of poverty and poor relief may help students interested in social and government studies. The history of poverty in its moral, social, economic and political aspects can offer illuminating analogies and indicators to a range of contemporary problems intrinsic to the issue of poverty. Although much of the theoretical debate on poverty and welfare schemes in the social sciences is of limited relevance for the analysis of the cyclical character of poverty in medieval and early modern Europe, there are common and distinctive features of this perennial problem which deserve more attention by those interested in the origins of the modern welfare state.

We have tried to shed some light on various, interrelated problems concerning poverty in early modern Europe: the perceptions of poverty, the causes of impoverishment, the sheer numbers of the poor, social policy and welfare programmes, and what since Oscar Lewis has been known as the 'culture of poverty'. All of them seem to be subject to change and may have a different quality in the early modern period than they have today in an industrialized society.

First, poverty in the *ancien régime* cannot be reduced to a socio-economic phenomenon. A social-control and political-economy model would not do justice to the complex reality and perceptions of poverty in the period for which we have used the convenient shorthand term 'early modern'. Today poverty is usually no longer considered a natural or God-given phenomenon for which there is no remedy. Social scientists and politicians believe that the question is only to find the proper strategy in the 'war' which most western nations have declared on poverty. Theories are advanced which place the responsibility for poverty with the society or with social and economic forces which condition the uneven distribution of wealth and resources. According to these theoretical and ideological assumptions, the elimination of poverty therefore requires not so much the reform, education or rehabilitation of the individual but social engineering. The commonly held view of nature unquestionably shapes the response to human need. A belief in the feasibility of social policy and welfare programmes becomes a basis for a completely different approach to poverty.

In the early modern period, however, the attitude towards poverty and the poor still had many medieval features, although modern elements were already present. The condition of poverty was not yet understood solely in economic terms. For Catholics as well as for Protestants the life and example of Christ was still an important guideline in the perception of social order. The notion of poverty was therefore different. Despite the rather complex and ambivalent connotations which characterize the concept of poverty after the Reformation it never lost completely its religious value or background. Things were, however, no longer as simple as in the Middle Ages, when the poor were predominantly seen as a means of salvation for the rich. The latter were required by the Church to act charitably, while in return the poor were obliged to pray for the soul of the alms-giver. Even some decades before the Reformation a far-reaching change can be noticed: since then the poor had been considered both blessed and condemned by God, virtuous and sinful, industrious and lazy. The Church had also split on the issue of 'merits'. Alms-givers could no longer count on the fact that their charitable acts would be reckoned to their credit on the Day of Judgment. The 'charitable imperative' (Colin Jones) might have gained momentum in post-Tridentine Catholic Europe, but one should not overlook the fact that Lutheran theologians also encouraged charity. Within the Protestant Church, *caritas* was no longer to be located in gestures of humility or of mercy, but was an expression or outward sign of Christian brotherly love which could also change its traditional form and acquire a slightly different religious and symbolic meaning.

Not for the Church, but for early modern governments and magi-strates, the poor were mainly a problem of public order, and only to a lesser extent of public relief. In contemporary political and economic writing, the poor represented a labour-reserve that might in the future be useful as a 'productive resource' (J. O. Appleby). During the economic process which has been labelled 'proto-industrialization' by some historians, the poor, men and women, presented themselves to welfare officials as well as to entrepreneurs as two separable categories: persons capable and willing to work on the one side, and idle persons on the other. This dichotomy remained the ideological basis for most of the schemes propounded for employing the poor, from the sixteenth up to the eighteenth century.

In the 1960s and 1970s a number of studies appearing in Britain, the United States, Germany and other western countries showed that despite post-war social reform and rather low levels of unemployment there was large-scale poverty among old people, fatherless families, the unem-ployed and the sick. Official studies found substantial numbers of people living below subsistence standards which society had approved. Michael Harrington's trail-blazing book *The Other America* (1959) made clear that, according to modern definitions of deprivation, more than a fifth of the population were living in conditions of poverty in a country proud of its democratic constitution that safeguards the 'pursuit of happiness' by every citizen. But poverty is something different in an affluent society such as the United States than in the poorest developing countries. There is agreement nowadays among social scientists that needs which are not satisfied can be defined only in terms relative to the society in which they are found or expressed. Distinctions made between 'absolute' and 'relative' poverty or between 'basic' or 'cultural' are therefore difficult to apply to pre-industrial Europe for which there is not only the lack of quantitative information over many aspects of social and economic life, but also the problem of selecting criteria according to which a historical comparison can be made.

An analysis of the numerical and spatial distribution of poverty in early modern Europe reveals several distinctive patterns. All early modern European societies have contained a core of permanently poor unable to sustain themselves and their family, as well as large number of 'potential' poor. The first category of poor, incapable of earning a living for reasons of age, illness or physical handicap, amounted to between 5 and 10 per cent of the population in most European towns from the fifteenth to the eighteenth century. The second category consisted of all those who were dependent on low wages and casual employment and hence were immediately affected by fluctuations in bread prices causing a severe subsistence crisis – a phenomenon which can still be noticed in developing countries until today but existed in western Europe only till the end of the *ancien régime*. This group amounted up to about 20 to 30 per cent of the urban population and represents the so-called 'crisis level' (Paul Slack) of poverty. Finally, one should not forget that there was also a 'background level' of poverty, which altered only in the medium to longer term during the early modern period. This rather large group of people, including as many as 50 to 80 per cent of all households, can be identified with urban artisans and small retailers assessed at minimum taxes, who could easily fall from self-subsistence to poverty. The figures relating to the number of the poor in the countryside show almost the same picture. There was the small core of the structurally poor followed by a second, much larger, concentric circle of poor peasants and farm-workers who belonged to the migratory and smallholding rural population. Their proportions in each region varied over the centuries, and could include as much as a third, maybe half of the peasantry.

Population expansion, economic stagnation, wars and natural calamities are traditional explanations of poverty which are still used in discussing the manifestations and causation of poverty in less developed countries today. Compared to modern industrial societies, poverty was experienced at many social levels in early modern Europe, although the lower classes in particular were prone to life-threatening deprivation. Not only day-labourers, smallholders and wage-earners but also artisans, middle-ranking peasants and even the lower nobility were at risk. Anyone could fall victim to ill-fortune (illness, accidents, premature death of breadwinners, captivity, etc.) from which recovery in an age which did not yet know social insurance was more difficult and therefore could lead in many cases to impoverishment or even destitution.

Another major cause – as in developing countries today – was population growth. The steadily rising population throughout the early modern period – a trend which was interrupted only by demographic twists such as plague, famine and war – led to the well-known pressure on limited resources that failed to grow as quickly and therefore brought about a steady rise in prices. In general the consequence of high food prices was not necessarily starvation but large-scale impoverishment. However, there were crisis years in the sixteenth, seventeenth and eighteenth centuries when, as in Somalia or Bangladesh today, people died in the streets of starvation and exhaustion. Another variable which is particularly relevant to pauperization is the structural changes the European economy underwent from the late fifteenth to the early nineteenth century. The general crisis of feudalism and the manorial system resulted in social disorder and serious economic hardship for many, especially agricultural labourers and smallholders forced from the land. The growth of international commerce and trade as well as the rise of a money economy with its new elements of capital investment, credit, interest, rent and wages also affected the incidence and nature of poverty. So too did proto-industrialization, which had in some urban centres, despite the advantageous long-term effects of industrialization and mechanization, a detrimental short-term impact on the traditional textile industry, causing massive unemployment in this important sector of the early modern economy. Although the dimensions and extent of pauperism varied according to short-term conjunctures and long-term transformations of the pre-industrial economy, the causes of poverty at the individual or family level nevertheless display a remarkable continuity across the centuries. Today, as in past centuries, the majority of those labelled as poor consist of children under fifteen, old people and households headed by females.

The basic tenets and programmes of any poor relief system reflect the values of the society in which the system functions. Therefore, one cannot understand or judge current social policy without first comprehending the foundations on which the modern social welfare system was built. Chronologically a number of types of reactions of the non-poor to poverty can be distinguished, although the traditional terms 'charity' and 'philanthropy', and the concepts for which they stand, continued to play a decisive role in help for the needy throughout the period under study. Among the traditional forms of poor relief, already practised in Antiquity and in the Middle Ages, was in addition to personal and unorganized alms-giving the distribution of food-stuffs, clothing, fuel and other goods by various charitable institutions (hospitals, monasteries, confraternities, guilds, etc.). Outdoor relief was financed primarily from charitable bequests, donations, and in some cases also from tithes. In the sixteenth century first attempts were made to introduce a compulsory poor rate to finance the expenditure on the relief of the growing number of needy people. Similar advanced attitudes towards outdoor relief were shown in various European countries by the creation of *monti di pietà*, communal banks offering cheap loans for the poor.

Another important source of aid to the needy during the Middle Ages and even more so from the sixteenth century onwards was the hospital. Early modern hospitals did not provide in the first place care and medical assistance for the ill; rather they housed and cared for pilgrims, travellers, orphans, the aged and the destitute, and in general provided a variety of services for all those a still predominantly Christian society considered in need. With the rise of the modern state, civil authorities gradually became responsible for administering the institutional relief conducted in the Middle Ages by church officials. Not all of the basic principles of public assistance did, however, originate in the early sixteenth century, for poor relief had been a matter of municipal concern long before that time. The long road to social security started in the fifteenth century, or perhaps as early as the fourteenth century in the case of the Italian city-states.

Modern attitudes towards poor relief manifested themselves from the sixteenth century onwards primarily in another field. Everywhere in early modern Europe we find a new emphasis on the obligation to work. Labour became the new medicine for poverty. The Reformation effected a new appraisal of labour. This was not a mere coincidence. Along with the growing awareness of the economic importance of labour went a new and even stronger emphasis on the duty of every man to work prescribed by divine law. With a few exceptions begging became despised and was no longer considered a proper means to overcome destitution. As a result of this changed perception of the able-bodied poor, labour in the eyes of poor relief reformers meant punishment of the idle as well as training and education. In the sixteenth century we can see already in an embryonic stage the ideas which are behind most of the schemes propounded for employing the poor during the rest of the early modern period. And even today welfare reformers still argue that the state must create more jobs and more opportunities of upward mobility for the individual in order to fight poverty. Modern welfare programmes no longer put the blame entirely on the victim; nevertheless they are devised to cajole and deter.

The intellectual debate of the sixteenth to the eighteenth centuries over the need to provide work and the expediency of compelling the poor to find jobs soon yielded to practical results, as, for example, the workhouse movement. When from the seventeenth century onwards most western European countries began to experiment with this new type of institutional relief, the earlier quality of labour as the means to fight the supposedly main cause of poverty, viz. idleness, had been overlaid by a more pragmatic concept in which confinement and compulsory labour were seen as the appropriate instrument of penal correction of beggars and other deviants. Thus, the paternal state of the late *ancien régime* attempted to combine social discipline with economic gains. Consequently, the workhouse became the distinctive feature of poor relief right to the nineteenth century, even if this English institution and its European adaptations and mutations failed to meet the high expectations of contemporaries.

Underlying this interpretation of poor relief was an ideology that saw charitable relations still as multi-faceted, paternalistic and reciprocal, morally as well as economically. In modern times things have changed.

These ties have become simpler, less personal and more bureaucratic. Now the government agencies dominate the welfare sector, and there a new spirit reigns. This development, which culminated in the modern welfare state, had already started in the sixteenth century, when personal contacts with the poor were gradually eliminated, and a more distant relationship, regulated by rules, stripped of moral and religious content, slowly took its place. This change in the quality of the relations between the poor and those who provided relief derived from sweeping changes in early modern society. Social relations lost their moral content as a result of the transition from feudalism to capitalism. From the end of the eighteenth century onwards the ideals of liberalism dominated social policy in the West, stressing economic and social values such as self-help and equality. With advancing industrialization and democratization of political power surveys of poverty in various countries helped to stir once again the social conscience of the middle and upper classes. Economic and social change brought about new attitudes towards the poor. The right of the poor to relief and work was no longer considered in paternalistic terms as an obligation of the state. Social security became instead the right of the individual.

To the changing attitudes towards the poor already discussed should be added the types of reactions of the poor to poverty. Apparently the connection between poverty and delinquency (theft, vagrancy, prostitution) was clearer in the early modern period than in modern times. Whatever the sources or the mode of analysis, most researchers are ready to admit that crime had a different quality and quantity in pre-industrialized societies. Certainly violence was not yet the prerogative of the slum subculture which is regarded by modern criminology as its most usual environment. The same applies to crimes against property. One offence was particularly important, namely theft. And in contrast to modern crime statistics, women played a minor role in this category of crimes. Historians of crime have suggested that women in early modern society were provided for in a way that men could not expect. There is at least some evidence that in a traditional society a poor woman could expect more assistance from her neighbours and from the magistrates than a poor man. A persistent hypothesis often tested and in the meantime more and more criticized is based on the dichotomy between crimes against poverty and crimes against persons. In its simplest form, the theory holds that the development of modern societies is accompanied by a modernization of crime. Criminality in pre-industrialized Europe is thus characterized more by violence against persons than by property crimes such as theft. Modern society by contrast is thought to experience more theft than violence. The *vol-violence* thesis still preoccupies historians of crime, but it is difficult to find a quantifiable relation between such phenomena as property crime, poverty and the modernization theory. The fact that often the condition of the poor pushes them into marginality and criminality has however been amply and sensibly supported by modern sociological research as well as by comparative historical studies. The only difference between then and now is that in a more affluent society theft of food for immediate consumption, a typical crime of the poor in the early modern period, plays only a rather minor role.

One of the major questions which has troubled both sociologists and historians since the 1960s is that of the existence of a 'culture of poverty'. This theory refers to the way of life of the poor, who are seen as being different from the non-poor not only economically, but in many other respects as well. The experimental air surrounding the pioneers of research into the history of poverty and deviance has allowed hypotheses to flourish. As studies on sociological data and historical documents have progressed, sensitivity to the possibilities and limitations of the evidence has gradually evolved. We now have a deeper understanding of the position of the poor within a given social structure, the attitudes and the actions of the non-poor towards the poor and deviant sectors of the population, and the effect of these upon the poor and the socially marginal groups themselves. In summary, the current state of research into the past and present problems of poverty and deviance gives evidence that the 'culture of poverty' is not an independent subculture, but rather a dependent and relational one. Or as an American sociologist, Chaim Isaac Waxman, has put it in a nutshell: 'It is a subculture that develops and persists along with the stigma of poverty as part of a vicious circle.'

Appendix I: Chronology

The following time-chart of poor relief reform in early modern Europe refers mainly to decisions and events which were of more than local importance. Abbreviations have been used to indicate the countries concerned: England and Scotland (GB), Germany (D), Low Countries (NL), France (F), Italy (I), Spain (E), Denmark (DK), Sweden (S), Finland (SF), Switzerland (CH)

1495　An Act Against Vagabonds and Beggars (GB)
1496　Ordinance by Charles VII which commissions the French courts to put vagabonds to the galleys (F)
1497　Imperial Diet decrees that each community should take measures to care for its own poor (D)
1509　The *Liber vagatorum* pictures the evil practices of sturdy beggars (D)
1522　Poor relief reform in Nuremberg (D)
1523　Luther composes the Poor Law Ordinance for the little Saxon town of Leisnig (D)
1525　Poor relief reform in Ypres (NL)
1526　Juan Luis Vives's *De subventione pauperum* published in Bruges (NL)
1529　Venetian Poor Laws (I)
1530　Imperial Police Ordinance entrusts communities with the relief of the poor in the Holy Roman Empire (D)
1531　Decision of the Sorbonne Faculty of Theology in favour of the poor relief reforms undertaken by the town of Ypres (F)
1531　Poor relief reform in the Low Countries initiated by Emperor Charles V (NL)
1531　Foundation of the *Aumône général* in Lyon (F)
1531　Vagrancy and poor relief act (GB)
1534　'Society of Charity' founded by Gian Matteo Giberti in Verona (I)

1535   Ignatius of Loyola, the founder of the Jesuit order, organizes poor relief reform in his native town (E)

1536   An Act for Punishment of Sturdy Vagabonds and Beggars (GB)

1536   Council of Cologne advocates reform of charitable institutions in one of Germany's largest archbishoprics (D)

1539   Rome establishes a *monte di pietà* (pawn shop for the poor) (I)

1540   Proclamation of the Castilian Poor Law (E)

1543   Royal supervision over the charities in France (F)

1544   Foundation of the Grand Bureau des Pauvres in Paris (F)

1545   Controversy between the two Spanish theologians Juan de Medina and Domingo de Soto on how to relieve the poor (E)

1545   Royal proclamation that able-bodied beggars should be forced to public works (F)

1546   Ordinance for the reform of the hospitals (F)

1547   An Act for the Punishment of Vagabonds and for the Relief of the Poor and Impotent Persons (GB)

1551   Paris is the first French town to introduce a poor rate (F)

1551   The Swiss cantons agree that the communities should be in charge of assisting the poor (CH)

1552   Act for the Provision and Relief of the Poor (GB)

1558   Publication of a royal decree that obliges all Danish parishes to put up a common box (DK)

1560   Edict on the administration of hospitals and other charitable institutions (F)

1563   Council of Trent enacts reform of charitable institutions (I)

1563   An Act for the Relief of the Poor (GB)

1563   Compulsory poor tax introduced by the cities of Rennes, Nantes and Vitré (F)

1565   Enactment of new poor laws by the Cortes of Castile (E)

1565   Cardinal Borromeo puts the reform plans of the Council of Trent into practice in Milan (I)

1566   Royal Ordinances of Blois postulate a system of parish responsibility for poor relief in France (F)

1572   An Act for the Punishment of Vagabonds and for the Relief of the Poor and Impotent (GB)

1576   An Act for the Setting of the Poor on Work, and for the Avoiding of Idleness (GB)

1579   Scottish Poor Law Act (GB)

1592   New Scottish Poor Law Act (GB)

1593   Proclamation on the appointment of hospital administrators and directors of other charitable institutions (F)

1596   Ordinance for the poor and beggars in Brandenburg-Prussia (D)

1596 Foundation of the Amsterdam house of correction (*rasphuis*) (NL)

1597 An Act for the Punishment of Rogues, Vagabonds and Sturdy Beggars (GB)

1604 Act for Punishment of Rogues, Vagabonds and Sturdy Beggars (GB)

1622 The General Hospital in Lyon becomes the first French institution to experiment with the 'Great Confinement' (F)

1625 Congregation of the 'Mission' (or 'Lazarists') founded by St Vincent de Paul (F)

1633 Foundation of the 'Daughters of Charity' by Louise de Marillac (F)

1649 Scottish Poor Law Act (GB)

1656 Foundation of the Paris General Hospital (F)

1662 Settlement Act (GB)

1662 Royal Proclamation order that a general hospital should be established in every French town (F)

1698 Uniform poor rate enacted in Sweden and Finland (S, SF)

1703 Poor Law in Brandenburg-Prussia (D)

1708 Danish Poor Law (DK)

1723 Knatchbull's Act permits unions of parishes and sanctions the refusal of relief to paupers who are unwilling to enter a workhouse (GB)

1724 Royal decree launches the 'Great Confinement' in France (F)

1724 Silesia orders the deportation of all sturdy beggars and vagabonds (D)

1736 Poor Law Act for the duchy of Holstein (D)

1768 Royal workhouses (*dépôts de mendicité*) founded in France (F)

1769 Spanish crown initiates a poor relief reform (E)

1782 Gilbert's Act on Workhouses (GB)

1788 Foundation of the General Poor Relief Agency in Hamburg (D)

1789 Benjamin Thompson alias Count Rumford invents the famous 'Rumford soup' which changes the diets in many European workhouses and charitable institutions (D)

1795 Introduction of the Speenhamland system (GB)

1797 F. M. Eden publishes his influential survey 'State of the Poor' (GB)

1798 Publication of Thomas Malthus's famous work 'Essay on the Principle of Population', which gives a demographic explanation to the causes of pauperism (GB)

Appendix II: Concise biographies of important poor relief reformers

Bertier de Sauvigny, Louis-Bénigne-François (murdered 1789): As the *intendant* of Paris he had already acquired a reputation in royal councils as a humanitarian reformer and as an indefatigable administrator, before he became in charge of the large-scale operation on mendicity undertaken by the French government in the 1760s. He was appointed *commissaire de la mendicité*. He also carried on the interests of his father, from whom he had inherited the office of an *intendant*, in agricultural improvement, public health, and the promotion of charitable establishments, including alms bureaux. One of his many charitable projects, the 'companies of provincial workers', also known as *corps de pionniers*, was intended to complement the function of the *dépôts de mendicité*, the French version of the 'houses of correction' for beggars, of which he was officially in charge.

Borromeo, Charles (1538–84): Archbishop of Milan and poor relief reformer. In addition to his life-time devotion to the poor, Borromeo had played an important part in forming the charitable regulations of the Council of Trent (1545–63). He was also the first one to put the charity legislation of this important council into practice. Before he took up his residence as Archbishop of Milan, Cardinal Borromeo, assisted by St Philip Neri (s.v.), had repaired and re-endowed the asylum for the insane S. Maria di Pietà dei Poveri Pazzi and opened a house for young women whose chastity was endangered. Borromeo left Rome for Milan in 1565. In their enforcement of the Tridentine poor relief reforms, he and his suffragans felt the need of secular assistance. In 1568 St Charles was able to open a new institution of charity in the city, known as a 'house of succour'. In spite of the many practical reforms of the ecclesiastical system of poor relief which he had initiated in Milan, the plague which struck the city and diocese in late 1576 proved that many weaknesses remained to be corrected. The three great works of charity which grew out of the experience with the plague catastrophe of 1576/7 in Milan became a lasting memorial for the greatness of its Archbishop.

Bucer, Martin (1491–1551): Eminent Protestant reformer and author of *De regno Christi* (1550) who by his sermons, letters and books influenced poor relief reform in Strasbourg, Ulm and the territory of Hesse. His ideas spread also to England, where his 'Treatise, How by the Worde of God, Christian mens Almose ought to Be distributed' was published posthumously in the late 1550s. In this tract he argues for the establishment of a common chest and the supervision of poor relief by deacons. Obviously influenced by the municipal poor relief reforms on the Continent, which took place in the 1520s and 1530s, he makes the point that every city is responsible for the relief of its own poor.

Bugenhagen, Johannes (1485–1558): Protestant reformer and theologian who set up the Poor Ordinance at Wittenberg. Thereafter his practical revisions were accepted by many north German cities (Brunswick, Lübeck, Hamburg). He maintained Luther's central principle of poor relief, namely the common chest. The changes he made pertained to administration and financing. Bugenhagen's reorganization was, however, not limited to poor relief, but extended to the entire organization of the Protestant Church. Owing to his influence many Protestant territories and city-states incorporated poor relief regulations in their new Church orders.

Burn, Richard (1709–85): English legal writer and topographer. He was a justice of the peace for the counties of Westmorland and Cumberland. He published an important handbook for *The Justice of the Peace and Parish Officer* (1755), dealing also with many practical matters of poor law administration by local government officials. In the 1770s he proposed a new poor law bill. Burn was the author not only of an often quoted pamphlet on poor relief reform, but also of one of the best legal treatises on this matter, besides being an active magistrate in his county who was very familiar with the everyday work of the overseers of the poor.

Calvin, John (1509–64): French theologian and religious reformer who influenced poor relief reform in Geneva. He saw social relations as being firmly based on God's law of love. Calvin proposed that the ministerial church élite and state officials work together towards the relief of poverty. The Church Ordinance of 1541 which he had set up recognized the lay hospital governors of Geneva as deacons of the Church. The poor relief system established during his life-time in Geneva was based on the deacons. It was their duty to receive all voluntary alms, ecclesiastical rents and other revenues, and to minister to the poor out of these funds.

Campomanes, Pedro Rodriguez Conde de (1723–1802): Spanish lawyer, politician and economist. Like many other mercantilist authors of eighteenth-century Spain, the Count of Campomanes advocated the creation of workhouses as a means of forcing the indigent into occupations useful to the state. He wrote, for example, that 'idleness must be suppressed in every country that wishes to develop its industry'. This view of the economic benefits to be obtained from the poor was given widespread popularity in Spain by the work of a fellow-countryman, Bernardo Ward, a minister of Ferdinand VI, which was published in 1782. In his own writings, Campomanes often resorted to long excerpts from Juan de Medina (s.v.) to refute contemporary objections to confinement. He argued that religious education would also be provided to the inmates of the so-called *hospicios*, and that the church would benefit from this spiritual welfare as well. He laid down specific regulations for the separation of the poor in the *hospicios*, observing that 'the very first rule must be to separate the innocent from those living in vice'. He also gave detailed instructions for the seizure of mendicants and warned that violence must be avoided in apprehending beggars and paupers.

Coornhert, Dirck Volkertsz (1522–90): Dutch writer on poor relief who came from a family of cloth merchants. He worked for fifteen years as an engraver and was employed later as a secretary at Haarlem and Gouda. He is mainly known as a writer and uncompromising advocate of religious toleration. His major work is a treatise called *Boeventucht* (1567/87). Its subtitle indicates the purpose of this booklet: 'means for reducing the number of harmful persons'. With his proposal Coornhert revealed himself as a representative of the new secular spirit in dealing with begging and poverty-related crime. Idleness, according to Coornhert, was the root of poverty and crime. His suggestion was to find a remedy for wandering rogues that was even more bitter then death. The solution was compulsory labour which was the opposite of the vagrant's life of leisure and freedom. He proposed three types of forced labour: galley servitude, various forms of public works, and the practice of several trades in penitentiaries or prisons, which had to be established in each town and rural district for this purpose. His treatise certainly influenced the magistrates who founded the first house of correction on the Continent in Amsterdam in the 1590s.

Echter von Mespelbrunn, Julius (1545–1617): Bishop of Würzburg and founder of the local university. In 1573, when he became Bishop of

Würzburg, he remarked that 'half the town would not be large enough for a hospital which admitted all those who wanted to enter'. Thus the first rule of the hospital which he founded in the city of Würzburg in 1579 was that only the really sick and poor were to be admitted. Being both bishop and princely ruler he also encouraged poor relief reforms in the major towns of his territory. His influence is obvious in such poor ordinances and hospital regulations as, for example, those of Gerolshofen, Dettelbach, Mellrichstadt, Würzburg, Königshofen and Volkach.

Eden, Sir Frederick Morton (1766–1809): English writer on the state of the poor. He was one of the founders and was afterwards chairman of the Globe Insurance Company. His claim to fame, however, is the investigation which he made into the state of the labouring poor in England. He was led to the subject by the high prices of 1794 and 1795. He performed the survey with great thoroughness. He visited and studied several parishes personally, and relied on information from many correspondents all over England. The three volumes which he published under the title *State of the Poor* in 1797 form one of the classical works in economic literature. The first volume contains the treatise on the poor, the second parochial reports relating to the administration of workhouses and houses of industry, friendly societies, etc. The third volume continues the parochial reports and also has an appendix, containing tables of prices and wages.

Geiler von Kaysersberg, Johannes (1445–1510): Well-known cathedral preacher in Strasbourg. As early as 1498, and frequently thereafter, he advocated that the civil authorities should be responsible for the poor and their relief. Geiler was vehement in exhorting the citizens themselves to give assistance to their poor neighbours and not to allow the whole burden of such work to fall upon the few clerical and municipal administrators of poor relief. He also advocated that work should be provided for those able to work, and that the children of the poor should be taught some useful trade in order to be able to earn their living once they came of age, and thus to avoid becoming dependent solely upon charity. His sermons moved the Strasbourg citizens to endow one of the earliest hospitals for poor syphilitics in the Holy Roman Empire.

Giberti, Gian Matteo (1495–1543): Italian papal official, later Bishop of Verona (from 1528) and friend of Pope Clement VII. He is known for this constructive plan of poor relief for Verona. One of his first works in his bishopric was the erection of a large hospital for the numerous sick, poor and orphaned children. While he was still in Rome, he had organized a *societas pauperum* to combat the problem of mendicity. His greatest contribution to the work of poor relief was in founding a 'society of charity' in 1534 which brought both clerical and lay citizens together in religious-fraternal administration of relief.

Giginta, Miguel de (1534–?): Spanish theologian who was awarded the canonry of Elna. From 1576 to 1588 he wandered about the Iberian peninsula attempting to convince prelates, monarchs and magistrates of the utility of his plans for poor relief reform. He also propagated his ideas in Portugal. Back in Combria he published his influential tract *Tratado de remedio de los pobres* (1579). This treatise belongs among the most noteworthy attempts at organization and discipline in sixteenth-century Spain. His plans received a warm reception in many Spanish cities, particularly in Barcelona where the city council and the Jesuits joined together in 1583 to establish a beggars' hospital.

Gilbert, Thomas (1720–98): English politician and poor relief reformer. In 1782 he introduced three bills in the House of Commons. The first two, on the amendment of the laws relating to houses of correction, and for enabling two or more parishes to unite together, passed into law, but the third for reforming the enactments pertaining to vagrants miscarried. In 1787 he introduced another poor law bill, grouping many parishes together, taxing dogs, and imposing an additional charge for the use of turnpikes on Sundays. Gilbert's publications on his various schemes of reform were numerous. In 1775 he published *Observations upon the Orders and Resolutions of the House of Commons with Respect to the Poor*. This publication was followed in 1781 by *A Plan for the Better Relief and Employment of the Poor in England*.

Hackfurt, Lucas (*c.* 1495–1554): Cleric, teacher and poor relief administrator in Strasbourg. In 1523 the magistrates entrusted him with the administration of the new poor relief scheme. He remained in charge of the municipal relief system (*Gemeines Almosen*) until his death. He was a fervent supporter of Protestantism and had allegedly some connections with the Anabaptist movement in Strasbourg. He was one of the first and most successful professional poor relief administrators in Germany in the first half of the sixteenth century. Having a university degree and some years' experience in various ecclesiastical offices, he represents the new type of poor relief administrator who often had given up an ecclesiastical career and had become a civil servant instead. Hackfurt's achievements reflect the advantages of the incipient professionalization of poor relief in the sixteenth century.

Harman, Thomas (n.d.): English author who wrote *A Caveat for Common Cursitors* (1566), in which he depicted the tricks of vagrants and sturdy beggars. Harman seems to have been Commissioner of the Peace in Kent. He obviously kept close records of the wayfarers who stopped at his door to beg. There seems now little doubt about the authenticity of his book on Elizabethan rogues which includes a detailed portrayal of various kinds of vagrants as well as an enlightening dictionary of beggars' cant.

Herrera, Cristóbal Pérez de (died 1620): Born and educated in Salamanca, he became a crown physician (*protomedico*) in 1577, and worked for some years as a doctor in the Spanish galleys. In 1595 he embarked on a career as writer and project-maker (*arbitrista*). So far as many schemes for relieving the poor are concerned, his ideas are most fully elaborated in the treatise *Amparo de pobres* (1598). Like many of his contemporaries who wrote about poor relief reform he assumed that work was available for beggars if they only chose to take it. Practical adjustments to plans previously propagated by Miguel de Giginta (s.v.) were put into practice when a beggars' hospital was established in Madrid in 1596.

Hyperius, Andreas (1511–64): Protestant theologian who agreed with Martin Bucer on many doctrinal issues. He stayed in England in 1537–41 and was later Professor of Theology at the first Protestant university in Marburg. He is the author of the Hessian Church Ordinance of 1566, which contained important regulations on poor relief. He also wrote an influential tract on poor relief which was translated into English in 1572 under the title *The Regiment of the Povertie*. His ideas and proposals influenced the poor relief reforms in the Hanseatic town of Bremen and probably even in England. Hyperius believed that it belongs jointly to the ecclesiastical and lay authorities to care for the poor. He distinguished between worthy and undeserving poor and advocated the punishment and disciplining of sturdy beggars.

Ignatius Loyola (1491–1556): Spanish soldier and ecclesiastic, founder of the Society of Jesus. In 1535 he persuaded the city council of his native town, Azpeitia, to adopt a plan to eliminate public begging. According to his proposals the sick, disabled, widowed and orphaned were to be separated from the sturdy and idle. A cleric and a layman would collect alms for the poor and distribute them according to a list of the needy persons drawn up by two deputies. The prohibition of begging and organization of alms-giving was but one reform accomplished during Loyola's stay in Azpeitia. The entire programme included a moral reform, pertaining among others to those who lived in mortal sin, card players and improperly dressed females.

Karlstadt, Andreas von (alias Bodenstein) (*c.* 1480–1541): Radical Protestant reformer who reorganized poor relief at Wittenberg in 1522. In his tract on begging he argues that poor relief reform is a Christian social responsibility. The civil authorities are therefore called upon to enforce a ban on begging and to be diligent in assisting the poor who dwell in their cities. The means for implementing this reform were according to his opinion already at hand, viz. Luther's common chest. Recent research has made clear, however, that there can be no longer any doubt of the historical priority of Luther (s.v.) over Karlstadt in the formation and implementation of poor relief reforms in Wittenberg in 1522/3.

Linck, Wenceslaus (1483–1547): Protestant preacher and reformer who established a new poor relief system in the town of Altenburg similar to the one already existing in Wittenberg. In 1523 he wrote a small treatise *Von Arbeit und Betteln*, in which he complained that poor relief reform in Altenburg had suffered drawbacks despite all his efforts from the pulpit. He, like Luther, blamed the rulers because they did not fulfil their duty 'to the best of their ability to provide for the poverty of the masses'. From 1525 to his death in 1547 he served as a preacher at the municipal hospital in Nuremberg.

Lorenzana, Francisco Antonio de (1722–1804): Archbishop of Toledo and Primate of Spain from 1772 to 1797. He supported restrictions on begging and the confinement of the poor through sermons and pastoral letters. He put his ideas into practice by establishing a workhouse in Toledo at his own expense. Cardinal Lorenzana took his own episcopal colleagues to task, as he debunked the time-honoured image of the pious bishop who achieved a reputation for sanctity and heard the 'vivas and acclamations for the poor' for kindness towards the indigent. Such generosity was in his opinion only the 'cheapest form of charity' and merely allowed the undeserving poor to continue lives of idleness at the expense of the Church. He saw the *hospicio* (the eighteenth-century Spanish workhouse) as a 'seminary of good vassals and neighbours, of useful artisans and well-educated Christians'. Like many other eighteenth-century poor relief reformers he believed that such an institution would not only educate the poor in their religious duties but would also provide the vocational training necessary for them to obtain decent employment upon their release.

Luther, Martin (1483–1546): Founder of Protestantism and important poor relief reformer. In his famous *Letter to the Christian Nobility of the German Nation* (1529) Luther demanded that each town should care for its own poor and that no one should be allowed to beg. Luther's principles of relief were first put into practice at Wittenberg, where his disciple Karlstadt (s.v.) reorganized the municipal poor relief. In 1523 Luther composed the Poor Ordinance for the little Saxon town of Leisnig. This scheme of relief was based on the common chest. Luther's idea was practically that of a trust, comprising all the wealth of the congregation. Only a part of this trust fund was to be devoted to the relief of the poor. Most of the money was to be used to defray the expenses of the Lutheran pastor and to maintain schools and church buildings. In 1528 Luther wrote the preface to a new edition of the *Liber vagatorum*, pointing out that he himself had been deceived in the past by fraudulent beggars and vagrants.

Malthus, Thomas Robert (1766–1834): English writer and curate of Albury in Surrey in 1798. From 1803 until his death he held a sinecure as rector of Walesbury in Lincolnshire. Stimulated by William Pitt's Poor Law Bill of 1796, he supported a proposal for children's allowances, but was already expressing unease at the current idea that an increase in population was desirable. In 1798 he published the first edition of his famous work *An Essay on the Principle of Population*, in which he argued that population would soon increase beyond the means of subsistence and that checks on this increase are necessary. He used information gathered on his travels in Europe. For example, he correlated the poverty of fishermen in Trondheim with their earlier marriages and larger families in contrast with the people of the interior parts of Norway – without considering other possible variables. This work aroused a storm of controversy and exerted a powerful influence on social thought in the nineteenth century. Malthus's next publication, *The Present High Prices of Provision* (1800), dealt particularly with the problems of poor relief.

Marillac, Louise de (1591–1660): A widow of the erstwhile secretary to Marie de Medici, after 1625 Louise de Marillac pledged her life to the service of the poor. Authorized by Vincent de Paul (s.v.) to offer to women spiritual instruction as well as practical training in confraternities of charity, she founded the religious society known as The Daughters of Charity in 1634. Despite initial suspicion and hostility even from among the poor, her charitable institutions soon snowballed in France. The Daughters of Charity were thus established against a background of strong ecclesiastical and social pressures in favour of the cloistering of the female religious. The Daughters of Charity were a company or society rather than a female order. Its members were required to imitate Christ and to perform a multiform activity in bringing spiritual and material aid to the poor, to hospital inmates, to foundlings, and so on.

Marshall, William (n.d.): English author who is known as the English translator of the Ypres regulations on poor relief. He advocated an income tax to pay for public works organized by a 'council to avoid vagabonds'. His ideas might have influenced early Tudor poor law legislation, especially the Acts of 1531 and 1536.

Medina, Juan de (died 1572): Abbot of the Benedictine monastery of San Vicente in Salamanca, whose book *De la orden que en algunos pueblos de España se ha puesto en la limosna* (1545) was an answer to a treatise by the eminent Spanish theologian, Domingo de Soto (s.v.) published in the same year. Medina suggested that public alms were to be given with discrimination while private individuals were to give indiscriminately. Morally corrupt or idle persons should thus be excluded from public assistance. Poor relief was to be administered and implemented by the clergy and not by laymen. After the 1545 debate Juan de Medina was appointed by the Inquisition to serve as censor of the writings of the unfortunate archbishop of Toledo, Bartolomé de Carranza.

Neri, Philip (1515–95): Consultant of many popes and saintly priest who devoted his life and work to the poor. He was deeply affected by the poor relief reforms which were instituted by various popes during the sixteenth century, and was always personally active in caring for the poor, whether he met them on the street, or visited them in hospitals or in their homes. In 1548 he founded the Confraternity of the Holy Trinity in Rome, which cared for sick and destitute pilgrims who flocked into Rome. He worked with Charles Borromeo (s.v.) and was a close friend of Ignatius Loyola (s.v.). He preached continually to the people of Rome that they should interest themselves more in their own poor. Only a few decades after his death, in 1622, he was sanctified by the Catholic Church.

Olavide, Don Pablo Antonio José (1725–1803): Spanish statesman, economist and writer on poor relief who contributed also to the expulsion of the Jesuits from Spain. While he served as ambassador, he advocated the secularization of poor relief in Spain, arguing that it was the prerogative of the Prince to be a *pater familias* of the nation and to care in this function for all who were in need. Olavide did not completely rule out religious and private charitable activities but allowed them only on the condition that they were under the authority and supervision of the Prince.

Philipp, Landgrave of Hesse (1504–67): German territorial ruler who supported the Reformation at a very early stage. Less known are his poor relief reforms which he introduced in his territory in the late 1520s and early 1530s. His public welfare policy included, for example, the foundation of four *Landespitäler* (Haina, Merxhausen, Hofheim and Gronau) which were the rural counterparts of the civic hospitals in German towns which mushroomed during and after the Reformation. These charitable institutions which cared for the mentally ill, the sick and the old in the Hessian countryside were quite unique at the time of their foundation. Philipp also invited prominent Protestant theologians to Marburg (e.g. Andreas Hyperius, s.v.) in order to help him with the reorganization of poor relief and the setting up of church ordinances which included paragraphs on welfare administration.

Renaudot, Théophraste (1586–1653): French physician and journalist, founder of the first French newspaper. Born in Loudun, he settled in Paris in 1624 where he became physician to the king. Appointed commissary general for the poor, he started an information agency for them, which in 1631 became a regular journal, *Gazette de France*. He opened a free medical clinic in 1635, with free dispensaries, and also opened the first pawnshop in Paris in 1637. The free medical aid to the lower classes of Paris brought him into trouble with his fellow physicians and the members of the Faculty of Medicine, who were afraid of the competitor on the medical market and who envied him because of the tremendous success of his policlinic in which he employed fifteen physicians. He was the author of several books relating to poor relief. The most famous one is *Traité des pauvres*. In 1644 his enemies won a decisive victory. Renaudot was no longer allowed to practise medicine and his clinic which had done tremendous service to the poor was ordered to shut down.

Rochow, Friedrich Eberhard von (1734–1805): German nobleman and retired officer of the Prussian army who was interested in educational reform and poor relief. He wrote many popular books on education as well as a less known tract on the repression of begging and institutional relief (1786). On his estate at Reckahn he founded the first German industry schools. In education he saw a splendid tool with which to combat poverty. There the children of the lower classes would learn reading, writing and arithmetic, and receive a moral education. At the same time, they would be instructed in spinning and other kinds of manual work.

Soto, Domingo de (1494–1560): An eminent Dominican theologian who was opposed to the municipal poor relief reform in Spain. His famous tract *Deliberación en la causa de los pobres* (1545) which sparked off the famous controversy with Juan de Medina (s.v.) questioned the necessity of mounting such a complicated operation as the new poor laws just to extirpate the disreputable lot of beggars deserving punishment. He agreed in principle with Medina that giving alms was an act of mercy, but made it quite clear that mercy had nothing to do with judgments concerning the merits of the recipients. Soto objected to the new Spanish poor laws also because they excluded foreigners from permanent relief. He suggested that the richer provinces and cities of Spain had an obligation to help the poorer ones. Poor relief should be administered by the clergy and the role of the secular authorities was to be limited to meting out punishment to vagabonds. The Dominican friar was aware of the poor relief reforms in Flanders, Italy and Germany, but he rejected them with the simple argument that what is done in other countries cannot be used as an adequate example for Spain.

Taintenier, François-Joseph (1729–76): Belgian economist and writer on poor relief. After having served as an officer in the cavalry for some time, Taintenier became a prolific writer and economist. In 1760 he published his first treatise on pauperism, which was soon reprinted. In 1775 followed another important tract on the same subject called *Supplément au traité sur mendicité*. The poor relief scheme which he had developed was put into practice later on by the magistrates of the cities of Ath and Tournai. His economic ideas were influenced by the French physiocrats. Being familiar with the poor relief system operating at Yverdon in the county of Vaud, Taintenier suggested that assistance should be given only to the resident poor and the distribution of relief should be done by *bureaux de charité*. He also believed that in order to combat poverty one had to establish schools in the countryside for the children of the poor.

Thompson, Benjamin (Count Rumford) (1753–1814): Anglo-American administrator, poor relief reformer and scientist. In 1784 he entered the service of Bavaria. He reformed the army, drained the marshes, established a common foundry and military academy, planned a poor law system, spread the cultivation of the potato and disseminated a knowledge of domestic economy. He also laid out the the English Garden in Munich. For these services he was made head of the Bavarian war department and count of the Holy Roman Empire. Faced with the problem of feeding the inmates of workhouses and soldiers in the army, he studied the science of nutrition. He developed a theory of nutritional value of water and introduced soup as the staple diet. His recipe for a hearty soup for the poor (*Rumford Suppe*) changed the diet in workhouses and charitable institutions in many European countries. He also experimented with many cheap foods for mass feeding of the poor. In connection with the workhouses set up to produce military clothing in Bavaria, Thompson studied the efficiency of illumination, inventing the shadow photometer which bears his name.

Vincent de Paul (1581–1660): French priest and founder of two Roman Catholic orders. He considered that the able-bodied poor were in need of work as well as food, and suggested the creation of useless labour for them rather than leaving them unemployed. In 1625 he founded the Congregatio Missionis (its members were also known as 'Lazarists'), which not only organized missions, for example in Corsica and Madagascar, but also unfolded a number of charitable activities for prisoners, galley-slaves, beggars, war refugees, and so on. From 1617 Vincent de Paul developed the organization of confraternities of charity, in which women within a parish joined together for mutual spiritual edification and for the practice of good works, most notably by caring for the poor. After 1625 his Lazarists were instructed to establish such charities in all villages where they held missions. From the early 1630s he worked together with Louise de Marillac (s.v.), who founded the female congregration known as the Daughters of Charity.

Vives, Juan Luis (1492–1540): Humanist and poor relief reformer. A Spaniard by birth, he spent the last years of his life in Bruges. His famous treatise about poor relief (*De subventione pauperum*, 1526) was dedicated to the magistrates of Bruges but soon gained a European audience. Vives was very much in favour of civil supervision of all poor relief. His scheme of municipal poor relief is based upon two principles: first, the poor who are fit to work by age and condition of health should be employed, and second, all poor should be registered in a census. He also advocated hospital reform and made vague suggestions about financing institutional and outdoor relief. Money was to be contributed by prelates, collected in poor boxes, bequeathed by testators, or earned by the labour of the poor. Vives can be credited with influencing the discussion on poor relief reform in the Low Countries and elsewhere, although the actual impact of his ideas on new schemes introduced in some cities (Bruges, Ypres) may have been rather limited.

Voght, Caspar von (1752–1839): Hamburg merchant and co-founder of the General Relief Agency in this Hanseatic town in 1788. He was a pioneer in poor relief reform of the late eighteenth century and maintained a keen interest in such reform projects until his death at age eighty-six. Far more than any of his German contemporaries, he was involved in poor relief reform throughout Europe. Early in the nineteenth century he master-minded schemes for the Holy Roman Emperor in Vienna, for the King of Prussia, and later on for Napoleon in France and Italy. Voght perceived his civic duty in works of a practical nature, regarding 'all knowledge that could not be turned to humanitarian purposes ... vain and empty'. As recognition for his services in reforming poor relief in Austria, he was ennobled by the German Emperor in 1801.

Select bibliography

INTRODUCTION

Assistance et assistés de 1610 à nos jours. Actes du 97e congrès national des sociétés savantes, Nantes 1972, vol. I (Paris, 1977)

Fischer, Wolfram *Armut in der Geschichte: Erscheinungsformen und Lösungs-versuche der 'Sozialen Frage' in Europa seit dem Mittelalter* (Göttingen, 1982)

Geremek, Bronislaw *Geschichte der Armut* (Munich and Zurich, 1988)

Gutton, Jean-Pierre *La Société et les pauvres en Europe (XVIe–XVIIIe siècles)* (Paris, 1971)

Hunecke, Volker 'Überlegungen zur Geschichte der Armut im vorindustriellen Europa', *Geschichte und Gesellschaft* 9 (1983), 480–512

Lindgren, Uta 'Europas Armut. Probleme, Methoden, Ergebnisse einer Unter-suchung', *Saeculum* 28 (1979), 396–418

Lis, Catharina and Hugo Soly *Poverty and Capitalism in Pre-industrial Europe* (Hassocks, Sussex, 1979)

Mollat, Michel (ed.) *Etudes sur l'histoire de la pauvreté (Moyen Age–XVI siècle)*, 2 vols. (Paris, 1974)

Riis, Thomas *Pauvreté et développement urbain en Europe XVe–XVIIIe/XIXe siècles: Une bibliographie* (Odense, 1981)

Riis, Thomas (ed.) *Aspects of Poverty in Early Modern Europe*, 3 vols. (Stuttgart etc., 1981–1990)

Woolf, Stuart *The Poor in Western Europe in the Eighteenth and Nineteenth Century* (London and New York, 1986)

LANGUAGE OF POVERTY

Chartier, Roger *Figures de la gueuserie* (Paris, 1982)

Geremek, Bronislaw 'Gergo' *Enciclopedia Einaudi*, vol. 6 (Turin, 1979), pp. 724–46

Himmelfarb, Gertrude *The Idea of Poverty: England in the Early Industrial Age* (London, 1984), ch. 13

Jütte, Robert *Abbild und soziale Wirklichkeit des Bettler- und Gaunertums zu Beginn der Neuzeit: Sozial-, mentalitäts- und sprachgeschichtliche Studien zum Liber vagatorum (1510)* (Cologne and Vienna, 1988)

Roch, Jean-Louis *Les Mots aussi sont de l'histoire: vocabulaire de la pauvreté et marginalisation* (*1450–1550*) (Doctorat 3ème cycle, University of Paris IV, 1986)

Stein, André L. *L'Ecologie de l'argot ancien* (Paris, 1974)

Woolf, Stuart *The Poor in Western Europe in the Eighteenth and Nineteenth Century* (London and New York, 1986), ch. 6

VISUALIZATION OF THE POOR

Barrell, John *The Dark Side of the Landscape : The Rural Poor in English Painting* (*1730–1840*) (Cambridge, 1980)

Deyon, Pierre 'A propos du paupérisme au milieu du XVIIe siècle: peinture et charité chrétienne', *Annales ESC* 22 (1967), 137–53

Feinberg, Anat 'The representation of the poor in Elizabethan and Stuart drama', *Literature and History* 12 (1986), 152–63

Garnier, François 'Figures et comportements du pauvre dans l'iconographie des XIIe et XIIIe siècles', in Henri Dubois, Jean-Claude Hocquet and André Vauchez (eds), *Horizons marins itinéraires spituels (Ve–XVIIIe siècles)* (Paris, 1987), pp. 303–18

Sachße, Christoph and Florian Tennstedt (eds) *Bettler, Gauner und Proleten : Armut und Armenfürsorge in der deutschen Geschichte : Ein Bild-Lesebuch* (Reinbek, 1983)

Sudeck, Elisabeth *Bettlerdarstellungen am Ende des XV. Jahrhunderts bis zu Rembrandt* (Strasbourg, 1931)

Wandel, Lee Palmer *Always Among Us. Images of the Poor in Zwingli's Zurich* (Cambridge, 1990), ch. 3

ACCIDENTAL CAUSES

Abel, Wilhelm *Massenarmut und Hungerkrisen im vorindustriellen Europa : Versuch einer Synopsis* (Hamburg and Berlin, 1974)

Corvisier, André 'Anciens soldats oblats, mortes-payes et mendiants dans la première moitié du XVII siècle', *Actes du 97e congrés national des sociétés savantes*, Nantes 1972 (Paris, 1977), *Histoire moderne*, vol. I, pp. 7–29

Fisher, F. J. 'Influenza and inflation in Tudor England', *Economic History Review* 2nd series 18 (1965), 120–9

Fissell, Mary E. *Patients, Power, and the Poor in Eighteenth-Century Bristol* (Cambridge, 1991)

Kahan, A. 'Natural calamities and their effect upon the food supply in Russia', *Jahrbücher für Geschichte Osteuropas*, n.s. 16 (1968), 353–77

Kamen, Henry 'The economic and social consequences of the Thirty Years War', *Past and Present* 39 (1968), 44–61

Patzelt, E. 'Pauvreté et maladies', *Povertà e Richezza nella Spiritualita ei Secoli XI e XII* (Todi, 1969), pp. 163–87

Scribner, Robert W. 'Mobility: voluntary or enforced? Vagrants in Württemberg in the sixteenth century', in Gerhard Jaritz and Albert Müller (eds), *Migration in der Feudalgesellschaft* (Frankfurt am Main and New York, 1988), pp. 65–88

CYCLICAL CAUSES

Abel, Wilhelm *Agricultural Fluctuations in Europe: From the Thirteenth to the Twentieth Centuries* (New York, 1980)

Appleby, Andrew 'Grain prices and subsistence crises in England and France 1590–1740', *Journal of Economic History* 39 (1979), 865–87

Schofield, Roger and Johan Walter (eds) *Famine, Diseases and the Social Order in Early Modern Society* (Cambridge, 1989)

Snell, K. D. M. *Annals of the Labouring Poor: Social Change and Agrarian England, 1660–1900* (Cambridge, 1985)

STRUCTURAL CAUSES

Borscheid, Peter *Geschichte des Alters. 16.–18. Jahrhundert* (Münster, 1987)

Laslett, Peter 'Family, kinship and collectivity as systems of support in pre-industrial Europe: a consideration of the "nuclear-hardship"-hypothesis', *Continuity and Change* 3 (1988), 153–75

Lombardi, Daniela *Povertà maschile, poverta femminile: L'ospedale dei mendicanti nella Firenze dei Medici* (Bologna, 1988)

Newmann-Brown, W. 'The receipt of poor relief and family situation', in Richard M. Smith (ed.), *Land, Kinship and Life Cycle* (Cambridge, 1985), pp. 405–22

Pelling, Margaret 'Old People and poverty in early modern towns', *The Society for the Social History of Medicine Bulletin* 34 (1984), 42–7

Sokoll, Thomas 'The pauper households small and simple? The evidence from listings of inhabitants and pauper lists of early modern England reassessed', *Ethnologia Europaea* 17 (1987), 25–42

FISCAL POOR

Arkell, Tom 'The incidence of poverty in England in the later seventeenth century', *Social History* 12 (1987), 23–47

Blockmans, W. P. and W. Prevenier 'Poverty in Flanders and Brabant from the fourteenth to the mid-sixteenth-century: sources and problems', *Acta Historiae Neerlandicae* 10 (1978), 20–57

Meyer, Jean 'Pauvreté et assistance dans les villes bretonnes de l'ancien régime', *Actes du 97e congrès national des sociétés savantes*, Nantes 1972 (Paris, 1977), vol. I, 445–60

Roeck, Bernd '"Arme" in Augsburg zu Beginn des 30jährigen Krieges', *Zeitschrift für bayerische Landesgeschichte* 46 (1983), 515–58

RECIPIENTS OF POOR RELIEF

Bog, Ingomar 'Über Arme und Armenfürsorge in Oberdeutschland und in der Eidgenossenschaft im 15. und 16. Jahrhundert', *Jahrbuch für fränkische Landesforschung* 34/35 (1974/75), 983–1001

Cavallo, Sandra 'Conceptions of poverty and poor-relief in the second half of the eighteenth century', in Stuart Woolf (ed.), *Domestic Strategies: Work and*

Family in France and Italy 1600–1800 (Cambridge and Paris, 1991), pp. 148–200.

Clasen, Claus-Peter 'Armenfürsorge in Augsburg vor dem Dreißigjährigen Kriege', *Zeitschrift des Historischen Vereins für Schwaben* (1984), 65–115

Pullan, Brian, 'Poveri, mendicanti e vagabondi (secoli XIV–XVII)', in *Storia d'Italia. Annali I. Dal feudalesimo a capitalismo* (Turin, 1978), pp. 988–97

CENSUSES OF THE POOR

Fischer, Thomas *Städtische Armut und Armenfürsorge im 15. und 16. Jahrhundert: Sozialgeschichtliche Untersuchungen am Beispiel der Städte Basel, Freiburg i. Br. und Straßburg* (Göttingen, 1979)

Slack, Paul *Poverty and Policy in Tudor and Stuart England* (London and New York, 1988), ch. 4

Woolf, Stuart *The Poor in Western Europe in the Eighteenth and Nineteenth Centuries* (London and New York, 1986), ch. 4

TOPOGRAPHY OF POVERTY

Boulton, Jeremy *Neighbourhood and Society: A London Suburb in the Seventeenth Century* (Cambridge 1987)

Deyon, Pierre *Amiens, capitale provinciale* (Paris, 1969), ch. 25

Rappaport, Steve *World Within Worlds: Structures of Life in Sixteenth-Century London* (Cambridge, 1989), ch. 6

Roeck, Bernd *Eine Stadt in Krieg und Frieden: Studien zur Geschichte der Reichsstadt Augsburg zwischen Kalenderstreit und Parität* (Göttingen, 1989), ch. 7

Romon, Christian 'Le monde des pauvres à Paris au XVIIIe siècle', *Annales ESC* 37 (1982), 729–63

Trenard, Louis 'Pauvreté, charité, assistance à Lille 1708–1790', *Actes du 97e congrès des sociétés savantes*, Nantes 1972 (Paris, 1977), vol. I, 473–98

DOMESTIC ENVIRONMENT

Benscheidt, Anja R. *Kleinbürgerlicher Besitz: Nürtinger Handwerkerinventare von 1660 bis 1840* (Münster, 1985)

Dinges, Martin 'Materielle Kultur und Alltag – Die Unterschichten in Bordeaux im 16. und 17. Jahrhundert', *Francia* 15 (1987), 257–79

Dirlmeier, Ulf *Untersuchungen zu Einkommensverhältnissen und Lebenshaltungskosten in oberdeutschen Städten des Spätmittelalters (Mitte 14. bis Anfang 16. Jahrhundert)* (Heidelberg, 1978)

Klonder, Andrzej 'Majatek ruchomy podopiecznych elbaskiego szpitala Sw. ducha w XVII wieku', in J. Sztetyllo (ed.), *Nadza i dostatek na ziemiach polskich od sredniowiecza po wiek* [Poverty and Affluence in Poland from the Middle Ages to the Twentieth Century] (Warsaw, 1992), 141–50

Roche, Daniel, *The People of Paris: An Essay in Popular Culture in the 18th Century*, translated by Marie Evans (Leamington Spa, 1987)

Scheftel, Michael *Gänge, Buden und Wohnkeller in Lübeck: Bau- und sozial-*

geschichtliche Untersuchungen zu den Wohnungen der ärmeren Bürger und Einwohner einer Großstadt des späten Mittelalters und der frühen Neuzeit (Neumünster, 1988)

NUTRITION

Appleby, Andrew B. 'Diet in sixteenth-century England: sources, problems, possibilities', in Charles Webster (ed.), *Health, Medicine and Mortality in the Sixteenth Century* (Cambridge, 1979), pp. 97–116
Camporesi, Piero *Food and Folklore* (Cambridge, 1992)
Jütte, Robert 'Diets in welfare institutions and in outdoor poor relief in early modern western Europe', *Ethnologia Europaea* 16 (1988), 117–35
Krug-Richter, Barbara 'Alltag und Fest. Nahrungsgewohnheiten im Magdalenenhospital in Münster 1558–1635', in Trude Ehlert (ed.), *Haushalt und Familie in Mittelalter und früher Neuzeit* (Sigmaringen, 1991), 71–90
Shammas, Carole 'The eighteenth-century English diet and economic change', *Explorations in Economic History* 21 (1984), 254–69
Teuteberg, Hans J. and Günter Wiegelmann *Der Wandel der Nahrungsgewohnheiten unter dem Einfluß der Industrialisierung* (Göttingen, 1972)

CLOTHING

Cunnington, Philis and Catherine Lucas *Charity Costumes* (London, 1978)
Jütte, Robert 'Windfang und Wetterhahn. Die Kleidung der Bettler und Vaganten im Spiegel der älteren Gaunersprache', in Harry Kühnel (ed.), *Terminologie und Typologie mittelalterlicher Sachgüter: Das Beispiel der Kleidung* (Vienna, 1988), pp. 177–204
Roche, Daniel *The People of Paris: An Essay in Popular Culture in the 18th Century*, translated by Marie Evans (Leamington Spa, 1987), ch. 6
Sievers, Kai Detlev *Leben in Armut: Zeugnisse der Armutskultur aus Lübeck und Schleswig-Holstein vom Mittelalter bis ins 20. Jahrhundert* (Heide, 1991), ch. 3
Simon-Muscheid, Katharina 'Die Kleidung städtischer Unterschichten zwischen Projektionen und Realität im Spätmittelalter und in der frühen Neuzeit', *Saeculum* 44 (1993), 47–64

NETWORKS

Bossy, John 'Godparenthood: the fortunes of a social institution in early modern christianity', in Caspar von Greyerz (ed.), *Religion and Society in Early Modern Europe, 1500–1800* (London, 1984), pp. 194–201
Boulton, Jeremy *Neighbourhood and Society: A London Suburb in the Seventeenth Century* (Cambridge, 1987)
Garrioch, David *Neighbourhood and Community in Paris, 1740–1790* (Cambridge, 1986)
Heal, Felicity *Hospitality in Early Modern England* (Oxford, 1990)
Klapisch-Zuber, Christiane *La Maison et le nom: Stratégies et rituels dans l'Italie de la Renaissance* (Paris, 1990)

Laslett, Peter 'Family, kinship and the collectivity as systems of support in pre-industrial Europe: a consideration of the nuclear hardship hypothesis', *Continuity and Change* 3 (1988), 153–75

Medick, Hans and David Warren Sabean (eds) *Interest and Emotion in Family and Kinship Studies: A Critique of Social History and Anthropology* (Cambridge, 1984)

Sabean, David Warren *Property, Production, and Family in Neckarhausen, 1700–1870* (Cambridge, 1990)

Smith, Richard M. (ed.) *Land, Kinship, and Life-cycle* (Cambridge, 1984)

Woolf, Stuart (ed.) *Domestic Strategies: Work and Family in France and Italy 1600–1800* (Cambridge and Paris, 1991)

SELF-HELP

D'Cruze, Shani 'The family and self-help through the evidence of diaries and autobiographies', paper prepared for International Perspectives on Self-help Conference (Lancaster 2–4 July 1991)

Dinges, Martin 'Self-help, assistance, and the poor in early modern France', paper prepared for International Perspectives on Self-help Conference (Lancaster 2–4 July 1991)

Finzsch, Norbert *Obrigkeit und Unterschichten: Zur Geschichte der rheinischen Unterschichten gegen Ende des 18. Jahrhunderts und zu Beginn des 19. Jahrhunderts* (Stuttgart, 1990)

Flynn, Maureen *Sacred Charity: Confraternities and Social Welfare in Spain, 1400–1700* (London, 1989)

Frölich, Sigrid *Die soziale Sicherung bei Zünften und Gesellenverbänden* (Berlin, 1976)

Holderness, B. 'Credit in English rural society before the nineteenth century, with special reference to the period 1650–1720', *Agricultural History Review* 24 (1976), 97–109

Macfarlane, Alan *The Family Life of Ralph Josselin: A Seventeenth-Century Clergyman* (Cambridge, 1970)

Newman-Brown, W. 'The receipt of poor relief and family situation: Aldenham, Hertfordshire 1630–90', in Richard M. Smith (ed.), *Land, Kinship and Life-Cycle* (Cambridge, 1984), pp. 405–22

Pelling, Margaret 'Old age, poverty, and disability in early modern Norwich: work, remarriage, and other expedients', in Margaret Pelling and Richard M. Smith (eds), *Life, Death and the Elderly: Historical Perspectives* (London and New York, 1991)

Walter, John 'The social economy of dearth in early modern England', in John Walter and Roger Schofield (eds), *Famine, Disease and the Social Order in Early Modern Society* (Cambridge, 1989), pp. 75–128

Wrightson, Keith and David Levine *Poverty and Piety in an English Village: Terlin 1525–1700* (London, 1979)

REORGANIZATION OF POOR RELIEF: IDEAS AND CONCEPTS

Alves, A. A. 'The Christian social organism and social welfare: the case of Vives, Calvin, and Loyola', *Sixteenth Century Journal* 20 (1989), 3–22

Dinges, Martin 'Attitudes à l'égard de la pauvreté aux XVIe et XVII siècles à Bordeaux', *Histoire, Économie et Société* 10 (1991), 360–74

Fideler, Paul A. 'Christian humanism and poor law in early modern England', *Societas* 4 (1974), 269–85

Himmelfarb, Gertrude *The Idea of Poverty: England in the Industrial Age* (London, 1984)

Jütte, Robert 'Poor relief and social discipline in early modern Europe', *European Studies Review* 11 (1981), 25–52

Pullan, Brian 'Catholics and the poor in early modern Europe', *Transactions of the Royal Historical Society*, 5th series, 26 (1976) 15–34

Scherpner, Hans *Theorie der Fürsorge* (Göttingen, 1962)

Steinbicker, Carl *Poor-Relief in the Sixteenth Century* (Washington, 1937)

REORGANIZATION OF POOR RELIEF: EXAMPLES

GERMANY

Fischer, Thomas *Städtische Armut und Armenfürsorge im 15. und 16. Jahrhundert: Sozialgeschichtliche Untersuchungen am Beispiel der Städte Basel, Freiburg i. Br. und Straßburg* (Göttingen, 1979)

Jütte, Robert *Obrigkeitliche Armenfürsorge in deutschen Reichsstädten der frühen Neuzeit: Obrigkeitliches Armenwesen in Frankfurt am Main und Köln* (Cologne and Vienna, 1984)

Katzinger, Willibald 'Zum Problem der Armut in den Städten Österreichs vom Spätmittelalter bis ins 18. Jahrhundert', in Thomas Riis (ed.), *Aspects of Poverty in Early Modern Europe II: Les Réactions des pauvres à la pauvreté* (Odense, 1986), 31–47

Lindemann, Mary *Patriots and Paupers: Hamburg, 1712–1830* (New York and Oxford, 1990)

SWITZERLAND

Hausmann, Karl Eduard *Die Armenpflege in der Helvetik* (Basel and Stuttgart, 1969)

Head, Anne-Lise and Brigitte Schnegg (eds) *Armut in der Schweiz, 17.–20. Jahrhundert* (Zurich, 1989)

Wandel, Lee Palmer *Always Among Us: Images of the Poor in Zwingli's Zurich* (Cambridge, 1990)

LOW COUNTRIES

Bonenfant, Pierre 'Les Origines et le caractère de la réforme de la bienfaisance aux Pays-Bas sous le règne de Charles Quint', *Revue Belge de Philologie et d'Histoire* 5 (1926), 887–904, 6 (1927), 207–30

Haesenne-Peremans, N. *Les Pauvres et le pouvoir : assistance et répression au pays de Liège (1685–1830)* (Kortrijk-Heule, 1983)
Mentink, G. J. 'Armenzorg en armoede in de archivalische bronnen in de Noordeligke Nederlanden 1531–1851', *Tijdschrift voor Geschiedenis* 88 (1975), 551–61

ITALY

Assereto, M. 'Pauperismo e assistenza. Messa a punto di studi recenti', *Archivico Storico Italiano* 141 (1983), 253–71
Rosa, M. 'Chiesa, idee sui poveri, e assistenza in Italia dal Cinque al Settecento', *Societá e Storia* 10 (1980), 775–806
Pullan, Brian 'Support and redeem : charity and poor relief in Italian cities from the fourteenth to the seventeenth century', *Continuity and Change* 3 (1988), 177–208

SPAIN

Callahan, William J. 'The poor, the privileged and the church in eighteenth century Spain', in R. E. Morton and J. D. Browning (eds), *Religion in the 18th Century* (New York and London, 1979), pp. 103–16
Flynn, Maureen *Sacred Charity : Confraternities and Social Welfare in Spain, 1400–1700* (London, 1989)
Martz, Linda *Poverty and Welfare in Habsburg Spain : The Example of Toledo* (Cambridge, 1983)
Soubeyrox, Jacques *Paupérisme et rapports sociaux à Madrid au XVIIIe siècle* (Lille and Paris, 1978)

FRANCE

Davis, Natalie Zemon 'Poor relief, humanism and heresy: the case of Lyon', *Studies in Medieval and Renaissance History* 5 (1968), 217–75
Dinges, Martin *Stadtarmut in Bordeaux, 1525–1675 : Alltag – Politik – Mentalitäten* (Bonn, 1988)
Gutton, Jean-Pierre *La Société et les pauvres. L'Exemple de la généralité de Lyon 1534–1789* (Paris, 1971)
Hickey, Daniel 'Changing expressions of charity in early modern France: some hypotheses for a rural model', *Renaissance et Réforme* 2 (1978), 12–22
Jones, Colin *The Charitable Imperative : Hospitals and Nursing in Ancien Régime and Revolutionary France* (London and New York, 1989)

ENGLAND AND SCOTLAND

McIntosh, Marjorie K. 'Local responses to the poor in late medieval and Tudor England', *Continuity and Change* 3 (1988) 209–45
Mitchison, Rosalind 'The making of the old Scottish poor law', *Past and Present* 63 (1974), 58–93

Oxley, Geoffrey W. *Poor Relief in England and Wales 1601–1834* (London and Vancouver, 1974)

Slack, Paul *Poverty and Policy in Tudor and Stuart England* (London and New York, 1988)

SCANDINAVIA

Dahlerup, Troels 'Den sociale forsorg og reformationen in Danmark', *Historie* n.s. 13 (1979/80), 194–207

Nielsen, M. H. 'Fattigvaesenet i Danmark 1536–1708', *Aarbog for dansk Kulturhistorie* (1897), 69–124

Riis, Thomas (ed.) *Aspects of Poverty in Early Modern Europe III. La Pauvreté dans les pays nordiques 1500–1800* (Odense, 1990)

CRIME AND POVERTY

Dübeck, Inger 'Poor women's criminality in 18th-century Denmark and Norway', in Thomas Riis (ed.) *Aspects of Poverty in Early Modern Europe II* (Odense, 1986), 193–206

Geremek, Bronislaw 'Criminalité, vagabondage, paupérisme: la marginalité à l'aube des temps modernes', *Revue d'Histoire Moderne et Contemporaine* 21 (1974), 337–75

Hufton, Olwen H. *The Poor of Eighteenth-Century France 1750–1789* (Oxford, 1974), chs. 8–12

VAGRANCY

Beier, A. L. *Masterless Men: The Vagrancy Problem in England 1560–1640* (London and New York, 1985)

Hufton, Olwen H. 'Begging, vagrancy, vagabondage and the law: an aspect of poverty in eighteenth-century France', *European Studies Review* 2 (1972), 97–123

Küther, Carsten *Menschen auf der Straße: Vagierende Unterschichten in Bayern, Franken und Schwaben in der zweiten Hälfte des 18. Jahrhunderts* (Göttingen, 1983)

Meneghetti, Casarin F. *I Vagabondi, la società e lo stato nella republicca veneta alla fine del '700* (Rome, 1984)

THEFT

Beattie, J. M. 'The pattern of crime in England 1600–1800', *Past and Present* 64 (1974), 47–95

Reinhardt, Steven G. 'The selective prosecution of crime in ancien régime France: theft in the Sénéchaussée of Sarlat', *European History Quarterly* 16 (1986), 3–24

Schwerhoff, Gerd *Köln im Kreuzverhör. Kriminalität, Herrschaft und Gesellschaft in einer frühneuzeitlichen Stadt* (Bonn, 1991), ch. 8

Vanhemelryck, F. 'Pauperisme en misdadigheit in Brabant in de XVIIIde eeuw', *Tijdschrift voor Geschiedenis* 88 (1975), 598–612

SMUGGLING

Bourquin, Marie-Helène and Emmanuel Hepp *Aspects de la contrebande au XVIIIe siècle* (Paris, 1969)

Dufraisse, Roger 'La Contrebande dans les départements réunis de la rive gauche du Rhin à l'époque napoléonienne', *Francia* 6 (1978), 508–36

Finzsch, Norbert, *Obrigkeit und Unterschichten: Zur Geschichte der rheinischen Unterschichten gegen Ende des 18. und zu Beginn des 19. Jahrhunderts* (Stuttgart, 1990), ch. 3

PROSTITUTION

Benabou, Marie-Erica *La Prostitution et la police des mœurs au XVIII siècle* (Paris, 1987)

Otis, Leah Lydia *Prostitution in Medieval Society: The History of an Urban Institution in Languedoc* (Chicago, 1985)

Perry, Mary-Elizabeth '"Lost women" in early modern Seville: the politics of prostitution', *Feminist Studies* 4 (1978), 195–214

Roper, Lyndal 'Mothers of debauchery: procuresses in Reformation Augsburg', *German History* 6 (1988), 1–19.

Schuster, Peter *Das Frauenhaus: Städtische Bordelle in Deutschland, 1350 bis 1600* (Paderborn, 1992)

STIGMATIZATION

Gibbs, Jack P. 'Conceptions of deviant behavior: the old and the new', in Mark Kefton *et al.* (eds), *Approaches to Deviance* (New York, 1968), pp. 44–55

Hergemöller, Bernd-Ulrich (ed.) *Randgruppen der spätmittelalterlichen Gesellschaft* (Warendorf, 1990)

Jütte, Robert 'Stigmasymbole: Kleidung als identitätsstiftendes Merkmal bei spätmittelalterlichen und frühneuzeitlichen Randgruppen (Juden, Dirnen, Aussätzige, Bettler)', in Robert Jütte and Neithard Bulst (eds), *Zwischen Sein und Schein: Kleidung und Identität in der ständischen Gesellschaft* (Freiburg/Breisgau, 1993), pp. 65–89

Waxman, Chaim Isaac *The Stigma of Poverty: A Critique of Poverty Theories and Policies* (New York, 1977)

SEGREGATION AND EXPULSION

Graus, František 'Randgruppen der städtischen Gesellschaft im Spätmittelalter', *Zeitschrift für historische Forschung* 8 (1981), 385–437

Hartung, Wolfgang 'Gesellschaftliche Randgruppen im Spätmittelalter. Phänomen und Begriff', in Bernhard Kirchgässner and Fritz Reuter (eds), *Städtische Randgruppen und Minderheiten* (Sigmaringen, 1986), pp. 49–114

Smith, A. E. *Colonists in Bondage* (1947, new edn Gloucester, Mass., 1965)

CONFINEMENT

Finzsch, Norbert and Robert Jütte (eds) *The Prerogative of Confinement : Social, Cultural and Administrative Aspects of the History of Hospitals and Carceral Institutions in Western Europe and North America 1500–1900* (New York and Cambridge, forthcoming)

Foucault, Michel *Discipline and Punish : The Birth of the Prison*, translated by Alan Sheridan (New York, 1979)

Schwartz, Robert M. *Policing the Poor in Eighteenth-Century France* (Chapel Hill, 1988)

Sellin, Thorsten *Pioneering in Penology : The Amsterdam Houses of Correction in the Sixteenth and Seventeenth Centuries* (Philadelphia, 1944)

Stekl, Hannes '"Labore et fame". Sozialdisziplinierung in Zucht- und Arbeitshäusern des 17. und 18. Jahrhunderts', in Christoph Sachße and Florian Tennstedt (eds), *Soziale Sicherheit und soziale Disziplinierung : Beiträge zu einer historischen Theorie der Sozialpolitik* (Frankfurt am Main, 1986), pp. 119–47

SUBCULTURE

Chartier, Roger 'Les Elites et les gueux. Quelques représentations (XVIe–XVIIe siècles)', *Revue d'Histoire Moderne et Contemporaine* 21 (1974), 376–88

Forster, Robert and Orest Ranum (eds) *Deviants and the Abandoned in French Society* (Baltimore, 1978)

Jütte, Robert, *Abbild und Wirklichkeit des Bettler- und Gaunertums zu Beginn der Neuzeit. Sozial-, mentalitäts- und sprachgeschichtliche Studien zum Liber vagatorum (1510)* (Vienna and Cologne, 1988)

McMullan, John L. 'Criminal organization in sixteenth and seventeenth century London', *Social Problems* 29 (1981), 311–23

Vincent, Bernard (ed.) *Les Marginaux et les exclus dans l'histoire* (Paris, 1979)

REBELLION

Hobsbawm, Eric J. *Bandits* (Harmondsworth, 1972)

Mousnier, Roland *Peasant Uprisings in Seventeenth Century France, Russia and China*, translated by Brian Pierce (New York, 1971)

Rudé, George *The Crowd in History : A Study of Popular Disturbances in France and England 1730–1848* (New York, 1964)

Schulze, Winfried *Bäuerlicher Widerstand und feudale Herrschaft in der frühen Neuzeit* (Stuttgart, 1980)

Walter, John 'The geography of food riots 1585–1649', in A. Charlesworth (ed.), *An Atlas of Rural Protest in Britain 1548–1900* (London, 1983), pp. 72–80

(E)MIGRATION

Altman, Ida and James Horn (eds), *'To Make America' : European Emigration in the Early Modern Period* (Berkeley, 1992)

Beier, A. L. *Masterless Men : The Vagrancy Problem in England 1560–1640* (Oxford, 1985), ch. 3

Jaritz, Gerhard and Albert Müller (eds), *Migration in der Feudalgesellschaft* (Frankfurt am Main and New York, 1988)
Mandrou, Robert 'Les Français hors de France aux XVIe et XVIIe siècles', *Annales ESC* 14 (1959), 662–7

OUTLOOK

Achenbaum, Andrew W. 'W(h)ither social welfare history', *Journal of Social History* 24 (1990), 135–41
Levine, Daniel *Poverty and Society* (New Brunswick, 1988)
Preußer, Norbert *Not macht erfinderisch: Überlebensstrategien der Armenbevölkerung in Deutschland seit 1807* (Munich and Vienna, 1989)
Rimlinger, Gaston V. *Welfare Policy and Industralisation in Europe, America and Russia* (New York, 1971)
Ritter, Gerhard A. *Social Welfare in Germany and Britain: Origins and Development* (Leamington Spa, 1986)
Sachße, Christoph and Florian Tennstedt (eds), *Soziale Sicherheit und soziale Disziplinierung: Beiträge zu einer historischen Theorie der Sozialpolitik* (Frankfurt am Main, 1986)
Williams, Karel *From Pauperism to Poverty* (London, 1981)

Index

NEW APPROACHES TO EUROPEAN HISTORY